Thomas Paine and the Literature of Revolution

Although the impact of works such as *Common Sense* and *The Rights of Man* has led historians to study Thomas Paine's role in the American Revolution and political scientists to evaluate his contributions to political theory, scholars have tacitly agreed not to treat him as a literary figure. This book not only redresses this omission, but also demonstrates that Paine's literary sensibility is particularly evident in the very texts that confirmed his importance as a theorist. And yet, because of this association with the "masses," Paine is often dismissed as a mere propagandist. *Thomas Paine and the Literature of Revolution* recovers Paine as a transatlantic popular intellectual who would translate the major political theories of the eighteenth century into a language that was accessible and appealing to ordinary citizens on both sides of the Atlantic.

Edward Larkin is Assistant Professor of English and American Studies at the University of Richmond. He received a B.A. from Harvard University in 1990 and a Ph.D. from Stanford University in 1998. He was awarded a Fulbright Fellowship to lecture on American studies and literature at Tallinn University in Tallinn, Estonia, during the 2004–05 academic year. Larkin is the editor of a new edition of *Common Sense* (2004) and has published articles in *Early American Literature* and the *Arizona Quarterly*.

Thomas Paine and the Literature of Revolution

EDWARD LARKIN

CAMBRIDGE
UNIVERSITY PRESS

CAMBRIDGE UNIVERSITY PRESS
Cambridge, New York, Melbourne, Madrid, Cape Town, Singapore, São Paulo

Cambridge University Press
40 West 20th Street, New York, NY 10011-4211, USA

www.cambridge.org
Information on this title: www.cambridge.org/9780521841153

© Edward Larkin 2005

First published 2005

Printed in the United States of America

A catalog record for this publication is available from the British Library.

Library of Congress Cataloging in Publication Data

Larkin, Edward, 1968–
Thomas Paine and the literature of revolution / Edward Larkin.
    p.   cm.
Includes bibliographical references.
ISBN 0-521-84115-1 (hardback)
1. Paine, Thomas, 1737–1809.   2. Political scientists – United States.
3. Revolutionaries – United States.   4. Paine, Thomas, 1737–1809 – Influence.
5. United States – Politics and government – 1775–1783.   6. Political
science – United States – History – 18th century.   I. Title.
JC177.A4L37   2005
320.51′092–dc22   2004027652

ISBN-13   978-0-521-84115-3 hardback
ISBN-10   0-521-84115-1 hardback

For Karen

Contents

Acknowledgments

I have many people and institutions to thank for making this project not only possible, but also a positive and rewarding experience. My first and greatest debt is to Jay Fliegelman, whose patience and personal attention were as important as his wonderful insights and savvy guidance. He has been a true mentor. At Stanford, where this project began as a doctoral dissertation, I also benefited from the critical acumen and humane treatment of Al Gelpi and George Dekker. Jay, Al, and George taught me a great deal not only about American literature and culture, but about how to be a scholar and a human being in the academy. During my graduate study, I was lucky to spend two terrific years at the Philadelphia Center for Early American Studies (now the McNeil Center), where Richard Dunn and Michael Zuckerman in particular made me feel welcome. At the McNeil Center I shared my work with a bright group of young historians to whom I am grateful for their friendship and intellectual camaraderie. At the risk of offending by omission, I must single out Edward Baptist, Liam Riordan, Konstantin Dierks, Jacob Katz Cogan, Sarah Knott, and Tom Humphrey. Beyond the confines of the Center, during my time in Philadelphia I was fortunate to get to know Christopher Looby and Jonathan Grossman, both of whom have read my work with care and offered not only insightful commentary, but much needed moral support. In Richmond, I am especially indebted to my friends and colleagues Tom Allen, John Marx, Kathy Hewett-Smith, Doug Winiarski, and Woody Holton. I could not have asked for a more thoughtful, intelligent, and generous group of fellow faculty members. I have also been fortunate to share my work and participate in the FLEA (Fall Line Early Americanists) reading group, where, in the tradition of the best eighteenth-century salons, Tom,

Doug, and Woody as well as Mark Valeri, Teri Halperin, Marion Winship, and Phil Schwarz continue to engage in a lively exchange of ideas.

In its early phases this project received generous fellowship support from both the Mellon Foundation and the Killefor dissertation fellowship at Stanford. Along the way, my work on Paine has also benefited from a grant at the American Philosophical Society, where Roy Goodman provided both a wealth of materials and good conversation. I also presented chapters at the McNeil Center and the Omohundro Institute for Early American History and Culture, where my work was read with remarkable care and attention. A version of Chapter 1 was published in *Early American Literature* and a version of Chapter 2 appeared in the *Arizona Quarterly*, where Maja-Lisa von Snidern provided exceptionally thoughtful editorial comments and suggestions. Portions of various chapters of this book also appeared in the Broadview Press edition of *Common Sense*, which I had the good fortune to edit. I thank the editors of these journals and press for permission to reuse these materials.

At Cambridge my editor Lewis Bateman provided a steady and patient guiding hand and found two of the best anonymous readers anyone could ask for. Both of my readers provided exemplary reports that helped me restructure significant portions of the argument. I thank them for their professionalism and generous attention to my manuscript. Before any of these institutions and wonderful people helped me through this process, I had the good fortune to be brought up by two terrific parents, Cati and John Larkin, who nurtured in me the passion for learning and the fascination with politics and literature that are the foundation of my work as a scholar. Finally, I owe an enormous debt of gratitude to my best friend and life-partner Karen Kaljulaid Larkin, who saw me through this project from start to finish: Your love and support have been essential to the completion of this work. This one's for you.

Introduction

Forty-five years after the Revolution, in an 1821 letter to a friend, Thomas Jefferson commented on the remarkable literary skills of his old friend and sometime political ally, Thomas Paine: "No writer has exceeded Paine in ease and familiarity of style, in perspicuity of expression, happiness of elucidation, and in simple and unassuming language."[1] Since then, Jefferson's observation about the unique character of Paine's prose has been reiterated time and again by scholars of the Revolution. In his 1976 monograph *Tom Paine and Revolutionary America*, Eric Foner sums up this most durable critical consensus: "What made Paine unique was that he forged a new political language. He did not simply change the meanings of words, he created a literary style designed to bring his message to the widest possible audience" (xvi). Paine himself recognized the novelty of his approach to political writing. At the beginning of *Rights of Man Part II*, he explains why his immensely popular response to Edmund Burke's *Reflections on the Revolution in France* had appeared in two parts: "I wished to know the manner in which a work, written in a style of thinking and expression different to what had been customary in England, would be received before I ventured further."[2] With a style specifically designed to appeal to a wide popular audience, Paine moved away from the dominant tradition of classical rhetoric, which was an integral part of an older exclusionary political discourse, and

---

[1] Jefferson to Francis Eppes. January 19, 1821. *Thomas Jefferson: Writings*, Ed. Merrill D. Peterson. New York: Library of America, 1984, 1451.
[2] Paine, Thomas, *Complete Works*, 2 Vols., Vol. I, 348–349. All further references will be noted in the text as CW followed by the volume and page numbers.

toward a new psychology of persuasion that would define the newly emergent public sphere.

The simplicity of Paine's language is only half the story, however. Scholarly emphasis on the popularity and unvarnished style of Paine's prose has led us to overlook how well versed he was in the very classical tradition that works such as *Rights of Man* overturned. Paine's writing does not simply abjure elite prose stylings so much as appropriate them for new ends. The apparent simplicity of Paine's language belies a subtle rhetorical gambit. Paine's success was largely predicated on his ability to present sophisticated political ideas to a general readership. When, for example, Paine states, at the beginning of the third section of *Common Sense*, that "In the following pages I offer nothing more than simple facts, plain arguments, and Common sense" (17), he emphasizes the essential accessibility of his arguments. Characterized as simple, plain, and common, his ideas are available to all readers. At the same time, however, it soon becomes difficult to separate facts from arguments, and arguments from what he insists are the intuitive and self-evident perceptions of common sense. This is precisely the point: By insisting that truth is by its nature simple and universal, Paine both manipulates and politically enfranchises a new popular audience by presenting what are actually complex and rhetorically sophisticated arguments as simple facts. This did not equate to dumbing down those arguments or voiding them of nuance, but rather in fashioning a new language that presented politics in a vernacular that artisans and other middling sorts were already accustomed to reading.[3]

By altering the form of political writing, Paine also altered its content. Democracy, for example, meant something quite different to one of Paine's earliest and most persistent critics, John Adams. Shortly after the publication of *Common Sense*, Adams anonymously published his *Thoughts on Government* where he quarrels with Paine's suggestion that the United States adopt a unicameral legislature. Adams and other more conservative advocates of independence perceived Paine's government as one too beholden to the will of the people. According to this camp, the

---

[3] For a recent exception to the tendency to disregard Paine's debt to classical rhetorical traditions see Robert Ferguson, "The Commonalities of *Common Sense*." Even Ferguson in his intensive examination of Paine's pamphlet has overlooked the popular origins of much of Paine's prose. Presenting a general intellectual history of the ideas and writing strategies in *Common Sense*, Ferguson does emphasize its attempts to reach a popular audience with the plain style and with various rhetorical strategies, but he never connects Paine's prose style to the periodical literature of the day, a literature that Paine had been trained in and that his readers were consuming in ever increasing numbers.

purpose of representative democracy (and of republican forms of government more generally) is to rein in the people and allow the leaders to restrain the mob and refine its crude notions of government and justice. The difference between Adams's and Paine's respective views is apparent in the very language that they use to discuss the role of government. Not only Adams's argument but also his rhetoric is designed to limit access to an elite group. "Thoughts on Government" begins with an address to the reader that implies that only a select few are capable of understanding the workings of government:

If I was equal to the task of forming a plan for the government of a colony, I should be flattered with your request, and very happy to comply with it; because, as the divine science of politics is the science of social happiness, and the blessings of society depend entirely on the constitutions of government, which are generally institutions that last for many generations, there can be no employment more agreeable to a benevolent mind than a research after the best. (3)

By suggesting that not even he – a Harvard-educated member of the incipient New England social and political aristocracy – is privy to such knowledge (which he further mystifies with references to a divine science) Adams implicitly counters the notion that ordinary citizens might be capable of understanding how governments work. Throughout the text, moreover, Adams's authority is often established through his ability to invoke key authorities from the past, such as "Confucious, Zoroaster, Socrates and Mahomet" in one instance, or "Sidney, Harrington, Locke, Milton, Nedham, Neville, Burnet, and Hoadly" in another (5, 7). Paine's strategy, on the other hand, is to open discussions of government to the general public by presenting his arguments as ones that he had arrived at through the use of simple logic and that were not contingent on access to privileged information or education. His writings strive to educate ordinary people in the workings of the state and thus redefine the relationship between such categories as "the people," "the state," and "democratic government."

The process of inventing a more accessible and appealing political language was anything but easy. It required knowledge of political theory and classical rhetorical traditions, as well as familiarity with contemporary popular modes of writing. This book explores how Paine constructed his new literature of politics and how he successfully represented himself as both a sophisticated political theorist and a popularizer. Herein lies the real novelty of Paine's prose: Instead of subscribing to the traditional binary that counterpoised the mob and the elite, he created an idiom where politics could be simultaneously popular and thoroughly reasoned. His writing made it possible to think of a public sphere that could be democratized outside the narrow confines of a literate bourgeoisie. Through his writings, in other words, Paine turns the people into thoughtful participants in the affairs of the nation and transforms democracy from a political system into a more broadly conceived social and cultural phenomenon involving the dissemination of ideas. In his version of democracy and the public sphere, which Adams and other leaders of the Early Republic saw as a serious threat to their power, everyone is equally capable of contributing to and participating in the nation's political and cultural life. This process of making politics accessible to ordinary people involved not only the invention of a new political language but, just as importantly, the fashioning of a new kind of political actor. The object of my study is often both Paine's prose and the persona he invents for himself in that prose, a persona who could serve as a model for others to emulate in the continuing effort to mediate the elite and the common.

I approach Paine as a professional writer who produced an important corpus of writings that integrates intellectual and literary trends from both sides of the Atlantic. Although this study explores his career from a distinctly American point of view, it also places him firmly in the context of a larger culture of exchange between England, the United States, and France. Paine offers a remarkable window into a transatlantic milieu in which he moved with ease and in which he achieved enormous success. In order to attain such recognition he had to construct an authorial persona whose voice would not become too intimately linked with a particular national identity. Paine, then, becomes the purveyor of a political language as thoroughly cosmopolitan as it was democratic. First, with *Common Sense*, he would import English and Continental ideas about democracy and the terms of public debate and integrate them into the American political scene. Then in *Rights of Man* he would export this new American democracy back to Europe where he would participate in a revolution in France and attempt to spark another one in England. Through Paine we see the traffic of ideas crossing the Atlantic in both directions but, most interestingly, we see how European ideas return to the Old World in a new shape after being refashioned and reimagined in the New World.

In spite of his central role in both the American and French Revolutions, Paine remains virtually unstudied as someone who sought to make his living by his pen. As a result of the impact of works such as *Common Sense* (1776) and *The Rights of Man* (1791), historians have studied Paine's role in the American Revolution and political scientists have evaluated his contributions to political theory, but he has been largely overlooked as a literary figure.[4] In large measure this oversight can be attributed to Paine's political reputation rather than his literary skills. Most of Paine's more prominent contemporaries were at best reluctant to pursue the radical egalitarian ideas that had driven the early stages of the Revolution and that he had come to represent.[5] After his involvement in the French Revolution and the publication of *Rights of Man* and *The Age of Reason*, American Federalists sought to discredit Paine's ideas with attacks on his character. Federalists, such as Peter Porcupine (William Cobbett), spread rumors about Paine because they were fearful of the popular support his ideas enjoyed. The success of those attacks on Paine mirrors the Federalists' success in containing the radicalism of the Revolution.[6]

Not only did his more conservative contemporaries succeed in limiting Paine's impact on the institutions of the day, but they managed to persuade future generations of his marginality.[7] Whether by raising questions about his character, his nationality, or the originality of his works, Paine's detractors have often succeeded in reducing one of the most important writers and thinkers of the eighteenth century to an atheistic, drunken, ill-mannered, unoriginal, unpatriotic propagandizer. Consequently, Paine appears only briefly in most histories of the American Revolution as the author of a pivotal but controversial pamphlet. Most recent histories acknowledge that *Common Sense* played a crucial role in the early days of the Revolution, but they emphasize its controversial aspects and its

---

[4] In "The Commonalities of *Common Sense*" Ferguson too notes the absence of a body of scholarship on Paine's literary abilities (465). Paine also plays a significant role in recent books by Elizabeth Barnes and Gillian Brown but on the whole his inclusion in the literary study of the American Revolution and Early Republic is the exception rather than the norm.

[5] See Gordon Wood, *The Creation of the American Republic* for an account of the more conservative agenda that propelled the supporters of the Constitution in the years following the War of Independence.

[6] On the conservative tendency of most early interpretations of the Revolution see Young, *The Shoemaker and the Tea Party* and Kammen, *Mystic Chords of Memory*.

[7] One measure of Paine's marginality in literary history can be seen in all the major anthologies of American literature where Paine occupies only a minor section of the text. Even though *Common Sense* is relatively short, no anthology (including specialized ones dedicated to early America) reprints more than a few excerpts from the text and for the most part the rest of his writings, with the exception of *Crisis No. 1*, are completely ignored. Considering the impact of *Rights of Man* and *The Age of Reason*, these telling omissions reflect a particular notion of what constitutes American literature in the Early National period.

popularity more than its intellectual content or its effectiveness.[8] Perhaps the most insidious of these categorizations of Paine has been the emphasis on his popular appeal. By aligning Paine's writing with "the popular," scholars have trivialized his contributions to American history and literature. The popular is implicitly set in opposition to the supposedly more important and real intellectual work of the Revolution done by Adams, Jefferson, Hamilton, and Madison, who are cast as enlightened patriarchs engaged in the allegedly more complicated questions of political economy and theory. Paine's contribution to the Revolution has thus been understood in terms that immediately relegate it to a secondary role.

If Paine challenges the distinction between the popular and the intellectual, the effect of reducing him to the role of a popularizer is to agree with the Federalists and other political and cultural elites who have succeeded over the years in making these two terms antithetical to one another. Paine exposes the limitations of that logic by exploding the distinction between high and low. That is to say, he denies the validity of the distinction between high and low suggesting that these categories refer to social rather than mental distinctions. Privileging reason and experience, Paine stigmatizes the idea of learnedness as fundamentally conservative. Where Adams establishes the authority of his ideas by reference to learned sources, Paine repeatedly appeals to the reader's capacity to reason for him/herself. For example, when he is discussing the "origin and rise of government" in *Common Sense*, Paine closes his case with an appeal to the reader's intuition: "And however our eyes may be dazzled with snow, our ears deceived by sound; however prejudice may warp our wills, or interest darken our understanding, the simple voice of nature and of reason will say, it is right" (68). The truth, in other words, is liable to be distorted by a number of our faculties, but it will always be available to our reason, which he strategically aligns with the voice of nature (as opposed, of course, to the voice of culture). Hence, reason itself becomes a commonly shared sense that everyone possesses by nature.

Given his skillful and persuasive assault on one of the key foundations of elite political and social power, the effort to discredit Paine should be understood less as a personal vendetta against him and more as an attempt to undermine his project of democratizing intellectual practice. In the late nineteenth century, no less a figure than Walt Whitman would identify this very issue regarding Paine's place in American history. Whitman,

---

[8] For example see Gordon S. Wood, *Creation of the American Republic*, 93–97, and Bernard Bailyn, *Ideological Origins of the American Revolution*, 287–291.

who would challenge divisions between elite and common in his poetry, recognized the importance of Paine's legacy and sought to promote Paine as a quintessentially American figure. In his conversations with Horace Traubel, Whitman discusses Paine repeatedly. On one occasion he comments in terms that capture a sense of the way Paine's writings had posed and continued to pose a serious challenge to elite power: "The most things history has to say about Paine are damnably hideous. The polite circles of that period and later on were determined to queer the reputations of contemporary radicals – not Paine alone, but also others ... I have always determined that I would do all I could to help set the memory of Paine right" (79). Although Whitman was unable to rescue Paine's reputation, his admiration for him, and the terms of his intellectual engagement with him, suggest the degree to which Paine had become a lightning rod for questions about the place of popular democracy in the Revolution and the nature of intellectual exchange in the nation. By obviating the distinction between high and low culture, Paine offers a way out of the central dichotomies of American intellectual life over the past two centuries. To recover Paine, as Whitman recognized, is to embrace the possibilities of a broadly democratic culture.[9]

It was precisely his ability to instill a sense of enfranchisement in a popular audience that had made Paine so extraordinarily successful: By 1791 he had sold more books than anyone else in the history of publishing, and he still had not published *The Age of Reason*.[10] Although sales are not

---

[9] One of the crucial differences between Whitman and Paine, however, is that Paine never invokes the language of genius that becomes such a paradox for Whitman. A Romantic, Whitman casts himself as simultaneously common and extraordinary. Although Paine can be remarkably self-serving in his writings, he never occupies the oracular position that Whitman employs in his poems. Perhaps this signals a cultural shift in the nineteenth century that reasserted the boundaries between high and low culture. In Whitman this longing to be both representative and exceptional represents an aspiration in American culture that continues to be present but cannot be realized. Paine was not yet saddled with the Romantic aesthetic that had transformed the author into genius. Hence, he could much more easily avoid becoming entangled in the role of visionary. Paine's ability to steer clear of some of the paradoxes Whitman faced was also due to the novelty of democracy in the United States. The structures of power were still being shaped in the new nation so that it was possible to imagine possibilities for the distribution of power in the late eighteenth century that would have evaporated by the second half of the nineteenth century, when American democracy had crystallized in to a particular set of institutions. It might even be that Whitman envied Paine's historical timing as much as he admired his tenacious advocacy of participatory democracy.

[10] In her dissertation, "Virtual Nation: Local and National Cultures in the Early United States," Trish Loughran shows that most of the commonly accepted accounts of the sales figures of Paine's writings are vastly exaggerated. Paine's most recent biographer

necessarily indicative of skill, Paine's texts not only sold, they shaped the major debates of the age. Even Adams, his lifelong political antagonist, admitted that Paine had exercised an unparalleled influence on the age:

I am willing you should call this the Age of Frivolity as you do, and would not object if you had named it the Age of Folly, Vice, Frenzy, Brutality, Daemons, Buonaparte, Tom Paine, or the Age of the Burning Brand from the Bottomless Pit, or anything but the Age of Reason. I know not whether any man in the world has had more influence on its inhabitants or affairs for the last thirty years than Tom Paine. There can be no severer satyr on the age. For such a mongrel between pig and puppy, begotten by a wild boar on a bitch wolf, never before in any age of the world was suffered by the poltroonery of mankind, to run through such a career of mischief. Call it then the Age of Paine. (Hawke, 7)

In spite of his profound dislike for Paine and his radical democratic ideas, Adams envied his fame, much as he did Jefferson's. More importantly, Adams recognized that in certain ways Paine had defined the revolutionary era. In one of his most brilliant rhetorical maneuvers, Paine had given his last major work a title that corresponded to the term that was emerging as the moniker for the era, thus ensuring that his name would be permanently linked with it. Paine's strategy of naming his text *The Age of Reason* also served to empty the term and the era of its association with high rational critique, instead connecting it to his own style of narrative critique where reason, rather than being identified with learning, is set in opposition to it.

Adams's characterization of Paine's influence on the era reveals the degree to which this is fundamentally an argument about the dissemination of knowledge and its implications for the exercise of power. As Adams would have recognized, Paine's purpose in *The Age of Reason* is once again to undermine a system of ideas and a language that is organized so as to limit access to a particular kind of knowledge (in this case, religious instead of political) to a select few. In 1806, when Adams writes these words in a letter to Benjamin Waterhouse, it clearly seemed to him that Paine had succeeded in his mission to democratize reason and religion. Although *The Age of Reason* had been denounced by the official channels of religion on both sides of the Atlantic, Paine had become a crucial icon for what Nathan O. Hatch has called "the democratization of American Christianity." Important religious leaders of the early nineteenth century, such as Lorenzo Dow and William Miller may have

John Keane credits Paine's own estimate of 120,00 to 150,000 as the number of copies sold. Even taking Loughran's more conservative numbers into account, his texts enjoyed unprecedented success.

ultimately disagreed with Paine's theological views, but they fully endorsed his critique of church authority, be it in the Roman Catholic, the Anglican, or the Methodist Church.[11] The irony is that Adams shared Paine's interest in rational religion, but like so many of his counterparts in the early Republic, he was concerned about the social and political repercussions of those ideas if they were spread to the masses.[12] Adams's references to Vice, Daemons, and the Bottomless Pit are thus designed to distance Paine's religious ideas from his own. As had been the case with *Common Sense*, Adams does not want his own more genteel and learned political and religious ideas to be confused with Paine's similar but more accessible versions of the same subjects, so he amplifies the distance between them by associating Paine with enthusiasm, disorder, and immorality.

In the midst of his insults Adams pinpoints one of the essential characteristics of Paine's writing that led to his success: His ideas did not conform to traditional categories of knowledge and discourse. The fact that Adams casts that quality as a mongrelization and employs metaphors – pig and puppy, wolf and boar – that associate Paine's writing with the barnyard is a fair indication that Adams sees Paine as someone who is diluting and bastardizing elite culture. Whitman, on the other hand, admires this quality and celebrates Paine as someone who is raising up the people and tearing down the artificial barriers that have traditionally kept ordinary people out of the public sphere. Despite their differing opinions of Paine and his role in U.S. history, Adams and Whitman agree that one of the most important distinguishing characteristics of Paine's thought and writing is that he refuses to accept the conventional dichotomies that underwrite traditional structures of authority. Not only does Paine reject

[11] In his closing observations to *The Democratization of American Christianity*, Hatch comments more broadly on Paine's cultural significance: "Nourished by sources as contradictory as George Whitefield and Tom Paine, many deeply religious people were set adrift from ecclesiastical establishments at the same time they demanded that the church begin living up to its spiritual promise" (225). In *Democratization* Hatch also discusses Lorenzo Dow's interest in Paine. On William Miller's deist phase see Wayne R. Judd, "William Miller, Disappointed Prophet." In *Joseph Smith and the Beginnings of Mormonism*, Richard Bushman points out that in his youth Smith studied Paine too.

[12] For an account of Adams's intellectual and religious commitments to the philosophical rationalism of the American Enlightenment see C. Bradley Thompson, "Young John Adams and the New Philosophic Rationalism." Through a careful analysis of Adams's diary, Thompson demonstrates that Adams, who has often been described by historians as a Puritan, actually "repudiated the orthodoxies of New England Puritanism" in favor of "a view of nature, man, and moral obligation that drew heavily on the enlightened views of Francis Bacon, Isaac Newton, and John Locke" (262).

the distinction between high and low culture, he also assails the binaries of public and private, entertainment and instruction, theoretical science (physics and astronomy) and common science (mechanics). Throughout his career Paine also denounces easy dichotomies in genre (that is, history, letter, narrative, and criticism), human psychology (feeling, fancy, understanding, passion, and reason), and, most spectacularly, reason and revelation.

Paine was not the first, or perhaps the most subtle and sophisticated, critic of any one of these dichotomies, but he intuited the links between them in ways that other thinkers had not. He did not see them as isolated instances, but rather as symptoms of a larger invisible system of thought. The principal purpose of these dichotomies was to exclude the mass of the people from power. Paine, therefore, would fuse the high and the low, politics and literature, reason and religion, and other such dichotomies as a means to dismantle the structures that underwrite elite intellectual and political power. The way to supplant the old divisions is to replace them with hybrid forms that reconnect the very elements the old forms had dichotomized. In a sense Paine's thinking represents the fusion of form and content writ large. This is precisely the point where literature and politics meet: where language directly shapes the exercise of power in the world. Paine writes texts that demonstrate how that language and those structures of power create an illusion of inevitabiltity to secure the status of the elites. They make it seem as if the current system is the product of a natural rather than an artificial process. In a fundamental sense, Paine's project partakes of the same philosophical and historical impulses that impelled Locke, Rousseau, Ferguson, and others to study the origins of the social and political systems in the eighteenth century.

At the same time that he denounces these essentialized dichotomies,[13] Paine insists upon simplicity as a fundamental value. At first blush, his appeal to simplicity may seem antithetical to the work of unmasking the falsity of the basic substructure of Western social, religious, and political authority, but his point, from *Common Sense*'s claims about the British constitutional monarchy to *The Age of Reason*'s account of revealed religion, is that these dichotomies have rendered the world (government, religion, politics, society, and so on) unnecessarily complex by creating a tangled web of artificial systems to prop up the elite's claim to preeminence. Reverting to common-sensical ideas of social and political relations

---

[13] Essentialized because they have become accepted as facts when, as Paine demonstrates, they are merely theories or constructs.

thus constitutes a simplification: It peels away all the layers upon layers of artifice that maintain the status quo. The most obvious and systematic example of Paine's effort to expose the fictions that prop up elite power is *The Age of Reason*, but that instance is only a crystallization of what he had been doing from the outset. He sets out to reveal how systems like the English constitution or institutional forms of Christianity organize the world through a series of pseudo-bureaucratic systems that in turn require other systems to explain the workings of the first iteration, and so on and so forth. Soon the distance from the original to the commonly disseminated version becomes so mediated that we can only see through a glass darkly. One of the most important effects of this structure of knowledge is that it then requires experts to decode, govern, and adjudicate how the rules of the system will work. In lieu of such arcana, Paine proposes models of government and religion that are transparent such that no specialized knowledge is required to understand and implement them. Thus the dichotomizers lose their power to shape the world and define themselves as the rightful possessors of the hidden laws of the universe.

Adams, to his credit, understood this about Paine before just about anyone else. This is why he would identify Paine as the chief architect of everything he abhorred about the late eighteenth century. Paine had to be demonized and dismissed because his ideas threatened the very foundations upon which Adams and his fellow elites' power was built. In spite of a recent surge of interest in him, Paine remains a minor player in contemporary political, historical, and literary interpretations of the Revolution in large part because he continues to pose as much of a threat to elite intellectual and political power today as he did in 1776.

Tracing Paine's career as a writer from his first days as the editor of the *Pennsylvania Magazine* through his enormous success with *Common Sense, Rights of Man,* and *The Age of Reason,* this book explores Paine's writings through their relationship to and role in many of the central cultural, social, economic, and political debates of the day. I focus principally on his participation in and relationship to the late eighteenth century transatlantic world of print, what has been called the Republic of Letters. Print culture and the Republic of Letters, while not exactly interchangeable, both refer more generally to the structures of exchange, production, and consumption of writing that took hold in the eighteenth century. Driven as much by the modernization of print technologies as by the rise of a culture of reading and transformations in political and social hierarchies, the new world of print that emerged during the enlightenment had its own rules of engagement and protocols for participation. The

Republic of Letters, as Dena Goodman has put it, "had a political culture constructed out of discursive practices and institutions that shaped the actions, verbal and otherwise, of the people to whose lives it gave structure, meaning, and purpose" (1). Paine's approach to writing can best be understood through an analysis of his participation in the various debates in which his texts are produced. Those debates, I am suggesting, are often just as much about authorship and the dissemination of ideas as they are about the nature of government.

The analysis presented here is guided not by chronological, ideological (in the sense of the history of ideas), or biographical concerns, but rather by the imperative to analyze Paine's writings as a series of public interventions. One of the meta-narratives of this study is Paine's relationship to the public sphere, as originally theorized by Jürgen Habermas and developed in an American context by critics such as Michael Warner and David Shields.[14] Paine's relationship to the public sphere was marked by a great deal of ambiguity. Throughout his career he would frequently critique the very public sphere that intellectuals like him helped to create. Thus, Paine's own interventions in the public sphere are often ambiguous and even incoherent. His rhetoric and the needs of his work pull him in different directions, sometimes toward an emphasis on the personal and others toward a focus on ideas. The tensions within Paine's relationship to the public sphere illustrate the degree to which in the late eighteenth century the public sphere had not solidified into a static ahistorical formation with clear rules of engagement and a coherent structure. Instead, Paine was a major participant in the vigorous and contentious debates over the shape of the public sphere that took place in the Early Republic as members of various different political, social, and economic interests competed for control over this important space. Each of the chapters of the book traces a particular concern or set of issues that Paine addressed at various points in his career and explores how those debates came to shape his rhetoric, arguments, and textual self-presentation.

A second strand organizing the chapters is the notion that he became interested in or engaged with a particular rhetoric – magazine writing,

---

[14] Let me clarify my use of the term "public sphere" here. The public sphere is Jürgen Habermas' term for the Republic of Letters. In Habermas' formulation it is set in opposition to the government and other forms of state-controlled media. I have chosen to use public sphere instead of Republic of Letters primarily because that is the term that has been used most persistently in the American context. As I will explain more fully in Chapter 2, I take the public sphere to represent an idea, perhaps even an ideal, more than an actual phenomenon.

historical writing, and scientific discourse – at given moments in his career.
This is not to say that there weren't other issues, ideological, political,
rhetorical, or otherwise, that shaped his writings, or that these issues didn't
persist across his career, but that at certain moments in his career Paine
became more intensely interested in particular rhetorical forms and those
come to influence his texts in specific ways. Therefore, I am suggesting
that Paine's prose was a product partly of his involvement in the key
debates of his era and also of his intellectual interest in various kinds of
popularly consumed writing. Through an analysis of his engagement with
these rhetorics and debates, around which I have organized the chapters
of this book, I investigate what was different about Paine's style and
language, and how he arrived at what he insisted, and his contemporaries
recognized, was a new mode of writing.

Chapter 1 challenges the remarkably persistent notion that Paine
emerged on the American scene as if from nowhere to publish *Common
Sense,* and then, just as suddenly, disappeared.[15] In truth, Paine first rose
to prominence as an editor of a magazine and did not leave Philadelphia
until over a decade later, when his desire to revolutionize Europe took him
back to the Old World in 1787.[16] In the opening chapter of the book I
examine the impact that Paine's tenure at the *Pennsylvania Magazine* had
on his approach to writing. The significance of his stint as an editor is perhaps the most overlooked aspect of Paine's emergence as a major figure in
revolutionary America.[17] It is difficult to imagine him writing *Common
Sense* without this earlier experience. Prior to arriving in Philadelphia in
1774, Paine had very little practice as a writer. While in England he had
been an active member of a voluntary association, The Headstrong Club,
where members debated current issues and probably circulated occasional

---

[15] In his article on Paine, even Ferguson marvels that "Somehow, after a scant twelve months
in colonial Philadelphia . . . he taught himself to write a previously unimagined story about
a better and decidedly new world" (472).
[16] Even after his return to Europe, however, he strongly identified with America, where he
would return after the conclusion of the French Revolution.
[17] For example, despite recognizing this period's crucial role in Paine's development as a
writer, Keane, who is most interested in Paine as a political figure, dedicates only a
brief section of his otherwise very thorough biography to assessing the impact of this
experience of Paine. Commenting on the significance of Paine's term as editor of Aitken's
magazine, Keane has observed, "Paine's involvement with *The Pennsylvania Magazine*
served as a literary apprenticeship. He was allowed to experiment with different ways
of writing, and his role brought him into contact with a rich variety of ideas and forms
of writing that stimulated his restless mind." Keane's discussion of Paine's editorship,
however, is largely bibliographical in nature, documenting which items were authored
by Paine and his motivations for writing them.

manuscripts. He also might have published a few minor items in the local Sussex newspaper.[18] His most significant work while in England was a pamphlet on behalf of his fellow excisemen appealing to the British government for improved wages and working conditions. While these experiences helped Paine establish his credentials, it was as editor of the *Pennsylvania Magazine* that Paine came to conceive of himself more seriously as a professional writer.

Not only did editing a magazine allow him to develop his rhetorical skills and acquire the knowledge about colonial American politics that would enable him to write *Common Sense*, but it also provided him with an audience, a public whose opinion he would manipulate and claim to represent. Just as much as his editorship of the *Pennsylvania Magazine* prepared Paine to write *Common Sense*, it prepared a public for his pamphlet. By the time *Common Sense* was published in January 1776, a key segment of Philadelphia readers had been educated in the rhetorical and argumentative modes Paine had learned to employ in the magazine. If *Common Sense* marked Paine's debut into the world of American politics, it also signaled his formal entry into the Republic of Letters. Although his writings in England and the *Pennsylvania Magazine* had constituted a contribution to the world of print, these were distinctly local interventions. *Common Sense* inaugurated Paine's career as a national and international voice.

Paine's ideas about print and the way it could structure social and political relations differed significantly from those of his mentor in Philadelphia, Ben Franklin. Paine, in fact, offers a remarkable contrast to Franklin, who has become the exemplary instance of the eighteenth-century American man of letters. Not only was Paine skeptical of the relationship between authors and printers, a subject he addressed with some frequency in both public and private writings, but he openly challenged the protocols of the Republic of Letters. In *The Letters of the Republic* Michael Warner offers an account of the development of the public sphere in the colonial and Early National period from the perspective of the printer.[19] In spite of our eagerness to claim Franklin as an early American author, we must not

---

[18] Keane, who identified some of these pieces in his biography, cautions, however, that there is no direct evidence that Paine authored these articles in the *Sussex Weekly Advertiser*. Their style and tone, however, correspond to Paine's. Keane also discusses Paine's participation in the Headstrong Club at greater length.

[19] Warner, for example, places a great deal of emphasis on the Zenger case and on Franklin's career. They serve as the crucial foundation for his later arguments about the belletristic texts that occupy the last couple of chapters of the book.

forget that he was first and foremost a printer. Paine, on the other hand, was first a writer and one who frequently felt oppressed by the demands of his printers. Consequently he viewed print culture and the public sphere very differently from Franklin, who had become quite wealthy thanks to his printing business. Franklin's best interests were served by a lively public debate wherein authority lay in the text and not in specific authors. Impersonality served the printer well because, ultimately, it shifted authority to them, and relegated the author to the part of a producer of words. To Paine, the polemical writer, it was crucial that authority be connected to the author.

When *Common Sense* unexpectedly became a sensation Paine suddenly turned into a significant figure in the Revolution. In the months following the publication of *Common Sense*, Paine's arguments came under intense attack in the Philadelphia press as a variety of loyalists attempted to counteract the success of Paine's pamphlet. He vigorously defended his arguments and in the process continued to build a public persona. That Paine was self-conscious about his self-representation is evident in the ways he foregrounded questions of authorial intent and sincerity in his *Forester's Letters* and in *The Crisis*. Chapter 2 focuses on the character of Paine's relationship to the press and the public. Paine was intensely aware of the degree to which the structure of the various relationships within the Republic of Letters (authors to printers, readers to authors, texts to printers, readers and authors, and so on) organized particular relationships of authority that could be more or less democratic according to how they were configured. Consequently, he would return to these issues throughout his career.

I begin by observing that in spite of the great success of his writings Paine never enjoyed much personal popularity. Unlike other major figures of the era, such as Franklin, Jefferson, and Madison, who were admired for their roles in the Revolution, Paine was more often an object of scorn and derision. I argue that Paine's failure to gain a cult of personality, ironically, stemmed from the same reason why he was so successful as a writer: that is, his unwillingness to accept one of the foundational principles of the Republic of Letters, the distinction between measures and men. Comparing his approach to public self-representation to Franklin's, I demonstrate that Paine's failure to adopt an impersonal mode of discourse when participating in political debates through the press doomed his public image. Paine recognized that separating a consideration of authors from the ideas they advance would allow the elites to retain control over the public sphere by encouraging the notion that they were disinterested writers. This was, after all, the republican public sphere and one of the fundamental tenets of classical republicanism was that only the wealthy, who were disburdened of the day-to-day financial concerns that affected the common people, were truly disinterested. Paine's refusal, however, to distinguish between measures and men and his insistent use of the *ad hominem*, made him an effective polemicist, but they also made him an easy target when his own character became the subject of public scrutiny. Thus, Paine's public political discourse led him to construct an authorial identity that was powerful for the immediate occasion but too personal for his own popularity. While he often succeeded in persuading other people to adopt the measures he supported, his methods insured that his success would not make him one of the heroes of the American War of Independence.

At the same time that he was working to create and control an effective textual persona, Paine was also eager to gain more control over the rights to his writings. In a print culture where authors were reduced to a secondary role in the commercial exchange between printers and readers, Paine became a strong advocate of the copyright.[20] In his efforts to secure copyright protection for authors, Paine repeatedly identifies his texts as literature. He articulates a broad understanding of literature in a footnote to the "Introduction" of the *Letter to Raynal* where he comments specifically on the place of literature and the role it has played in the United States. He attributes the dearth of writers in the new nation to the absence of any intellectual property laws:

The state of literature in America must one day become the subject of legislative consideration. Hitherto it has been a disinterested volunteer in the service of the Revolution, and no man thought of profits: but when peace shall give time and opportunity for study the country will deprive itself of the honor and service of letters and the improvement of science, unless sufficient laws are made to prevent depradations on literary property. (CW II, 213)

The "it" of the second sentence could just as easily be substituted with an "I," for Paine was very conscious of his financial situation since he had never sought remuneration for his writings at the time of publication. He had sacrificed personal gain in order to maximize the distribution of his texts, but now that he felt the cause had been successfully attained, Paine was eager to protect his interest as an author.

The notion of an author's right to his works was so important to Paine, who at this very moment was seeking compensation for his services on

---

[20] For a more comprehensive analysis of the structure of power and commercial relations in the eighteenth-century world of print see Mark Rose, *Authors and Owners*.

behalf of the American cause, because his writings and his ideas constituted the extent of his property. Two years earlier he had written to his friend Henry Laurens about his plan to publish a collection of his writings: "I intend this winter to collect all my publication, beginning with *Common Sense* and ending with the Fisheries, and publishing them in two volumes, octavo, with notes. I have no doubt of a large subscription" (1179). Broke and feeling unappreciated as a result of his controversial, and unsuccessful, attempt to expose Silas Deane for embezzling money from Congress,[21] Paine sees this as an opportunity to finally make a little money off of his hugely popular writings. Unfortunately, the dearth of paper in Philadelphia at the time insured that this plan would not come to fruition. Paine, however, was well aware of the fact that his literary talents were his best financial resource. In the course of this letter to Laurens, Paine also comments on his vocational status: "I know but one kind of life I am fit for, and that is a thinking one, and, of course, a writing one – but I have confined myself so much of late, taken so little exercise, and lived so very sparingly, that unless I alter my way of life it will alter me" (CW, 1178). Given his reliance on writing, it was only natural that Paine would vocally support protection for authors. Paine, thus, not only wrote popular and influential works, but he identified himself publicly as a professional writer.

Once the War of Independence had concluded, Paine was forced to seek ways to generate interest in his publications. One approach was to capitalize on his role in the Revolution by writing a history of it. For him this was not only a financial opportunity but also a political one. Although much of the rhetoric of *Common Sense* emphasized the colonists' right to independence on the basis of natural developmental and political representational concerns, to Paine the most important aspect of the Revolution was that it instituted a democratic government in place of the prior monarchical one. In order to insure that the fundamental change in form of government be recognized as the truly revolutionary part of the American War of Independence, he repeatedly emphasized the need for a proper history of the recent events, a project he wished to undertake. Chapter 3 argues that Paine's *Letter to Raynal*, although it has not been recognized as such, constitutes his history of the American Revolution. In order to write his own history of the Revolution, Paine

---

[21] For a more detailed analysis of Paine's notorious public dispute with Silas Deane, known at the time as the Deane Affair, and its impact on Paine's career and public image, see Chapter 2.

recast historiography as a form of literary criticism. Paine's preoccupation with history would later find its most potent expression in *Rights of Man, Part 1*. This chapter demonstrates how *The Letter to Raynal* anticipates many of the argumentative strategies Paine employed to great effect in *Rights of Man*.

The other major project that Paine undertook at this time in his ongoing effort to raise some income was to design a method for constructing iron bridges. Not only would these bridges be able to span wider rivers, but they would be more durable than the traditional wooden model. Thus, Paine, like many of his fellow American revolutionaries, actively pursued scientific endeavors. He spent most of the decade following the conclusion of the War of Independence attempting to perfect his design. As a result, he was very much aware of the important methodological changes taking place in science. In the eighteenth century, science had evolved from a private endeavor practiced exclusively by gentlemen to a more democratic and thoroughly public activity, with experiments being conducted for profit in coffeehouses and itinerant lecturers earning a living explaining Newtonian science to middling sorts. The popularization of science granted scientific language and metaphors a great deal of cultural authority in the eighteenth century. In Chapter 4, I demonstrate how mechanical and other scientific metaphors inform Paine's post-Revolutionary writings, especially *Rights of Man* and *The Age of Reason*. Paine, however, did not simply incorporate scientific and technological metaphors into his texts, these discourses reshaped his thinking. Rather than serving as an adjunct to his work, scientific reasoning occupies a central place in *Rights of Man* and *Age of Reason*, texts in which he attempts to elaborate a science of politics and of religion, respectively.

If the tale of Paine's arrival on the scene of American history has been characterized by mystery, his disappearance in the historical accounts of the era is equally intriguing. The reasons for Paine's marginalization, particularly in light of his remarkable impact, are intimately linked with the historical needs of the new nation and our continuing failure to move beyond the political and cultural agenda that was set in the early republic, specifically the project of constructing a native history and culture that would define the United States as fundamentally different from the rest of the world.[22] In order to construct the new nation as a unique historical

---

[22] For a more thorough account of early national interpretations of the Revolution see Alfred Young, *The Shoemaker and the Tea Party* and Michael Kammen, *Mystic Chords of Memory*.

case, historians of the early republic emphasized the differences between American society and European society in the years leading up to the revolution. This historical exceptionalism was accompanied by the attempt to identify cultural traditions distinct from European forms, in this case an American literature that would not be perceived as derivative of English letters.[23]

The nationalist aims of this cultural project also required that the authors of these particularly American works be readily identifiable as Americans. Paine suffered both because he was perceived to be an Englishman, not an American, and also because his radical political goals were international in nature and not limited to the British-American colonies' goal of independence. Furthermore, the reinterpretation of the Revolution as a less radical or threatening event almost necessitated his exclusion. Paine, in other words, did not fit into the grand narrative of American history and culture constructed in the early nineteenth century to differentiate Americans from their European counterparts, stabilize the elites' control of national politics, and underwrite the expansionist aims of the young republic. Instead, Paine repeatedly asserted the commonality between Europeans and Americans. One of his most famous aphorisms in *Common Sense*, "The cause of America is in a great measure the cause of all mankind" (CW 1, 3), implies precisely the kind of shared agenda that American exceptionalists have attempted to erase. Ultimately for Paine the American Revolution was important not for its nationalistic import but for its larger significance:

> The independence of America, considered merely as a separation from England, would have been a matter but of little importance, had it not been accompanied by a revolution in the principles and practice of governments. She made a stand, not for herself only, but for the world, and looked beyond the advantages herself could receive. (CW 1, 354)

In *Rights of Man* and *The Age of Reason* Paine essayed to extend the effects of the American Revolution to overcome cultural and social as well as national boundaries. If he was going to succeed in reproducing his American success in England and France, he needed to emphasize the similarities between Europe and the United States.[24]

---

[23] For an account of the enduring claims of American exceptionalism see Michael Kammen, "The Problem of American Exceptionalism: A Reconsideration," *American Quarterly* 45, 1 (March 1993): 1–43.

[24] Ironically, these similarities had made it possible for him to establish his voice as an advocate of democratic revolution in the American colonies in the first place because

Chapter 5 traces Paine's depiction in the various biographies of him published in the late eighteenth and nineteenth centuries in order to show how the process of writing him out of American history took shape. The first biography of Paine, commissioned by a British ministry eager to discredit the author of *Rights of Man*, was published in England in 1791 and it set the tone for most of the early accounts of his life. Like Adams' recollection of Paine in his journal, the strategy of this biographer is to emphasize Paine's commonness by focusing on his family's socio-economic origins, and his his allegedly coarse personal habits and mercurial character. These attacks are designed to ensure that Paine not be recognized in elite cultural and political circles. As the chapter will show, his biographers link his prose style and arguments to his person, thus implying that if the man is lowly, coarse, and vicious then so must his writings be. Although the controversial nature of his writings and his refusal to contradict the allegations made about his personal behavior may have contributed to his negative public image, I argue that Paine's status as a professional writer not only made him particularly vulnerable to personal attacks, but also led to his marginalization as a historical and literary figure.

In a similar vein, the book concludes with an Epilogue that explores how Paine was viewed by several key nineteenth-century American literary figures. Touching on Royall Tyler's and Walt Whitman's respective views of Paine, the focal point of the Epilogue is Herman Melville's *Billy Budd* where Paine, as the author of *The Rights of Man* in particular, makes a crucial appearance. My reading of *Billy Budd* foregrounds the references to Paine as a key to unlocking the political message of Melville's enigmatic tale. For Melville, Paine becomes emblematic of the inner conflicts of the Revolution and the nation's ultimate betrayal of the democratic ideals that had sparked the transformations of political and social systems on both sides of the Atlantic. More generally, the chapter shows how Paine's legacy, while sometimes in the background, persisted well into the nineteenth century.

My aim throughout this book is to reconstruct Paine's literary career and trace his development as a writer. Because studies of Paine have often focused on a particular text or debate in which he participated, we get the

---

they enabled him to readily understand the issues at stake in the colonial situation. Had the political and social atmosphere in eighteenth-century England been radically different from that of the British-American colonies, Paine would not have been able to make such a fluid transition into the political milieu of revolutionary Philadelphia.

impression that Paine emerged full blown with a completely developed prose style that he simply deployed over and over in his various publications from 1776 through 1806, when he stopped publishing. Instead, I hope to present the development of a clever and flexible writer whose prose evolved as a reflection of his changing interests, according to the issues at hand, and the audience(s) he wished to reach. Although this book often deals with questions of intellectual history and literary biography, it is fundamentally a study in the workings of print culture. By exploring the career of one of its most successful (and infamous) participants, we learn about what it meant to write and be a writer in the late eighteenth century republic of letters. From this perspective, although he did not primarily write fiction or poetry, the challenges Paine faced did not differ greatly from the obstacles Hannah Foster, Susanna Rowson, or Charles Brockden Brown encountered over the course of their literary careers. More importantly, studying Paine teaches us important lessons about the way ideas and books were exchanged, shaped, and disseminated at the time. My story begins with a novice magazine editor learning his craft in revolutionary Philadelphia.

I

Inventing an American Public

The Pennsylvania Magazine *and Revolutionary American Political Discourse*

The July 1775 issue of the *Pennsylvania Magazine*, edited by Thomas Paine, opens with an essay, "Observations on the Military Character of Ants," that purportedly investigates a new aspect of the nature of ants. The author, who writes under the pseudonym Curioso, observes that generally ants are cited only for their "industry and economy," but that "we have neglected to consider them as patriots jealous of their natural rights, and as champions in the defence of them" (295). He then relates his observations of the interactions between a colony of red ants and one of brown ants that inhabit his yard. The reds are portrayed as seeking to deprive the browns of their natural rights thereby forcing the browns to war,

A war which the browns were driven into by the overbearing insolence of the reds, and obliged to undertake for the protection of their settlement. Had they passively submitted, they might have again been treated in the same manner [deprived of their property], and have wearied out their lives in building cities for others to take from them. (299–300)

The red ants are clearly identified with the British redcoats in this article, which uses the author's observations about ants as an occasion to justify the American colonies' right to raise an army to defend their property. Curioso ends his article by providing the moral to this story of the conflict between the two ant colonies: "A nation without defence is like a handsome woman without virtue, the easiness of the approach invites the ravager. And for the same reason that we ought not to tempt a thief by leaving our doors unlocked, we ought not to tempt an army of them by leaving a country or a coast unguarded" (300). Curioso thus suggests that the colonies should protect themselves from the British, characterized as thieves and invaders, if they wish to retain their freedom and property. An army here also becomes a masculine analogue to female chastity, serving as a means of protection rather than aggression and, consequently, the call for the colonies to raise an army is translated into an act of virtue, or, more precisely, into virtue itself.[1]

A few pages later, an article seemingly about matters of domestic comfort, "An Easy Method to Prevent the Increase of Bugs," continues the analogy of the British with bugs. In this brief item the writer suggests that his method of eradicating household bugs might also be used as a tactic to defeat General Gage's army: "if the communication could be cut off between the bed and the floor and wainscot, these gentry, like Gen. Gage's army, by being excluded from fresh provision, would be starved out" (305). By this time fighting had begun in Massachusetts and General Gage, commander of the British army in that colony, had attempted to quell the rebel outbreak.[2] While neither article overtly states a political position, they each clearly express anti-British sentiments. Under Paine's editorship the articles printed in the *Pennsylvania Magazine* rarely engage the political events and issues of the time directly; instead, the writers displace them onto other subjects, such as natural history, thus employing a strategy that enables them to address the significant ideological issues of the revolutionary period allegorically. Insofar as it naturalized politics, by making it part of the everyday, this strategy was designed to render politics more accessible to certain readers. However, it did not reach all readers, as is illustrated by one reader's response to "An Easy Method." Noting the difficulty of the method proposed in the article, the anonymous letter writer suggests that his wife's method, namely cleanliness, would be a more effective solution to the problem. By focusing on the literal meaning of the article the reader has entirely missed the significance of the reference to General Gage's army in the original piece.

---

[1] In *Common Sense* Paine would return to this sexual analogy only to make the opposite point: "Can ye give prostitution its former innocence? Neither can ye reconcile Britain and America.... As well can the lover forgive the ravisher of his mistress, as the continent forgive the murders of Britain" (CW I, 30). Unlike Curioso's version of the feminized nation, where America can regain her virtue by raising an army, Paine's does not allow for a restoration of virtue. The difference, of course, is that Curioso's account focuses on each party's behavior, whereas Paine's deals with the nature of the relationship between them.

[2] On April 18–19 American rebels confronted General Gage's army when he attempted to seize rebel weapons and ammunition stored in Concord, just outside of Boston. In June of 1775 British and American troops faced one another in the Battle of Bunker Hill, generally considered the first battle of the Revolution.

Nevertheless, by contextualizing political discussion in such a way that it would not preclude the participation of any particular sector of the reading public, as editor of the *Pennsylvania Magazine* Paine attempted to make politics and political action available to a broader segment of the population than was previously thought desirable or imagined possible. For much of the eighteenth century access to the public sphere was largely restricted to the members of an elite class who were learned in the rhetorical forms appropriate for any discussion of civic affairs (Cmiel, 31). Prior to Paine, colonial American writers, most notably John Adams and John Dickinson, had advocated the need for an informed citizenry, but in *Common Sense* Paine would be the first to write to and for the common people as participants in the political issues of the day.[3] As Paine's most recent biographer has noted, through his works Paine "invented a plain style crafted to capture the attention, and secure the trust, of audiences previously accustomed to being pushed about or ignored, not being written for, talked about, and taken seriously as active citizens" (Keane, x). The key for Paine was to discover a way to mobilize these people. In essence, Paine sought to expand the "public" included under the rubric of the "public sphere" to make it more representative of the general population, that is, more democratic.

Paine, however, did not merely "secure the trust" of an already existing audience, he invented a public that he could then claim to represent in his writings. In his critique of Jürgen Habermas's description of the public sphere, Keith Michael Baker contends that " 'Public opinion' took form as a political or ideological construct, rather than as a discrete sociological referent" (172). Paine, it seems to me, bears out Baker's argument that the eighteenth-century version of public opinion, the tangible manifestation of the public sphere, should be understood as a political invention (Baker, 168). This chapter will explore how Paine went about constructing a particular version of the public, which would then provide him with a legitimating constituency. The public whose opinion Paine wished to represent and enfranchise was significantly different from the public that was typically included in eighteenth-century political debates. As Richard Brown has shown, in the middle of the eighteenth century the lower ranks were still generally denied a public voice in the political debates of the age:

---

[3] In *The Strength of a People* Richard D. Brown provides an insightful account of the process whereby common people were slowly included in the realm of politics. Regarding Paine's role in this process Brown notes, "The innovations in Paine's pamphlet presumed an audience of politically interested common men, not an elevated citizenry of gentlemen and masters of business" (64).

"Common people should be sufficiently educated so as to value subordination and deference over the siren calls of demagogues, but they should not be so well informed that they would dare to judge public affairs on their own" (43–44). In order to expand the public sphere to make it more accessible to common people, Paine had to invent a language that would represent them as legitimate participants in the public sphere. This chapter argues that Paine's acute understanding of the nature of the public sphere as an invention, and his ability to manipulate public opinion was by no means accidental; on the contrary, it was intimately linked to his training as a magazine editor, his conception of writing, and his self-identification as a professional political writer.

THE RISE OF THE MAGAZINE

As editor of the *Pennsylvania Magazine* Paine not only contributed to the continuing development of the magazine in America, he also inherited a tradition, however short, of a particular kind of writing with a specific goal. The magazine emerged in the eighteenth century out of the same circumstances that resulted in the rise of the novel. In *Before Novels*, his study of the literary historical context that led to the emergence of the novel, J. Paul Hunter discusses various new types of publications that were produced by the ferment of eighteenth-century print culture. Hunter observes that in early eighteenth-century England, "New readers, new modes of literary production, changing tastes, and a growing belief that traditional forms and conventions were too constrained and rigid to represent modern reality or to reach modern readers collaborated to mean – in the eyes of both proponents and critics – that much modern writing was taking radical new directions" (10). These alterations, Hunter notes, led to an explosion of new types of publications intended to take advantage of the potential new market of readers.

Strangely, Hunter does not include the magazine, one of the most popular and durable print inventions of the early eighteenth century, in his discussion of the novel publications of the era. The magazine exemplified many of the tendencies of the period that Hunter alludes to in his discussion of the changing world of print:

In the mixture of journalism and conversation, print record and loose talk, fiction and fact, informed opinion and baseless speculation, the oral and written cultures dramatically meet and interact in the coffeehouse milieu, reflecting changes in the larger world and demonstrating not only how quickly booksellers had learned to exploit the daily possibilities of print but also how 'talk' and the current opinion joined and enlarged the cycle of 'now' consciousness. (175)

Hunter's description of the results of the convergence of oral and written cultures could also be used to describe the early magazine, which sought to combine essays on a wide spectrum of subjects with entertainment. If the coffeehouse's combination of a cacophony of voices and a multiplicity of topics served as the ideal model for innovative publishers in the eighteenth century, then the magazine, whose distinguishing characteristics were precisely the broad spectrum of topics addressed, its numerous contributors, and its accessibility to the general public, provided a natural print analogue to the discourse of the coffeehouse.[4]

The magazine was invented in 1731, by Edward Cave, a London printer and publisher who had worked for various newspapers prior to setting up for himself. Cave, sometime printer, journalist, and postal clerk, purchased his own printing office in 1731, and shortly thereafter began publishing the *Gentleman's Magazine; or Trader's Monthly Intelligencer*. Cave's use of the word "magazine" to identify his publication was altogether new. Prior to 1731, the word "magazine," according to the OED, referred to "a place where goods are laid up; a storehouse or repository for goods or merchandise," whereas periodical publications were generally called journals or miscellanies. In the Introduction to the first issue of his magazine Cave refers to his new application of the word: "This Consideration has induced several Gentlemen to promote a Monthly Collection, to treasure up, as in a Magazine, the most remarkable Pieces on the Subjects abovemention'd, or at least impartial Abridgments thereof, as a Method much better calculated to preserve those Things that are curious, than that of transcribing them" (January, 1731, n.p.). Cave's magazine would thus share in the word's original meaning, but instead of containing goods or merchandise, his magazine would serve as a repository of a new kind of product, information, which had become an important commodity in eighteenth-century Europe.[5]

Cave's magazine took the form of a collection of information and entertainment ranging over a wide variety of topics and united under one cover.

---

[4] On the significance of coffeehouses and taverns in Early America see David W. Conroy, *In Public Houses*.

[5] In his *Structural Transformation of the Public Sphere* Jürgen Habermas attributes the expansion of print culture and reading audiences in the early eighteenth century to the growth of the European commercial empires, which, in turn, depended for their success on timely and accurate news. In Habermas's words, "For the traffic in news developed not only in connection with the needs of commerce; the news itself became a commodity" (21).

His motto for the *Gentleman's Magazine*, "E Pluribus Unum," captures this sense of his publication as a collection of diverse materials stored in one place.[6] Cave envisioned his magazine as a remedy for the problems created by the proliferation of newspapers during the period:

> Upon calculating the Number of News-Papers, 'tis found that (besides divers written Accounts) no less than 200 Half-sheets a month are thrown from the Press only in London, and about as many printed elsewhere in the Three Kingdoms; a considerable part of which constantly exhibit Essays on various Subjects for Entertainment; and all the rest occasionally oblige their Readers with matters of Public concern, communicated to the World by Persons of Capacity thro' their, Means: so that they are become the chief Channels of Amusement and Intelligence. But then being only loose Papers, uncertainly scatter'd about, it often happens, that many things deserving Attention, contained in them, are only seen by Accident, and others not sufficiently publish'd or preserved for universal Benefit and Information. (January 1731, "Introduction," n.p.)

More significant than its centralizing mission, however, was the *Gentleman's Magazine*'s inclusion of essays and news on a wide variety of subjects. The practice of anthologizing the best pieces from other publications was common by the first decade of the eighteenth century, but the literary miscellanies and historical journals that engaged in this practice only published essays that fell under the rubric of their respective areas of interest, be they politics, poetry, or historical essays. In other words, literary miscellanies did not print items from the news, or historical essays, and, likewise, historical journals did not print literary works; instead, each area of knowledge was treated separately in its own journals.

Cave, however, set out to produce a publication that would not be limited by subject or other forms of boundaries: His magazine would print interesting items on a broad range of subjects. The inclusiveness of Cave's publication is evidenced in his advertisement announcing the new *Gentleman's Magazine* where he lists the variety of subjects to be treated in it:

> Publick Affairs, Foreign and Domestick,
> Births, Marriages, and Deaths of Eminent Persons,
> Preferments, Ecclesiastical and Civil.
> Prices of Goods, Grains and Stocks.

[6] Cave borrowed the motto "E Pluribus Unum" from Peter Motteaux's earlier publication the *Gentleman's Journal*. For more on the connections between Cave and Motteaux's respective publications see Carlson's *The First Magazine*, 29–58. Jay Fliegelman has discussed the later adoption of Cave's publication's motto for the United States; see *Declaring Independence*, 173.

Bankrupts declar'd and Books Publish'd
Pieces of Humor and Poetry
Disputes in Politicks and Learning
Remarkable Advertisements and Occurrences.
Lists of the Civil and Military Establishment.
And whatever is worth quoting from the
Numerous Papers of News and Entertainment, British
and Foreign; or shall be Communicated
proper for Publication.
With Instructions for Gardening, and the Fairs for February.
(*Universal Spectator*, January 30, 1731)

Thus, the *Gentleman's Magazine* seeks to become a compendium of the useful knowledge of the day. In this regard, it shares the same fundamental purpose as Diderot's *Encylopedie*. The crucial difference, however, is that Cave's project is aimed at a general audience.

If his creative appropriation of the term magazine had helped Cave define his publication's mission, the first word in his publication's title, "gentleman," plays an equally important role in his literary project. Through the seventeenth and early eighteenth centuries the term "gentleman" referred to a very specific and strictly defined segment of the population in Britain, which was described in 1626 by Sir Henry Spelman: "Gentleman is the lowest class of the lesser nobility in England. The appellation, however, is fitting even for the greatest; but it applies to the former generically as being the threshold of nobility, to the latter specifically as the highest degree of the name" (qtd. in Beckett, 19). By the eighteenth century the term had evolved to the point that it no longer referred exclusively to the lesser nobility but was being used by wealthy individuals who did not possess a coat of arms. In theory, gentleman still referred only to members of the aristocracy, but in practice now wealthy individuals who were not members of the nobility, were also commonly identified as gentlemen. Although the group identified by the term "gentleman" now consisted of a larger segment of Britons in its expansion from the nobility to a landed and a monied aristocracy, an exclusive set of individuals still effectively controlled British politics. The aristocracy, Stephen Shapin has observed, "regarded themselves as the political nation, and, so far as having a voice in the sanctioned public forums was concerned, they *were* the political nation. It was their voices that were heard in national political deliberations; they effectively exercised their individual wills in economic, legal, and political deliberations; and they legally spoke for all the rest" (46).

While the aristocracy may have controlled British politics, their voices began to encounter increasing competition from the middle classes during the eighteenth century. The proliferation of information via the newspapers and the emergence of coffeehouse culture in the early part of the eighteenth century gave rise to the public sphere, which in turn validated public opinion as a legitimate voice in national politics. In Habermas's formulation the connection between literature and politics is crucial: "The public sphere in the political realm evolved from the public sphere in the world of letters; through the vehicle of public opinion it put the state in touch with the needs of society" (30–31). Habermas argues that the introduction of "critical reasoning" into the daily press in the form of "periodicals containing not primarily information but pedagogical instructions and even criticism and reviews" represented the crucial step that allowed private people to "compel public authority to legitimate itself before public opinion" (24–25). As public opinion became increasingly important in national politics, so the aristocracy's uncontested status as *the* political nation was diminished. And, although they managed to retain political control in England into the twentieth century, now they had to contend with the will of "the people."[7]

At the same time that public opinion was emerging as a legitimate voice in national politics, the category of gentleman, with its traditional interrelationship with honor, was increasingly under question.[8] Cave's use of the term "gentleman" in the title to his magazine reflects the changing notions about the definition of who qualified for membership in the group of people who could legitimately identify themselves as gentlemen. The interchangeability of gentleman and merchant suggested by the full title of Cave's magazine, *The Gentleman's Magazine; or Trader's Monthly Intelligencer*, reflects a new social ideology that does not see honor, which was understood to be the basis of gentility in the seventeenth century, as

---

7 I do not mean to suggest here that there was or is such a thing as a static or identifiable will of the people, but rather that politicians would now have to tailor their policies to account for a version of "the people" who could then be said to endorse those views. The more democratic the society the more a politician's success is contingent upon his or her ability to appear to represent the people which, paradoxical as it may seem, this chapter suggests is largely dependent on his or her ability to persuade the people to see themselves in a particular way. In other words, politicians don't so much alter their policies or views to correspond to the will of the people (although this can and does happen), but instead attempt to persuade the people to perceive themselves and their interests in the ways that the writer, representative or candidate wants them to see them.

8 In the fourth and fifth chapters of *The Origins of the English Novel, 1600–1740*, Michael McKeon traces the "gradual discrediting of aristocratic honor" that culminated in the middle of the eighteenth century (133). Also on the subject of the definition, role, and influence of the English aristocracy during this period see, Beckett, *The Aristocracy in England, 1660–1914*, and Stone, *The Crisis of the Aristocracy, 1558–1641*.

an inherited characteristic, and, moreover, that does not equate gentlemen with membership in the nobility or landed gentry. Implicit in Cave's title, then, is the notion that the status of a gentleman could be acquired, not just inherited. To this end, Cave reprinted various pieces from the London papers that dealt specifically with the qualities that one must obtain to become a gentleman. Not surprisingly, in one of the earliest issues, May 1731, Cave reprints an item from the *Weekly Register* describing the kinds of knowledge that a gentleman ought to possess:

> To make a perfectly good Companion, a Man should have so much Learning as to enable him to taste the Greek and Latin Authors; an Extensive and general Knowledge of Men and Things; Judgment, Wit, vivacity, Humour, good Nature, or a strong desire to please. But as all of these are not to be expected in one Man, 'tis however necessary he should have two of them, viz. Knowledge and good Nature. The more general our Knowledge is, the better. For he who is master of but one or two things is usually a pedant; wise in one thing, and a blockhead in everything else. Our Knowledge should be in the first place, that which is most useful, then that which is most fashionable and becoming a Gentleman, Moral Knowledge, or the Science of Life, is absolutely necessary for our own happy Conduct. Natural Philosophy entertains and fills the Mind with great and sublime Ideas of the first Cause. The History of Men in all Ages and Countries, their Manners, Customs and Laws; which to read with Advantage, 'tis necessary to understand Geography and Chronology. Bids us study the History of our own Country, and read Poetry to improve our Imagination and Language. (198)

It is, of course, no accident that most of the topics identified as indispensable knowledge for a gentleman in this piece correspond to those Cave had enumerated in the advertisement for his magazine five months earlier. The *Gentleman's Magazine*, therefore, served as an instrument in the identification and education of a new class of gentlemen in Britain. As aristocratic ideology lost much of its authority to define, and therefore to limit, the categories of gentry, gentility, and worth slowly began to supersede birth as the primary qualification for inclusion among the genteel, publications such as Cave's became instrumental in the definition of the nature and dissemination of the means of such worth.[9] By making a certain kind of compendious knowledge one of the basic requirements of a gentleman's character, Cave naturally promoted his own interests, for his magazine enabled readers to acquire precisely the kind of knowledge required by a gentleman.

If Cave's *Gentlemen's Magazine* provided a model of success, it also showed that in order to succeed the magazine had simultaneously to

[9] See McKeon, 133.

represent its audience and recreate it. Cave did not create the new category of gentlemen that emerged in the early part of the eighteenth century, but he certainly had a hand in reshaping the category as it continued to evolve over the course of the century. Paine, likewise, did not single-handedly create the *Pennsylvania Magazine* or its audience, but in order for it to be successful he would have to first identify his audience and then attempt to reinvent it. The audience that the *Pennsylvania Magazine* aimed to attract was somewhat different from Cave's.

In the absence of a proliferation of journals and other forms of serial publications that Cave's magazine had had to compete with in London, the two forms of publications that Paine and Aitken had to compete with in Philadelphia were the newspaper, of which there were several at that time, and the almanac. In many respects, the *Pennsylvania Magazine* was designed to inhabit a niche in between the more current-events orientation of the newspaper and the seasonal rhythm of the almanc. As it had been for Cave in London, the primary difference between the *Pennsylvania Magazine* and the *Pennsylvania Gazette* or *Poor Richard's Almanac* was more a matter of sensibility than of content. Although newspapers such as the *Pennsylvania Gazette* or the *Pennsylvania Evening Post* were certainly eclectic in content (especially be the standards of the modern newspaper), they tended to focus on local happenings and the political, social, and economic news of the day. Morphologically, the magazine bore more of a resemblance to the almanac than it did to the newspaper. A typical almanac primarily focused on pseudo-scientific information (primarily dedicated to a daily calendar predicting the weather for the year, but also including sections on various other natural phenomena such as eclipses, the location of the planets, the tides, and the rising and setting of the sun). Most almanacs, though, would also include various short essays on a wide range of subjects. In 1775, John Carter's *The New England Almanac, or Lady's and Gentlemen's Diary*, for example, prefaced each month's calendar with a brief essay, usually no longer than six lines. In addition it included a three page essay, "A Brief View of the Present Controversy between Great-Britain and America, with some Observations thereon." In 1776, *Poor Wills Almanac* called attention to its essay content on its title page by setting it off from the generic fare with a large type ALSO, under which appeared the following description: "Monthly Observations on Gardening, a Collection of Useful Receipts, and a Variety of Essays in Prose and Verse." By including a "Meteorological Diary" section in each issue, the *Pennsylvania Magazine* plays upon its resemblance to an almanac, simply shifting the emphasis from one section of the Almanac to another. The almanac's typical lower and middling sort of readership was precisely the audience Paine, the son of an artisan, would repeatedly attempt to politicize over the course of his writing career.

In the end, his job as editor of a magazine proved invaluable to Paine's formation as a writer because he soon discovered that the particular nature of the magazine made it especially well suited to promoting his political goals. It did not hurt, moreover, that the magazine he would edit was based in Philadelphia, which had become the political and mercantile center of the British colonies in America. As the busiest port in the colonies Philadelphia had the largest population of artisans and craftsmen in the colonies, most of whom supported the nonimportation agreements that went into effect on December 1, 1774, because they perceived the importation of British manufactures as an economic threat. One historian has suggested that "The politicization of the mass of Philadelphians – from the master craftsmen to a significant segment of the laborers and poor – was the most important development in Philadelphia's political life in the decade before independence" (Foner, 56). As editor of the *Pennsylvania Magazine*, Paine became an active participant in the process of that politicization by publishing essays intended to foment popular political action.[10] If, as one of his biographers has stated, "1775 was not the happiest year to begin a literary journal," the volatile political atmosphere in Philadelphia provided an ideal environment for Paine to develop his skills (Hawke, 27).

THE *PENNSYLVANIA MAGAZINE*

A couple of weeks before Paine arrived in Philadelphia, Robert Aitken had made public his proposal to publish a monthly magazine. By this time, sixteen different magazines had appeared and disappeared in the colonies. The last magazine published in Philadelphia, the *American Magazine and Monthly Chronicle*, edited by William Smith, had expired in October 1758,

---

[10] Paine's acute awareness of the magazine's audience is reflected in his choice of the essay on ants that directly appeals to a working class readership by raising questions about labor and the workers' right to the fruits of their labor. Along these lines, Jack P. Greene has suggested that Paine played a key role in what he calls "the modernization of political consciousness" (73). Greene argues that, "The result [of this modernization] was a wholly new political mentality for participants at all levels of the political process..." and that, "This transformation was accompanied by – and played a key role in bringing about – two crucial developments: the mobilization of large segments of society that had previously been inert, and the desacralization of the traditional political order" (74).

after a thirteen-month run. These early magazines had been American only by virtue of the fact that they were published in the colonies. According to the foremost historian of colonial American periodical literature, "Probably at least three-fourths of the total contents of [the magazines published in the colonies before 1794] were extracted from books, pamphlets, newspapers, and Other magazines, both English and American . . . Much of the larger part of the selections was, of course, English" (Mott, 39). In the November 21, 1774 issue of the *Pennsylvania Packet*, a Philadelphia weekly newspaper, Aitken presented his plan for the *Pennsylvania Magazine*, which was to be an "American Magazine" that would print original American essays and poetry, and not just reprint material from British publications.[11]

In an advertisement accompanying the proposal for the magazine in the *Packet*, Aitken further defined the role of his publication in broad moral terms: " 'being unalterably determined to conduct this Magazine upon a plan of the most extensive usefulness, and to admit nothing but what relates to the grand interests of *Learning, Virtue*, and our common *Christianity.*" Aitken also insisted that the magazine would remain strictly impartial in matters of politics and religion, an impartiality that the allegorical mode of the insect pieces both sustains and undermines. In the eighteenth century, as Stephen Botein has noted, printers were forced, by market conditions, to attempt to "please all customers at all times": "Usually unable to rely for a living on the favor of any one group among his neighbors, including those who wielded political power, a colonial printer by custom labored to serve diverse interests in the community. Unlike London, where large profits were sometimes to be had by making partisan commitments to one well-financed faction or another, colonial America was a place for printers to be studiously impartial" (19). So, while the *Pennsylvania Magazine* was pro-American, its challenge was to avoid the appearance of partisanship.

The combination of a volatile political atmosphere and the economic difficulties faced by a monthly journal's printer thus created the conditions that led to the choice of fables of one sort or another as the political writers' primary tool. But political subjects would not be completely

---

[11] In his "Proposal" published in the *Pennsylvania Packet* Aitken describes the first of the six sections of his new publication in the following manner: "A proportion of nearly the same number of pages in each Magazine will be set apart for original American productions, and the greatest attention given that none be admitted but such as are of real merit." The anxiety about the quality of the American pieces that is in evidence in this passage further underscores the novelty of such a proposition.

ignored by Aitken's magazine: "As to the subjects of these dissertations, they may extend to the whole circle of science, including politics and religion as objects of philosophical disquisition, but excluding controversy in both. Lest this should offend any, all the political controversy proper for this periodical publication will fall under the article of news" (n.p.). The *Pennsylvania Magazine* was to be divided into six separate sections with a definite emphasis placed on issues of particular interest to the American colonies: American essays, selected essays from British magazines, a list of new books with "remarks and extracts," a poetry section, news or "Monthly Intelligence," and a meteorological diary.

Aitken, who among other things had previously printed some of Benjamin Franklin's work, published the first issue of his *Pennsylvania Magazine; or, American Monthly Museum* in February of 1775, and hired Paine, who arrived in Philadelphia with a letter of introduction from Franklin, as his editor for the following month.[12] Paine's participation in the magazine, however, could more accurately be described as a contributing editorship since he also wrote a great deal of the material that was printed in the various issues he edited between February and August of 1775. Although Paine had only published a few minor pieces in England and had no experience as an editor, his impact on the sales of the *Pennsylvania Magazine* was dramatic and immediate. Just a month after accepting Aitken's offer to edit the magazine, Paine wrote to Franklin about his new venture: "a printer and bookseller here, a man of reputation and property, Robert Aitkin, has lately attempted a magazine, but having little or no turn that way himself, he has applied to me for assistance. He had not above six hundred subscribers when I first assisted him. We now have upwards of fifteen hundred, and daily increasing" (CW II, 1131). Paine had found both his audience and his voice. Under his guidance the *Pennsylvania Magazine* would attain the greatest circulation of any American magazine up to that time (Mott, 87).

Although he did not edit the debut issue of the *Pennsylvania Magazine*, Paine made two significant contributions to it, the "Publishers Preface" and an essay entitled "The Utility of this Work Evinced," in which he presents his vision of the role of the magazine.[13] The "Preface" begins with an apology for the deficiencies of the publication, which Paine

---

[12] Aitken was also the official printer for Franklin's American Philosophical Society, and had, among other things, also published Freneau's "Rising Glory of America," and James Burgh's *The Art of Speaking*.

[13] The "Publisher's Preface" and the lead article of the debut issue, "On the Utility of Magazines" are among the articles Aitken attributes to Paine in a letter to James Carey,

attributes first to its "infant state," and then perhaps more significantly, to the "present unfortunate, situation of public affairs" that has gained the attention of "those whose leisure and abilities, might lead them to a successful application to the Muses." Even as he states that "every heart and hand seem to be engaged in the interesting struggle for *American Liberty*," Paine reiterates Aitken's promise, from his proposal in the *Packet*, that the magazine remain impartial in order to "avoid giving offence to any by our publication." Nevertheless, Paine's involvement compromised Aitken's intentions from the outset because he brought what proved to be a decidedly political voice to the magazine.

In "The Utility of this Work Evinced," the lead article immediately following the "Publisher's Preface," Paine argues that magazines are useful because they provide the population with "the opportunities of acquiring and communicating knowledge" (9). He likens a "properly conducted" magazine to a "nursery of genius," which provides "exercise" for the mind so that it does not "fall into decay" (10). As a "nursery of genius" and a "market of wit" the magazine generically becomes an educational instrument that may be used to assist America as it "outgrow[s] the state of infancy." Thus the *Pennsylvania Magazine* becomes a parental mentor in the process of educating the people of the colonies, a process that, within the context of the post-Lockean developmental models of the period, inevitably leads to independence.[14] The mission of the magazine to educate its readership thus implicitly involves it in a revolutionary process.[15]

To Paine the utility of the magazine stems precisely from its capacity to mold a people: "there is nothing which obtains so general an influence over the manners and morals of a people as the press; from that, as from a fountain, the streams of vice or virtue are poured forth over a country: And of all publications none are more calculated to improve or infect than a periodical one" (10).[16] Once he has pointed out the power

---

the editor of an early two-volume compilation of Paine's writings. See Frank Smith "New Light on Thomas Paine's First Year in America, 1775."

[14] See Jay Fliegelman, *Prodigals and Pilgrims*.

[15] In *Revolution and the Word* Cathy N. Davidson argues that "Given both the literary insularity of many novel readers and the increasing popularity of the novel, the genre necessarily became a form of education, especially for women. Novels allowed for a means of entry into a larger literary and intellectual world and a means of access to social and political events from which many readers (particularly women) would have been otherwise largely excluded" (10). In 1775, I would argue, this was the role Paine imagined for the magazine.

[16] According to the OED, the term "infect," which Paine uses along with "improve" to describe the effects a magazine may have on its readers, was just shifting from its primary

of the press to shape moral character, Paine indicts British magazines, those "retailers of tale and nonsense," for corrupting their readers. In America, by contrast, magazines hasten a process of purging old world corruption: "The cottages as it were of yesterday have grown to villages, the villages to cities, and while proud antiquity, like a skeleton in rags, parades the streets other nations, their genius, as if sickened and disgusted with the phantom, comes hither for recovery" (9). Paine casts America as a haven from the corrupting influence of British thought, for he suggests that "There is a happy something in the climate of America, which disarms [foreign vices] of all their power both of infection and attraction" (10). Paine thus invokes the, by then, commonplace theory, derived from Montesquieu, that physical environment plays a crucial role in the character of an area's inhabitants. This notion led Montesquieu to propose that "If it is true that the character of the spirit and the passions of the heart are extremely different in the various climates, *laws* should be relative to the differences in the passions and to the differences in these characters" (*Spirit*, 231). At this point in his career Paine was not prepared to draw this conclusion regarding the fundamental relationship between the colonies and Great Britain. Nevertheless, he employs the environmental argument to suggest that the *Pennsylvania Magazine* will help to keep out foreign vices by printing mostly original essays written by Americans and minimizing the amount of British material. Paine thus extends the strategy of the nonimportation of British "articles" that was in effect in the commercial sector into the intellectual sphere.

Paine returns to the problem of the corrupting effect of British habits and customs that comes with the importation of British goods in an article in the next issue of the *Pennsylvania Magazine* (February 1775). Whereas Paine was concerned with the influence of British wit on the American mind, the author of "Substitutes for Tea," who writes under the pseudonym "A Philanthropist," at first seems merely to suggest that tea generally has a detrimental effect on people's physical and mental health. He cites various doctors who have claimed that tea "has much increased the diseases of a nervous and languid mature," and includes his own observation, "I never saw a man or woman, who, from their youth was fond of, and practiced drinking it freely, who was not rendered a weak, effeminate creeping valetudinarian for life" (74). We soon discover, however,

---

neutral to its more familiar negative sense. In the context of Paine's sentence the word could serve as an appositive for improve. In its neutral sense, however, the term could also be read negatively as a warning to his readers about the dangers of the British press.

that his quarrel is not with all teas, but rather solely with "India Teas," that is, those imported from India via Britain. He advises a substitution of those teas with teas produced from American plants:

But if we must, through custom, have some warm tea, once or twice a day, why may we not exchange this slow poison, which besides its other evils destroys our constitution, and drains our county of many thousand pounds a year, for teas of our own American medicinal plans: many of which may be found, pleasant to the taste and very salutary, according to our various constitutions. (75)

The real argument of this essay, then, proves not to be with tea itself, but with the practice of importing tea from Britain, for the idea is not to substitute tea with another kind of beverage, but rather to substitute one kind of tea for another.

Whereas in his essay on the utility of magazines Paine warns about the danger of "infection" from British wit, this writer exposes the danger resulting from British teas, as both become symbolic forms of poison to Americans. The issue is not health so much as financial and commercial independence that in the context of the nonimportation agreements of recent months had become a deeply political matter.[17] It is not the weakening of the body, but the debilitating effect the importation of tea from Britain has on the body politic, reinforced by his repeated use of the word "constitution," that truly concerns "A Philanthropist."[18] Small wonder that after pointing out the medicinal virtues of various sources of tea native to the colonies, "A Philanthropist" ends his essay by appealing to the American aristocracy, "the gentleman and ladies of the first rank," to "use their influence and example, to abolish this pernicious custom of drinking the Asiatic teas, and introduce and persevere in using their own; they will have the self pleasing satisfaction of having emancipated their country from the slavery and tyranny of an evil custom" (76).

Through articles such as this one the magazine fulfills its self-appointed mission of educating the American people in the path of independence ostensibly without making politics its primary subject. In particular, as Jay Fliegelman has observed, "Paine favored articles about marriage not

---

[17] On the connections between consumption and the revolution see T. H. Breen, "'Baubles of Britain': The American and Consumer Revolutions of the Eighteenth Century."

[18] The author of "Substitutes for Tea" draws on the discourse of luxury, that would have been all too familiar to his readers, but he subverts it by putting it in the service of a revolutionary agenda instead of its usual conservative aim. As John Sekora has shown, luxury was typically used in the eighteenth century to uphold traditional hierarchical structures in society. See Sekora, *Luxury: The Concept in Western Thought, Eden to Smollett.*

only in justification of his own [marital] separation, but because domestic politics addressed the same ideological issues as international politics" (Prodigals, 124). While the nature of the marriage bond was a subject of great interest during this era, it also served, like natural history in the insect articles, as an analogical context within which such broad ideological problems as consent and independence could be addressed without direct reference to the political relations between the colonies and Britain. To Paine, as the essay on the consumption of tea suggests, consent and independence were not only political issues; they were also essentially economic ones. One of the facets of marriage, therefore, that concerned Paine the most was its economic dimension.

Two columns, "The Old Bachelor" and "Reflections on Marriage," the former sometimes written by Paine, Francis Hopkinson, or one of the various regular contributors to the magazine, and the latter by John Witherspoon under the pseudonym Epaminondas, treated the subject of marriage on a regular basis. In addition to his contributions to the Old Bachelor series Paine, who left England after his separation from his second wife, also contributed various articles and poems on the subject. Both the Old Bachelor and Epaminondas celebrate the virtues of marriage, but simultaneously emphasize that only a happy marriage is worth preserving. In his first three numbers, appearing in the March, April, and May 1775 issues of the *Pennsylvania Magazine*, the Old Bachelor attributes his unhappiness and loneliness to his failure to marry. In a pseudonymous reply to the Old Bachelor, Paine sets out to demonstrate that the Old Bachelor "might have been as unhappy even in the desirable matrimonial state" (June 1775, 254). Paine writes the essay, "Consolation for the Old Bachelor," from the perspective of a local merchant whose wife insists that he take her and their six-year-old daughter to visit a "wealthy taylor" in New York. The ensuing tale recounts the trip, which soon becomes a catalogue of distress and misery as the wife complains endlessly and blames the merchant for everything that goes wrong while carelessly spending his hard-earned money.[19] The merchant, subjected to the tyrannical rule of

[19] For a more detailed analysis of the connections between gender and class in the formation of an American identity see Smith-Rosenberg, "Dis-Covering the Subject of the 'Great Constitutional Discussion,' 1786–1789." Smith-Rosenberg suggests that in order for the revolution to succeed patriot writers had to "constitute a new American identity, one that Virginia planters, Rhode Island merchants, Georgia farmers, and Pennsylvania artisans would internalize as their own and in that process become subjects of and to a new nation" (843). The magazine, she contends, played a crucial role in this effort to "constitute a new homo *Americanus*." Like Smith-Rosenberg's magazine editors and writers, Paine

his wife, emphasizes that his only recourse throughout is "silent patience" because his wife would not listen to him (257). Unlike Paine's merchant, the American colonists were no longer willing to wait silently while their pleas for representation were being ignored by the British crown.

In his column from this very same issue of the magazine, the Old Bachelor agrees with Paine when he asserts "No wife is better than a bad one and the same of a husband" (263). The Old Bachelor then sets up another critique of marriage "Reflections on Unhappy Marriages," that he claims to have found by accident, but which was almost certainly written by Paine. In "Reflections on Unhappy Marriages" Paine identifies marriage as the most important determinant of "the weal or woe of life" and warns his readers about the dangers of rashly entering into so critical a relation as marriage for the wrong reasons, those being primarily passion or money. Paine dedicates most of the essay to condemning marriages of economic convenience: "Matches of this kind are downright prostitution, however softened by the letter of the law; and he or she who receives the golden quaffing of youth and beauty, so wretchedly bestowed, can never enjoy what they so dearly purchased" (264). Paine concludes his argument with the words of an "American savage," who rejects Christian marriage because "not one in a hundred of them had anything to do with happiness or common sense" (265). The savage elaborates on this theme: "But if any should be found so wretched among us, as to hate where the only commerce ought to be love, we instantly dissolve the band: God made us all in pairs; each has his mate somewhere or other; and 'tis our duty to find each other out, since no creature was ever intended to be miserable" (265). In his innocence the savage becomes a source of common sense and, by implication, suggests that excessive cultivation leads to moral decay.[20] The savage's use of the term "commerce" to describe the marriage union only emphasizes the point that "mutual affection," and not economic gain, is the proper basis for this kind of relationship.

constructed a white, male, American identity through opposition to class, racial, and gender others, but Paine also sought to constitute an American identity that would be more politically inclusive to lower and middling sorts than its European counterparts.

[20] By using an American Indian as a rational commentator who can provide an unbiased assessment of European practices Paine draws on a tradition that dates back as far as Thomas Brown's *Amusements Serious and Comical*, originally published in 1700. In his *Amusements* Brown's narrator presents his Indian observer in similar terms to Paine's "American savage:" "Thus I am resolved to take upon me the *Genius* of an *Indian*, who had had the Curiosity to travel hither among us, and who had never seen any Thing like what he sees in *London*. We shall see how he will be amazed at certain things, which the prejudice of Custom makes to seem reasonable and natural to us" (13).

Paine thus uses the American savage as an advocate for divorce, arguing that no law should keep two people together who will only "double each other's misery." The savage prefers his customs to the Christian God's because in his people's customs marriages "last no longer than they bestow mutual pleasures" for they "oblige the heart" (265). Invoking a line of reasoning that Montesquieu had advocated fifty years earlier in his *Persian Letters*, Paine suggests that the true reason for marrying is not financial well-being or passion, but love, and if and when mutual affection subsides, as in the case of his relationship with his own wife, then the marriage should be terminated.[21] In a single issue of the *Pennsylvania Magazine* Paine uses "Consolation for the Old Bachelor" to depict the woes of an unhappy marriage, and "Reflections of Unhappy Marriages" to argue for the value of divorce as a means of ending marriages that are only making people miserable. In both cases the relationship has deteriorated because it has been reduced from an emotional or affectionate tie to a commercial or economic one. Shifting the analogy from marital to paternal relations, Paine would once again draw on this line of argument in *Common Sense* by repeatedly suggesting that Britain's interest in the colonies had sprung from economic motives rather than the affectionate concern of a parent. Paine even proposes that the parental analogy has been invoked for purely political ends: "the phrase *parent* or *mother country* hath been jesuitically adopted by the King and his parasites, with a low papistical design of gaining an unfair bias on the credulous weakness of our minds" (CW I, 19). Ultimately, Paine suggests that the relationship between the colonies and Great Britain has not devolved from an affectionate union into an economic one; instead, it has always been a purely economic union.[22]

POLITICAL FABLES

Many of the political ramifications implicit in the marriage articles come to the surface in a fable written by Paine for the April 1775 issue of the magazine. The fable would become one of Paine's favorite genres not

[21] In "Letter 116" of the *Persian Letters* Usbek describes the impact of outlawing divorce in Christian countries: "Not only did it take all the pleasure out of marriage, but it also discouraged its purpose. The intention was to strengthen the bonds of marriage, but they were weakened; and instead of uniting two hearts, as had been planned, they were separated forever" (209).

[22] Two paragraphs before condemning the parental analogy for colonial relations as a devious rhetorical ploy, Paine asserts that "We have boasted the protection of Great Britain, without considering, that her motive was *interest* not *attachment*" (CW I, 18).

only because it was already the most popular literary vehicle of religious instruction and political polemic during the first three quarters of the eighteenth century, but because Paine also recognized that it was well suited to the needs of a magazine. As one critic has noted, "Simplicity and brevity are paramount virtues in the fable, qualities which also permit the literary dilettante to dash off a specimen without being wearied by prolonged creative thought" (Noel, 13). The fable's wide appeal made an ideal vehicle for Paine's political goals: "Despite the emphasis both Locke and Fenelon place on the use of fables in elementary education, the eighteenth century did not limit the genre to young minds. Its very acceptance as a literary genre stemmed from the conviction that everyone could read fables for edification and enjoyment" (Noel, 10). In fact, Rousseau insisted in *Emile* that fables were only appropriate for adults because they might mislead the young: "Fables can instruct men, but the naked truth has to be told to children" (112). Whether for children or adults, the fable's combination of brevity, didacticism, and accessibility (both to readers and potential contributors) corresponded perfectly with the material and political needs of the *Pennsylvania Magazine* under Paine's editorship.

Writing as "Esop," Paine invents an "original" fable, "Cupid and Hymen," in which Hymen, the god of marriage, attempts to wed Ruralinda, a poor villager who is in love with another man, to a rich lord who has paid her mother in exchange for Ruralinda's hand. Cupid, the god of love, intervenes and asserts his authority over Hymen who, he claims, has no authority to conduct a marriage without his approval:

Know Hymen, said he, that I am your master. Indulgent Jove gave you to me as a clerk, not as a rival, much less a superior. 'Tis my province to form the union and yours to witness it. But of late you have treacherously assumed to set up for yourself. 'Tis true you may chain couples together like criminals, but you cannot yoke them like lovers.... At best you are but a temporal and temporary god, whom Jove has appointed not to bestow, but to secure happiness, and restrain the infidelity of mankind. (159–160)

In this fable Hymen has not only overstepped his authority, but he has betrayed Cupid and allied himself with Platus, the god of riches. Paine thus sets up a contest between love and money as the proper basis for the marital union. At first it seems as if the crucial drama of the fable will revolve around Hymen's "pretensions to independence": The subordinate Hymen rises up against his ruler, Cupid. However, the fable shows Hymen's revolt to be based upon a corruption of marriage. The focal point of Paine's fable then becomes its account of the nature of marriage, and, in particular, the subordination of commercial to sentimental considerations as the basis for such a relationship.[23] Hymen's misguided revolt hinges on a misunderstanding both of his role and of the nature of marriage. The central point of the fable derives precisely from Cupid's assertion of his authority over Hymen, for through Cupid, Paine asserts the primacy of love in the union of marriage. Without Cupid's approval, the union can only be temporary, because Hymen alone cannot create a permanent bond, especially when Ruralinda will not consent to the marriage. Ironically, Paine asserts the legitimacy of one hierarchical relationship (Cupid's rule over Hymen), in order to undermine another one (Great Britain's rule over the American colonies). The fable's implications for the relationship between Great Britain and its colonies in North America are clear enough: The bond should be based on mutual consent and affection, not on commercial interests. Moreover, the fable implies that there is a choice involved in the relationship. The parent-child metaphor typically had been used to naturalize the relationship between England and her colonies and reinforce the mother-country's claims to authority over her children. The marriage metaphor in "Cupid and Hymen" offers an alternative model for the relationship between England and America in which the terms of the union are contingent and contractual. Later, in *Common Sense* Paine will return to the parent-child metaphor, this time employing emerging theories of childhood development in an attempt to subvert the fixed hierarchy of the traditional parent-child relationship.

Paine's decision to invoke Aesop and represent his own political allegory of "Cupid and Hymen" must have seemed only natural, given their broad popularity and cultural resonance in the eighteenth century: "Few books sold more steadily in eighteenth-century America than Aesop in the imported English editions of Croxall and Draper" (Wolf, 46). In addition to its numerous British editions, Samuel Croxall's *Fables of Aesop and Others* (1722) went through four American editions between 1777 and 1800.[24] In fact, Aesop's *Fables* were commonly used in schoolbooks both in England and throughout the colonies for they had the "additional advantage of providing morals" (Wolf, 46). Samuel Croxall spells out the

---

[23] In *States of Sympathy* Elizabeth Barnes has argued, through a reading of *Common Sense*, that "Paine's rhetoric proposes sympathy as the basis of democratic society" (30). We can see an early version of the role that sympathy will play in Paine's later social and political arguments in these pieces on marriage.

[24] All in all, sixteen different editions of Aesop's *Fables* were published in the colonies between 1777 and 1800, three of which appeared in Philadelphia in 1777. In addition to Aitken's printing of Croxall's translation of the *Fables*, Robert Bell printed competing translations by Robert Burton and Robert Dodsley in 1777.

educational value of his version of Aesop in his dedication to the young George Lord Viscount Sunbury, Baron Halifax:

These Fables, My Lord, abound in Variety of Instruction, Moral and Political; They furnish us with Rules for every Station of Life; They mark out a proper Behaviour for us, both in respect to selves and others; and demonstrate to us, by a kind of Example, every Virtue which claims our best Regards, and every Vice which we are most concerned to avoid. (London, A3 verso)

In his applications Croxall explains the virtue to be emulated or vice to avoid that each fable addresses. While most of the fables deal with individual behavior, Croxall, as his dedication indicates, was well aware of the fact that more than a few political lessons are provided in them.

Croxall's version of Aesop, Annabel Patterson has, shown, "was designed ... to discredit [Roger L'Estrange] as one who had distorted his classical origins, and imposed upon them a political interpretation that was not only offensive to Whigs and libertarians, but incompatible with the fable's origins" (143). Leaving nothing to chance, Croxall ends his "Preface" to the *Fables* with an overt statement of his political beliefs and by extension, therefore, of the politics of his text: "Professing (according to the Principle on which the following Applications are built) that I am a Lover of Liberty and Truth; an enemy to Tyranny, either in the Church or State, and one who detests Party Animosities and factious Divisions, as much as I wish the [Peace] and Prosperity of my County" (n.p.). While he could never have foreseen it, several decades later Croxall's statement as well as his "Applications," in which he defended individual rights and freedom whenever possible, would have appealed greatly to American revolutionary readers. In 1777 none other than Paine's former employer and publisher Robert Aitken printed the first American edition of Croxall's *Fables* of *Aesop and Others*. Thus, with "Cupid and Hymen" and the other fables he published in the *Pennsylvania Magazine*, Paine continues a tradition of employing the fable as a genre ideally suited to oppositional political writing. In this respect, despite their political differences, Paine follows in the tradition of L'Estrange, for whom in the late seventeenth century the fable "was necessary as a vehicle of otherwise prohibited criticism" (Patterson, 140).

BECOMING AMERICAN

Thus, in articles on natural historical and domestic topics, essays on marriage, and fables, Paine repeatedly breaks down the division between the political and the nonpolitical realm even though the structure of the

Pennsylvania Magazine marks that difference by its overinsistent division between the documentary "Monthly Intelligence" section and the purportedly nonpolitical essays in the main body. Paine understood that these separate spheres, marked by separate sections in the publication, often overlapped and he exploited that tenuous boundary in ways few had before. On occasion, however, he would print an explicitly political essay. In the July 1775 issue Paine complemented the "Monthly Intelligence" item with "A Declaration by the Representatives of the United Colonies of North America, now met in General Congress at Philadelphia, setting forth the necessity of their taking up Arms," with essays such as "On the Military Character of Ants" and "Thoughts on Defensive War." As we have seen, Curioso's "On the Military Character of Ants" concludes by asserting the importance of national defense by casting the colonies in the role of a woman seeking to protect her virtue. In "Thoughts on Defensive War" Paine, writing under the pseudonym "A Lover of Peace," urges the Quakers to support the American colonies' cause and take up arms against the British stating that "America must suffer because *she* has something to lose. Her crime is property" (313, emphasis mine). Both pieces figure America as female and make chastity stand for all property, thus shifting the emphasis of war from a question of aggression to one of the protection of virtue. In order to persuade the Quakers, Paine also analogizes spiritual freedom and political liberty, thus appealing to the same concepts of liberty and property that Curioso makes central to his argument in the essay on ants.

The principal arguments of these two essays are also employed in the Continental Congress's "Declaration . . . Setting Forth the Causes and Necessity of Their Taking Up Arms" where once again consent and property become the major issues at stake for the colonies. After providing a brief history of the relations between the colonies and Britain, the document states: "We are reduced to the alternative of choosing an unconditional submission to the tyranny of irritated ministers or resistance by force. – The latter is our choice. – We have counted the cost of this contest, and find nothing so dreadful as voluntary slavery" (qtd. in *Pennsylvania Magazine*, 236). Like the brown ants in Curioso's article, the colonies present themselves as victims forced to defend themselves from enslavement. The document emphasizes that the sole reason for taking up arms is to defend their property rights and freedom and not to sever the union with Britain:

In our native land, in defense of the freedom that is our birthright, and which we ever enjoyed till the late violation of it – for the protection of our property, acquired solely by the honest industry of our fore-fathers and ourselves, against violence actually offered we have take up arms. We shall lay them down when hostilities shall cease on the part of the aggressors, and all danger of their being renewed shall be removed, and not before. (237)

In this passage the Continental Congress's statement not only echoes the rhetoric used by "Curioso" and "A Lover of Peace" to justify the use of military force to defend one's property, but it also recalls much of the rhetoric of the articles about marriage in its assertion that the Parliament has become tyrannical in its determination to establish specific measures without the consent of the colonies.[25] Therefore, just as he approves of divorce to remedy an unhappy marital relationship, Paine advocates revolution as a solution to the intolerable relationship between the colonies and Great Britain. What was implicitly political allegory in the articles on marriage, here becomes the explicit political agenda. The first two articles thus serve to prepare the audience for the last, and in so doing attempt to direct the reader's interpretation and reaction to it. Thus, in order to participate as a voice in the revolutionary process without becoming openly partisan, the *Pennsylvania Magazine* blurred the distinction between political and nonpolitical material. The difference between the articles in the main section of the magazine and the material in the "Monthly Intelligence" section is largely the difference between the overtly political and the covertly political.

Moreover, through allegory – either used directly in articles like "Observations on the Military Character of Ants," and "Cupid and Hymen," or more generally in the use of particular themes or subjects such as marriage – the *Pennsylvania Magazine* in effect redefined the political and geographical category of "American" by transforming it into a behavioral category. Being an American became a matter of acting and thinking in specific ways, and by extension participation in the revolution also became a matter of everyday life. For example, the simple act of consuming

---

[25] Paine had also provided evidence of prior instances of British ministers' exploitation of their colonial dominions in essays such as "Reflections on the Life and Death of Lord Clive" (March 1775). In this article, in which Paine documents Lord Clive's brutal actions in India and subsequent fame in England, Paine laments the fate of one of England's other colonial possessions, "But, Oh India! thou loud proclaimer of European cruelties, thou bloody monument of unnecessary deaths" (108). The simple substitution of England for Europe makes the parallel with the American colonists' situation evident. Paine further reinforces his point by referring to Clive's personal economic motives: "Resolved on accumulating an unbounded fortune, he enters into all the schemes of war, treaty, and intrigue" (108). This essay was followed immediately by the first installment of "The Old Bachelor."

tea, or any other home-grown product, enabled one to "emancipate their country from the slavery and tyranny of an evil custom" ("Substitutes for Tea"). This form of political action, as T. H. Breen has shown, enabled anyone and everyone to participate in the revolutionary process in their own way.[26] To the extent that these articles make the revolutionary experience an integral part of the reader's daily life, they create an atmosphere where every action or thought can be interpreted as either pro-American or pro-British. So, while not every article printed in the *Pennsylvania Magazine* directly addresses a political issue, everything in it takes on a political dimension insofar as it can be construed as a form of acting as an American rather than as a British subject. Paine seems to have sensed that creating a viable national identity for Americans other than through their customary association with Britain was a crucial part of the revolutionary process.

The *Pennsylvania Magazine* thus provides a perfect example of what John Adams meant in 1815 when, in one of his most famous letters to Thomas Jefferson, he suggested that the war was only the "Effect and Consequence" of the true revolution, which "was in the Minds of the People, and this was effected, from 1760 to 1775, in the course of fifteen Years before a drop of blood was drawn at Lexington" (455). Paine had been one of the first to understand that in order for a revolution to take place in the minds of the people, and for it to succeed, it first had to be made available to them. Even as the magazine aimed to educate colonial Americans and lead them down the path to independence, it also served as an apprenticeship for Paine as he perfected the political and rhetorical strategies that would propel him to prominence as a spokesman for the Revolution.

No one has been able to ascertain the exact date, but Paine seems to have ceased to work for Aitken sometime between August and September

---

[26] In "Baubles of Britain," T. H. Breen documents the "politicization of consumption," which took place in the American colonies during the 1760s and 1770s. Breen demonstrates how during these two decades, beginning with the Stamp Act of 1765 and culminating with the Tea Act of 1773, "Parliament managed to politicize consumer goods, and when it did so, manufactured items suddenly took on a radical new symbolic function" such that "before long it was nearly impossible for Americans to speak of imported goods without making reference to constitutional rights" (76, 91). Thus, Breen concludes, "a constitutional crisis transformed private consumer acts into public political statements" (88) thereby providing the colonies with a unifying "language for revolution," which also enabled those usually excluded from colonial politics to play a significant role in this new political arena.

of 1775, when they parted ways in a dispute over Paine's compensation.[27] After Paine's departure Aitken continued to publish his magazine, which he now also presumably edited, through July 1776, when the war made it impossible for him to keep publishing it. Meanwhile, Paine, who had essentially acquired a new profession through his work for Aitken, continued his new career as a writer by publishing various essays in the Philadelphia newspapers and writing *Common Sense*. Prior to editing Aitken's magazine Paine had only written an address to the British Parliament advocating an increase in wages for his fellow excisemen in England, "The Case of the Officers of Excise," which failed to persuade Parliament and cost him his job. It would not be until 1775, when he began working for Aitken that Paine would publish on a regular basis. In his account of his service to the American cause, presented to the Continental Congress in 1783 as part of his plea for monetary compensation, Paine denied ever having published prior to his arrival in America: "The first public work I undertook (and the first thing I ever published in my life except a few miscellaneous pieces in the *Pennsylvania Magazine* in the year '75 for in England I never was the author of a syllable in print) was the pamphlet *Common Sense* " (CW II, 1229). Paine seems to have wanted to convey the impression that he had emerged *ex nihilo* as a writer with a work of the magnitude of *Common Sense*. Perhaps he understood those earlier publishing experiences as a kind of apprenticeship. In any case, Paine connected his emergence as a writer to his relocation to America: becoming an American and becoming a writer were inextricably linked in his imagination.

It seems only appropriate, however accidental it may have been, that the last issue of the *Pennsylvania Magazine* was the July 1776 edition, for the Declaration of Independence, which was reprinted in that issue, provided concrete evidence that the people had learned the lessons Paine had been so eager to teach. As he would observe in his *Letter to the Abbé Raynal* six years later, "Our style and manner of thinking have undergone a revolution more extraordinary than the political revolution of the country. We see with other eyes, we hear with other ears; and think with other thoughts, than those we formerly used" (CW II, 243). Paine's goal as editor of the *Pennsylvania Magazine* and throughout most of his career as a writer, for which the magazine editorship prepared him, was to foster precisely such a revolution in the people's style and manner of thinking.

[27] Hawke, 34–35; Keane 103–104.

Not surprisingly, then, his most enduring and successful works, *Common Sense, The Rights of Man,* and *The Age Reason* all attest to his commitment to help his fellow men see with other eyes, hear with other ears, and think other thoughts. During his stint as editor of Aitken's magazine Paine had gained the literary skills necessary for him to "create a literary style designed to bring his message to the widest possible audience," and he would introduce that style a few short months after leaving the magazine (Foner, xvi). Paine's success at bringing about such revolutionary changes in the public sprang from his ability to persuade his readers to see themselves as he wanted them to; to use Paine's own words, they did see with other eyes for they now would see with Paine's eyes. In the case of the American Revolution, those who failed to be so educated could now expect more violent means of persuasion.

2

"Could the Wolf Bleat Like the Lamb?"

Paine's Critique of the Early American Public Sphere

> There never was a man less loved in a place than Payne is in this, having at different times disputed with everybody, the most rational thing he could have done would have been to have died the instant he had finished his Common sense, for he never again will have it in his power to leave the world with so much credit.
>
> Sarah Franklin Bache, January 14, 1781

When Thomas Paine arrived in Philadelphia in November 1774, he was an anonymous and penniless immigrant, who, after years of struggling in England as a staymaker, exciseman, teacher, and storekeeper, had decided to try his luck in the colonies. A year later, with the publication of *Common Sense*, Paine was the toast of Philadelphia. But Paine's popularity was never entirely uncontested. In fact, it would decline rapidly and not recover by his death thirty-four years later. As the epigraph demonstrates, Sarah Franklin Bache characterized Paine's dwindling reputation aptly in a 1781 letter to her father, Benjamin Franklin: From the outset Paine's public role was intricately linked with controversy; the dispute over *Common Sense* was only the first of Paine's many public battles during his career as a political writer in America. In 1783, in one of his various pleas for remuneration from the Confederation Congress, Paine recounts his initiation into the public arena in less than enthusiastic terms: "Scarcely had I put my foot into the Country but it was set on fire about my ears. All the plans or prospects of private life (for I am not by nature fond of, or fitted for a public one, and feel all occasions of it where I must act personally, a burden) all these plans, I say, were immediately disconcerted, and I was at once involved in all the troubles of the Country" (CW II, 1227). If Paine

49

was reluctant to participate in public affairs, he certainly did not show any signs of diffidence in his writing. On the contrary, the author seems to relish his role as a public figure. His decision to adopt the pseudonym "Common Sense" after the publication of his hugely successful pamphlet only emphasizes the degree to which he had embraced his public persona.

In this chapter I will argue that although Paine was a strong advocate of a public political discourse, what we have come to identify as the public sphere, he also became one of the public sphere's most strident critics. While critics of Michael Warner's account of an impersonal public sphere have pointed to the centrality of orality and performativity in late eighteenth-century America, Paine forces us to reexamine the political and class assumptions of the republican public sphere.[1] Translated into the political terms of the late eighteenth-century United States this means that the republican public sphere was not so much real, as an ideal espoused by the elites, the Federalists, in order to limit access to public political debates and retain control of the political arena.[2] Recognizing that the republican public sphere was by no means the inclusive, accessible, cacophonous realm that many of its proponents claimed it to be, Paine attempts to construct a version of the public sphere devoid of the exclusionary principles introduced by republican ideology with its emphasis on the connection between individuals' economic wealth and their capacity for civic virtue and disinterestedness. The main thrust of Paine's

---

[1] A growing body of work has studied the cultural significance of performativity and orality in early America. Arguing that "The elocutionary revolution [of the mid-eighteenth century] made the credibility of arguments contingent on the emotional credibility of the speaker" (2), in *Declaring Independence* Jay Fliegelman describes the emergence of a "culture of performance" during the revolutionary period, which "sought to replace artificial language with natural language and to make writing over into the image of speaking" (24). Along similar lines, in *Voicing America* Christopher Looby explores the central role that notions of orality played in shaping the revolutionary and federal periods, suggesting that "since [the United States'] legitimacy was explicitly grounded in an appeal to rational interest, not visceral passion-voice embodied a certain legitimating charisma that print could not" (4). More recently, in *Eloquence is Power* Sandra Gustafson traces the ways that early American writing and rhetoric is shaped by an ongoing dialectic with theories of eloquence.

[2] Commenting on the limitations of Habermas' conception of the public sphere, Nancy Frasier observes, "We can no longer assume that the bourgeois conception of the public sphere was simply an unrealized utopian ideal; it was also a masculinist notion that functioned to legitimate an emergent form of class rule" (116). Ironically, at the moment when we endorse the republican public sphere as historical fact, we are blinded to the true struggle it seeks to conceal, the struggle to control public politics and writing in the aftermath of the Revolution.

critique, as we shall see, was aimed at the distinction between public and private that underwrites the conception of the republican public sphere. He saw this distinction as an overtly ideological strategy employed by elites to conceal their political motives.[3]

In spite of his skepticism about the propriety of disconnecting the private from the public in matters political, Paine strongly advocated a vigorous and open discussion of public affairs that he hoped would include the widest possible range of voices. For Paine, the solution lay in making the public sphere more accessible to middling and lower sorts who were frequently excluded from the public discussion of matters of state.[4] Consequently, Paine's attempts to reform the public sphere often irritated the political and social elites who wished to retain control of the new nation's affairs. It should come as no surprise, therefore, that Paine's understanding of the nature of public debate, and the style of polemical writing he adopted as a consequence of that understanding, led to a curious disjuncture in his public career between his unparalleled success as a writer and his failure to gain the personal recognition and popularity among the public that other revolutionary figures had obtained. This chapter traces Paine's participation in and attitude toward the public sphere through three key controversies in which he played a central role. First, I examine his inauguration into public life in the debates surrounding *Common Sense*. Next, I focus on the controversy sparked by his allegations that Silas Deane had bilked the Continental Congress, and finally, I attend to the last major controversy Paine created with the publication, in 1796, of "The Letter to George Washington."

DISPUTING *COMMON SENSE*

Less than three weeks after the first advertisement for *Common Sense* appeared in the *Pennsylvania Journal* (January 10, 1776), Robert Bell advertised a second edition of the pamphlet in the *Evening Post* (January 27,

---

[3] Paradoxically, while classic republicanism held that disinterestedness was only made possible by economic prosperity – thus drawing a fundamental link between the public and the private – once achieved, disinterestedness implied that the individual could escape private interest in order to pursue the public good.

[4] As Geoff Eley has noted, "The virtue of publicness could materialize other than by the intellectual transactions of a polite and literate bourgeois milieu. Despite the best efforts of the latter precisely to appropriate such a function to itself and to establish exclusive claims on the practice of reason, 'private people putting reason to use' could also be found elsewhere" (304).

1776). Bell's advertisement also included an attack on the author of *Common Sense*, who remained anonymous throughout the dispute, because, unhappy with the financial arrangement with Bell and now knowing that his pamphlet was already exceptionally popular, Paine had taken his pamphlet to the Bradfords who agreed to print a competing edition. Bell was responding to the advertisement from two days earlier in which W. and T. Bradford of Philadelphia offered "a new edition of COMMON SENSE, addressed to the inhabitants of America, with large and interesting additions by the author," which Paine intended to supersede the Bell edition. In a brief notice "To the PUBLIC" the Bradford advertisement further notes that "The encouragement and reception which this pamphlet hath already met with, and the great demand for the same, hath induced the publisher of the first edition to print a new edition unknown to the author, who expressly directed him not to proceed therein without orders, because large additions would be made thereto."[5] Bell, however, claimed in his advertisement that "he neither heard nor received any such directions or orders" (EP, January 27, 1776). While the controversy between Bell and Paine, which was played out publicly in the press over the following several weeks, only served to draw even more attention to *Common Sense* and its now celebrated but still anonymous author, Paine's character also suffered in the debate.

In his advertisement responding to the competing Bradford edition, Bell questions the ethics of Paine's decision to seek a new printer for his popular pamphlet:

As soon as the printer and publisher discovered the capricious disposition of the ostensible author [Paine], he disclaimed all future connexion, and by the publication of a second edition, which he advertised in a news paper, immediately declared his desirable independence from the trammels of catch-penny authorcraft, whose cunning was so exceeding great as to attempt to destroy the reputation of his own first edition, by advertising intended additions before his earliest and best customers had time to read what they had so very lately purchased. (EP, January 27, 1776)

Turning the tables on Paine, Bell here appeals to the very principles Paine's argument espouses in *Common Sense*. The power of Bell's attack lay in his clever alignment of himself as printer and publisher with the cause of

---

5 *Evening Post*, Philadelphia. January 25, 1776. All further references will be noted in the text as EP.

independence and of the author with despotism and monarchy.[6] Furthermore, Bell's reference to writing as "author-craft" suggests a connection between writing and other sinister practices such as priestcraft and political craft. Bell invokes the political rhetoric of the period that focused on dispelling the notion of politics as an arcane science. While Paine never explicitly invokes it in *Common Sense*, his emphasis on the need to simplify the government, because "the more simple any thing is, the less liable it is to be disordered, and the easier repaired when disordered" (CW 1, 6), stems from the discourse of political craft that Bolingbroke had used so effectively in the 1730s in England.[7]

Three days later, the controversy between Paine and Bell occupied the entire back page of the *Evening Post*, where Bell's original attack is reprinted in the left column, and a response from Paine appears in the right column. Whereas Bell attacked Paine directly in a strident tone, Paine defends himself without attacking Bell personally, by appealing to his readers' sentimentality. Paine sets the tone of his response in the opening line where he presents his motive for writing: "The author, for the sake of relieving the anxiety of his friends, maketh the following declaration" (EP, January 30, 1776). Paine suggests that he is not so much interested in arguing with Bell, as he is in securing the respect of his friends. Paine's strategy of presenting himself as a sensitive, caring friend, culminates in his assertion that "he hath neither directly, nor indirectly, received, or is to receive any profit or advantage whatsoever from the edition printed by Robert Bell" and that he intended his portion of the profits to be used "for the purpose of purchasing mittens for the troops" who were then on their way to Quebec (EP, January 30, 1776). Paine's sentimental and patriotic appeals present an innocent disinterested public servant who has been wronged by Bell, and who, unlike Bell, will not stoop to an *ad hominem* attack. It is only as a consequence of the reader's belief in Paine's

---

[6] In *Declaring Independence* Jay Fliegelman remarks of Bell's rhetorical strategy: "Here is the American Revolution recast (and inverted) as the conflict between author and publisher" (79). My own reading of the dispute between Paine and Bell is indebted not only to Fliegelman's analysis, but also to James Green's treatment of the subject in his 1993 Rosenbach Lectures in Bibliography.

[7] Fifty years earlier, Caleb D'Anvers, the fictional editor of Bolingbroke's opposition newspaper, *The Craftsman*, explained that publication's title stating that, "The purpose of the venture...was to expose corruption and craft in all professions. The mysteries of state and political craft were the most mischievous of these corruptions, and the paper dedicated itself to unraveling and exposing the dark secrets of political craft" (Kramnick, 19). Paine does not mention Bolingbroke in *Common Sense*, but he does cite Dragonetti on the "science of the politician" (CW I, 29).

innocence, that Bell's meanness becomes apparent in Paine's account of their transactions. Paine's decision not to attack Bell's character directly only reinforces the image of himself that Paine seeks to project in these advertisements.

In February Bell retaliated by publishing a new book, *Additions to Common Sense*, an attempt to cash in on Paine's success, which, as Bell notes in his advertisement, "consist of Pieces taken out of News Papers, and not written by the Author of COMMON SENSE" (EP, February 20, 1776). The various authors of the essays in Bell's compilation simply repeat many of the arguments made in *Common Sense* without the rhetorical or argumentative power of its original.[8] Ironically, in spite of his banking on the continued popularity of *Common Sense* to ensure the success of this new text, Bell accompanied the advertisement for *Additions* with a new attack on Paine. This time Bell characterizes Paine as a mysterious and evil scoundrel intent on the destruction of his enemies:

The envious Mr. ANONYMOUS, the shadow of an author, with his murdering MASK and his DARK LANTHORN, fully equipped for the ruffian business of assassination (like unto a villanous THIEF, whose voracious cravings for PREY constrain him to forget the fears which forced him so lately to scamper away) hath once more crept into the field to ROB and to DESTROY the reputation of authors, whose literary abilities OUT-SHINE his, as far as the blaze of a torch OUT-SHINETH the glimmering of a candle. (EP, February 24, 1776)

Unlike his previous attack, in which he questioned the motives of Paine's actions, Bell now impugns Paine's character directly. Once again, Bell builds on the image of the author as a sinister figure: The contrast between light and dark in Bell's imaginative construction of Paine serves to reinforce the association of his anonymity with an evil nature. Even though his readers would surely recognize the hyperbole of Bell's description, it effectively raises doubts about the credibility of the still nameless author of *Common Sense*.

No sooner had Paine's public quarrel with Bell over the possible profits resulting from the unprecedented popularity of Paine's pamphlet subsided, than several responses to *Common Sense* began to appear in the newspapers and in pamphlets. In March, just two months after he had originally published Paine's pamphlet, Bell printed and published *Plain Truth*, the first response to Paine's massively popular pamphlet.[9] Bell also attached

---

[8] The authors of the items contained in *Additions to Common Sense* remain unknown.

[9] The first advertisement for *Plain Truth* appeared in the *Pennsylvania Gazette* for March 13, 1776.

a work of his own, "The Printer to the Public: On the Freedom of the Press" to *Plain Truth*. In his one page item Bell, tacitly acknowledging the impact of Paine's text and its popularity, defends his right to publish this new work:

Having very lately, without any other authority than the THE LIBERTY OF THE PRESS, ushered into the hands of the public, certain speculations

FOR AMERICAN INDEPENDENCY.

By the same authority, viz, THE LIBERTY OF THE PRESS: ROBERT BELL, Provedore to the Sentimentalists; hath printed, published, and is now selling (Price Three Shillings) to all who are capable of practising so much impartiality, as to give a hearing to the other Side, by lending their attention towards certain speculations.

AGAINST AMERICAN INDEPENDENCY. (*Plain Truth*, n.p.)

To support his decision to print *Plain Truth* Bell cites several passages from the popular Junius' *Free Letters* and De Lolme's *Essay on the English Constitution*. Following these selected extracts, on the verso of the title page, as if to reaffirm his commitment to the liberty of the press, Bell includes an advertisement for the latest edition of *Common Sense*. As a printer Bell could ill afford to take sides in a political debate (although that did not impede him from demonizing one of the participants in the debate); instead, his impartiality allowed, even encouraged, him to profit from both sides of the dispute.[10] *Plain Truth*, written by James Chalmers under the pseudonym Candidus, however, could compete with *Common Sense* neither in sales nor in argumentative power. As with most of the attempts to respond to Paine's arguments, *Plain Truth* did not really stand a chance. Failing to grasp the emotional power of Paine's text, Candidus, citing Montesquieu repeatedly, attempts to respond to each of Paine's arguments with rational and empirical arguments. In so doing he not only allows Paine to set the terms of the debate, but he fails to counter the sentimental power of *Common Sense*. Candidus appeals to the reader's reason, where *Common Sense* owed much of its success to Paine's appeal to his readers' passion and imagination, as well as their reason.

Paine's appeal to his reader's imagination in *Common Sense* is evidenced most explicitly in his use of phrases such as "The cause of America is in a great measure the cause of all mankind" (CW I, 3), which give the reader a sense of involvement in an epic struggle. While Paine makes such

---

[10] For an excellent account of the role and limitations of printers during the American Revolution, see Stephen Botein, "Printers and the American Revolution."

sweeping generalizations, he carefully avoids any kind of explicit statement of the larger argument of *Common Sense*. His assertion regarding
the magnitude of the American cause itself benefits from a lack of speci-
ficity as to the nature of that cause, for it appears before Paine has even
stated the main thesis of his text. Thus, by making them feel they are
part of a larger, irresistible movement, Paine attempts to win over his
readers to his argument in favor of independence, even before he has
stated it. This strategic combination of generalization and evasion allows
Paine a degree of freedom, both in his range of subjects addressed and
in his rhetoric throughout his text, that those attempting to answer his
arguments would fail to duplicate.

Paine clearly senses a need to prepare his readers for his open call for
a declaration of independence before explicitly urging them to revolution. Nothing on the title page to *Common Sense* suggests that it will
endorse a permanent separation from England. The title page's list of
"subjects" to be discussed in the pamphlet – "I. Of the Origin and Design
of Government in general, with concise remarks on the English Constitution. II. Of Monarchy and Hereditary Succession. III. Thoughts on the
present State of American Affairs. IV. Of the present Ability of America,
with some miscellaneous Reflections." – suggest, rather, that this is a
study of the contemporary political and economic conditions in Britain
and America.[11] Paine does not even raise the issue of independence as
a viable option until the third section of the pamphlet when he rather
defensively offers his motivation for supporting such a course of action:
"I am induced not by motives of pride, party or resentment to espouse
the doctrine of separation and independence; I am clearly, positively, and
conscientiously persuaded that it is the true interest of this continent to be
so" (CW I, 24). Thus, when Paine finally announces the central argument
of his pamphlet, he downplays its significance by shifting attention away
from the argument itself and onto his reasons for supporting it. Recognizing the controversial nature of his argument Paine allows his readers
to sidestep the issue of whether they agree with his conclusion or not by
focusing on his reasoning process instead of on the conclusion reached.

Paine's rhetorical strategy also involves allowing his readers to infer the
conclusions to be drawn from his arguments. In *Common Sense* he does
not spell out a specific course of action for his readers until the end of the

---

[11] I have consulted the American Philosophical Society's copy of Bell's 1776 edition. In his
Bibliographical Check List of Common Sense, Richard Gimbel also reproduces facsimiles
of the title page of various editions of *Common Sense*.

pamphlet when he lays out his conclusion: "To CONCLUDE, however strange it may appear to some, or however unwilling they may be to think so, matters not, but many strong and striking reasons may be given to show, that nothing can settle our affairs so expeditiously as an open and determined DECLARATION FOR INDEPENDENCE" (CW I, 38–39). By this time, however, his assertion that this is the only proper course of action is a foregone conclusion. Yet even this call to action is contained within a different argument about the potential sources of unity among the residents of the various colonies and their local governments. The effect of Paine's style of argumentation, therefore, is to give the impression that his conclusions follow rationally and inevitably from the evidence presented. In *Plain Truth*, where Candidus insists upon the folly of independence before presenting the evidence to support his point of view, the sense conveyed is that the evidence has been put in the service of the argument rather than the conclusion following naturally upon the evidence.

In a series of letters that he published under the pseudonym Cato, William Smith, the Provost of the College of Philadelphia and a noted Anglican minister, responds more effectively to *Common Sense* precisely because, for the first three letters at least, he avoids the pitfall of a point by point refutation of the arguments of Paine's pamphlet. Instead, Cato simply asserts his support for reconciliation without addressing the details of Paine's arguments or even referring to *Common Sense* directly. From the outset, it is clear, nonetheless, that his letters are motivated by the effectiveness of Paine's arguments in favor of independence. Cato states his position clearly in the second letter: "I am bold to declare, and hope yet to make it evident to every honest man, that the true interest of America lies in reconciliation with Great Britain, upon constitutional principles, and I can truly say, I wish it upon no other terms" (*Pennsylvania*, March 11, 1776).[12]

Acknowledging Paine's pamphlet, if only indirectly, for the first time, Cato sets up his role as he remarks upon the lack of responses to the arguments for independence:

Why the many publications in favor of independency, with which our presses have lately groaned, have passed hitherto unnoticed, I am not able to determine. But there are certainly times when public affairs become so interesting, that every man

---

[12] Portions of *Cato's Letters* were printed in various Philadelphia newspapers. Although it was not the first newspaper to print the first letter, for the sake of consistency, I am citing them as they appeared in the *Pennsylvania Packet*, which along with the *Gazette* published the entire series.

becomes a debtor to the community for his opinions, either in speaking or writing. Perhaps it was thought best, where an *appeal* was pretended to be made to the COMMON SENSE of this country, to leave the people for a while to the free exercise of that good understanding which they are known to possess.... If little notice has been taken of the publications concerning independence, it is neither owing to the popularity of the doctrine, the unanswerable nature of the arguments, nor the fear of opposing them, as the vanity of the author would suggest. I am confident that nine-tenths of the people of Pennsylvania yet abhor the doctrine. (March 11, 1776)

Openly declaring himself the spokesman for the cause of reconciliation with Great Britain, a cause he suggests hardly needs his assistance, Cato flatters his readers for their ability to discern the proper course of action in this matter. At the same time, he subtly calls for more responses to *Common Sense* by arguing that the outcome of the current debate concerns everyone, and under these circumstances all interested parties ought to make their opinions known. Cato cleverly invokes the language of commercial relations, an issue that was also at the center of the debate over the implications of independence, to enjoin others to express publicly their opinions regarding the proper relationship between the colonies and Britain, which would naturally have important consequences for the colonies' economy as well as for their government. Paradoxically, then, Cato employs an economic argument in favor of the democratic process, seemingly advocating that the people's voice become the final authority to support his argument in favor of the British monarchical system of government.

Although Cato expresses faith in the people's judgment here, in his next letter, "Cato III," he acknowledges the need for a direct response to Paine's pamphlet, lest the people be deceived: "The people generally judge right, when the whole truth is plainly laid out before them; but through inattention in some, and fondness for novelty in others, when but one side of a proposition is agitated and persevered in, they may gradually deceive themselves, and adopt what cooler reflection and future dear-bought experience may prove to be ruinous" (March 25, 1776). Cato thus applauds his audience's capacity to judge in these matters, while cautioning them about the possibility of deception. Appropriately, not until this third letter, where he questions Paine's motivation for writing his pamphlet, does Cato actually begin to address *Common Sense* directly. He begins by attacking its author rather than his arguments: "these proofs ought to be more pure than what can flow through the foul pages of interested writers, or strangers intermeddling in our affairs, and avowedly pressing their republican schemes upon us, at the risk of all we hold valuable" (March 25, 1776). Cato's attempt to impeach Paine's voice on the basis of his nationality posed a unique problem because while Paine was indeed a recent emigrant to the colonies, he was an Englishman. To estrange Paine for being an Englishman suggested precisely the kind of breach that Paine was trying to delineate in *Common Sense*, for if Paine was a stranger to America by virtue of being English, then surely Americans were also strangers to Britain. So while this particular attack on Paine might have served to alienate Paine from an American audience, it also implied a growing distance between the colonies and the mother country that ultimately could be used to undermine Cato's larger argument.

Cato's *ad hominem* assault conforms to his larger tactic of not addressing the specific arguments of *Common Sense*, choosing instead to attack the general argument for independence, and supplementing that argument by attacking the credibility of its foremost advocate. This approach, as Cato well understood, placed him in the difficult position of attempting to deny Paine's larger argument without belittling the colonies' strengths as Paine had described them in *Common Sense*. Cato's anxiety about this predicament manifests itself in his fourth epistle, "Not a word shall be drawn from me to discredit our own strength or resources, altho' the accounts given of them, by the author of Common Sense, appear incredible to some. I will even go beyond him in expressing my good opinion of our situation" (March 25, 1776). Cato knew that regardless of the veracity of Paine's assessment, Paine's opponents had to be careful not to alienate their audience by denigrating its social and economic capacity. Unfortunately for Cato, the problem was that the economic and military disadvantages of the colonies when compared to those of Britain constituted perhaps the best argument against independence. Indeed, as had Paine's other critics, Cato eventually attempts a reasoned answer to Paine's specific contentions about the colonies dependence upon Britain. In this letter Cato notes that Paine has effectively led him to this trap: "He has called repeatedly for *answers*, and announced his second edition to the world in the following strain of self-adulation, 'That as no answer hath yet appeared it is now presumed that none will,' and therefore as may be fairly implied, that he is unanswerable" (March 25, 1776). Cato then commences his critique of the details of *Common Sense*, which predictably enough raises many of the same questions about Paine's pamphlet as Candidus does in *Plain Truth*. Forced to rely on the same facts (for example, colonial dependence), Cato fails to match the ethical and pathetic appeal of Paine's pamphlet.

FRANKLIN'S DIFFIDENCE AND PAINE'S DIRECT STYLE

Paine's triumphant inaugural experience in the arena of public politics, however, would prove to be atypical for him because more often than not in the next three decades he would find himself on the losing end of public opinion. The reasons for his setbacks varied in great measure according to the specific circumstances of the matters debated, but one factor that hurt him repeatedly was his personal approach to these debates, an approach that contrasted sharply with that of his mentor, Benjamin Franklin. Throughout his political life Paine repeatedly looked to Franklin as a patron, a guide, and even as a father figure.[13] He first met Franklin in 1774, when Franklin was in England and Paine had gained some measure of success with his "Case of the Officers of Excise."[14] When he decided to emigrate to America he procured a letter of introduction from Franklin, which greatly facilitated his settling in Philadelphia, and enabled him to find employment almost immediately. As soon as he was established in Philadelphia, Paine wrote the first letter of what would become a long and friendly correspondence with Franklin. More than their friendship, however, the most illuminating aspect of this relationship is the contrast between their respective approaches to politics and political writing, and their resulting public images.

Early in *The Autobiography*, in a frequently studied passage, Franklin discusses his early exposure to the Socratic Method, which he learned from an English Grammar he was studying:

I continu'd this Method some few Years but gradually left it, retaining only the Habit of expressing my self in Terms of modest Diffidence, never using when I advance any thing that may possibly be disputed, the Words, *Certainly, undoubtedly*, or any others that give the Air of Positiveness to an Opinion; but rather say,

---

[13] Upon arriving in America Paine wrote to Franklin and noted that he did not have the time to make a fair copy of the letter because he had to write to his father. Thus, at this pivotal moment in his life, Paine writes to Franklin before he writes to his father. That Franklin returned Paine's affection is evident from a letter he wrote to Paine in 1785: "Your kind Congratulations on my safe Return give me a great deal of Pleasure; for I have always valu'd your Friendship.... Be assured, my dear Friend, that instead of Repenting that I was your Introducer to America, I value my self on the Share I had in procuring for it the Acquisition of so useful and valuable a citizen."

[14] Paine, then employed as an exciseman in Lewes, England, wrote the "Case" in 1772 at the behest of his fellow excisemen who felt their working conditions and wages were unacceptable. The pamphlet, directed at Parliament, did not succeed at its purpose and it cost Paine his job, but it made it possible for him to become acquainted with Oliver Goldsmith and Benjamin Franklin, both of whom regarded him highly (Hawke 16–18, Keane 72–79).

I conceive, or *I apprehend* a Thing to be so or so, *It appears to me*, or *I should think so and so for such & such Reasons*, or *I imagine* it to be so, or *it is so if I am not mistaken*. – This Habit I believe has been of great Advantage to me, when I have had occasion to inculcate my Opinions & persuade Men into Measures that I have been from time to time engag'd in promoting. (1321–1322)

The rhetorical strategy Franklin advocates in this passage is almost diametrically opposed to Paine's approach to argumentative writing. Whereas strategic diffidence was the governing principle of Franklin's rhetorical style, certainty and confidence, at times even arrogance, often characterized Paine's writing. The difference in Paine and Franklin's respective approaches to public exchange reflects a more fundamental difference in their views of the relationship between human reason and truth. As the previous passage implies, Franklin does not believe that individuals have access to an essentialized truth. He is careful, for example, not to identify his beliefs as truths, instead calling them opinions. As Michael Warner has suggested, Franklin understands rhetoric and rationality to be inextricably intertwined: "Rhetoric ceases to be duplicitous masking in Franklin's rationality because the negative self-relation of the instrumental rhetorician *is* the structure of rationality. Rhetoric is rational because rationality is rhetorical" (81). In other words, Franklin's diffidence is the product of a conviction that knowledge is the product of dialogue but because dialogue is ongoing, knowledge is always only temporary or contingent. Certainty is anathema to this formulation, both because it ends dialogue and because it presumes that individuals can have direct access to truth.

Paine, who insists on the simplicity of the world, believes firmly that there is one essential truth. Certain of his knowledge of this truth, Paine writes in order to communicate it to his contemporaries. At the same time, he insists that everyone, if they are willing to free their minds of prejudice (or custom as he often calls it), can access that truth; it is not a mystery that requires specialized knowledge to be understood. His prose and thought reflect a profound sense of certainty because he is simply reporting, rendering transparent, truths that are immanent in the world. We can see this sense of certainty in the first paragraph of *Common Sense*: "Perhaps the sentiments contained in the following pages, are not *yet* sufficiently fashionable to procure them general favor; a long habit of not thinking a thing *wrong*, gives it a superficial appearance of being right, and raises at first a formidable outcry in defence of custom. But the tumult soon subsides. Time makes more converts than reason" (CW I, 3). If the "perhaps" at the beginning of the statement suggests any diffidence in the writer, it soon vanishes as it becomes apparent that Paine is sure about the truthfulness of his argument despite his anticipating a "formidable outcry" against it. When he urges his readers to free themselves of the tyranny of the past "custom," in order to be able to act in the present, Paine provides his readers with a psychological explanation for their resistance to his argument. Paine uses that psychology to transform the reader's resistance into a form of proof as to the truthfulness of his contentions. That is, his contentions are true precisely because at first they seem to be wrong. According to Paine's logic, only those that succeed in escaping the powerful hold of the past will see the reasonableness of his arguments. Nowhere is this clearer than in his statement of purpose in *Common Sense*:

In the following pages I offer nothing more than simple facts, plain arguments, and common sense: and have no other preliminaries to settle with the reader, than that he will divest himself of prejudice and prepossession, and suffer his reason and his feelings to determine for themselves: that he will put on, or rather that he will not put off, the true character of a man, and generously enlarge his views beyond the present day. (CW I, 17)

Bringing his invocation of fashion in the "Introduction" full circle, Paine characterizes the ability to resist the fashionable as a manly quality. Paine thus stigmatized any opposing arguments as not only unthinking and/or reactionary, but also effeminate.

Paine's tendency to explain disagreements or resistance to his views through personal psychology further reinforces the fundamental difference between him and Franklin. Interactions between audiences and authors are always complicated. Where Franklin places the onus on the author, Paine prefers to make the reader responsible for opening his mind to the ideas presented by the writer. From this perspective, we might say that Franklin assumes a reader such as himself, one who reflects on ideas and is open to persuasion, and Paine assumes a reader who needs to be pushed and prodded, and, most importantly, who is reluctant to examine and reconsider his/her assumptions about the world. Franklin, following Warner's reading, would contend that Paine's rhetoric generates the reader's resistance to the ideas presented in the text by transforming the debate into a personal battle of wills. However, it is hard to argue with Paine's success at reaching and provoking the widest possible audience. Would *Common Sense* or *The Age of Reason* have been as influential if they had been written in the tones of modest diffidence advocated by Franklin? On the other hand, Franklin's approach enabled him to engage with a much broader spectrum of voices in the cacophony that was

Revolutionary Philadelphia (for example, he counted both the radical Paine and the conservative William Smith among his many friends).

Franklin could mediate the competing political positions of the day because he never invested himself personally in any of them. As Warner has argued, Franklin did not see himself as personally implicated in his thoughts: "By characterizing thinking itself as manipulation of thought, it postulates a manipulating self that does not coincide with thought, that is not even imminent in it" (79). Warner goes on to note that this dissociation of the self and thought is further mediated in Franklin by his conception of writing, because Franklin "envisions writing as the scene of pure socialization, and even of a social erotic, paradoxically because it is freed from the localization of the personal, the bodily, the corruptible" (87).[15] Paine, who like most of his contemporaries, was incapable of such self-negation, became the representative voice of a particular political position. This made it impossible for him to compromise in the ways that would make Franklin legendary. If Paine recognized alternative views, he could never quite accommodate them in his thinking. This was partly because he was convinced that that world was simple (and polyphony is complicated), but also because he had become strongly identified with a specific set of ideas. This isolated Paine and contributed to his downfall because, in Franklin's terms, Paine's ideas may have appealed to a broad audience, but they always remained emphatically his. They were overly entangled with his person. Unlike Franklin, who seeks to persuade without seeming to persuade, Paine seeks to convince his reader and says so. But, of course, that's part of what made Franklin a skilled politician and Paine an unparalleled polemicist. For a polemical writer such as Paine the diffidence Franklin advocates would undermine much of his argumentative power. What we might miss in a celebration of either of these approaches is the degree to which each needed the other. More generally, to be successful the Revolution required both people like Paine to produce strong opinions and provoke debate and people like Franklin to work his magic and find common ground.

---

[15] In Warner's study, Franklin epitomizes the new relationship to print that arose in the early eighteenth century (xiii). Warner characterizes this relationship as "normally impersonal": "the reader does not simply imagine him- or herself receiving a direct communication or hearing the voice of the author. He or she now also incorporates *into the meaning of the printed object* an awareness of the potentially limitless others who may also be reading" (xiii). Therefore, "The meaning of public utterance, for both [author and reader], is established by the very fact that their exchange can be read and participated in by any number of unknown and *in principle unknowable others*" (40).

Just as Franklin had studied and rejected the personalized approach Paine would employ, Paine had pondered the depersonalized approach to public debate and found its reliance on the distinction between public and private unsatisfactory. In the "Introduction" to *Common Sense*, Paine invokes that distinction when he observes that, "In the following sheets, the author has studiously avoided every thing which is personal among ourselves. Compliments as well as censure make no part thereof. The wise and the worthy need not the triumph of a pamphlet; and those whose sentiments are injudicious or unfriendly will cease of themselves, unless too much pains is bestowed upon their conversions" (CW I, 3). Paine's reference to the wise and the worthy undermines his statement of disinterestedness, insofar as it returns to the personal in the very act of rejecting it as a proper basis for establishing an argument's validity. In other words, it is only because of the strength of his character, his wisdom, and his worthiness that he does not depend on the success of his pamphlet to prove himself. While Paine generally avoided personal attacks in *Common Sense*, as he became more involved, and personally invested, in the political world of the Revolution and Early Republic, his attitude shifted and he began to appeal to the testimonial or character-based arguments and attacks he had disclaimed at the beginning of his breakthrough pamphlet.

We can see Paine's approach to public debate changing in the series of letters he wrote in response to Cato. Paine published his "Foresters Letters" in various Pennsylvania newspapers in April and May of 1776. Perhaps in response to Cato's insinuations about the author of *Common Sense*, Paine's tendency to personalize arguments now manifests itself openly in these letters. Paine, however, understands the value of distinguishing between individuals and arguments. Dena Goodman has described the notion that one should consider policies or ideas independently of the individual proposing them as an issue that obtained particular resonance in the second half of the eighteenth century: "Although the distinction between personal insult and the criticism of ideas may not have been new, the need to disentangle them in practice took on a new urgency in the Enlightenment Republic of Letters" (*Republic*, 96).[16] Indeed, in the first installment of "The Forester" Paine reiterates his commitment to the notion that policies and not the individuals espousing them should be the subject of debate: "To be *nobly wrong* is more manly than to

---

[16] While Goodman's study focuses on France, these developments, as she points out, crossed national borders.

be *meanly right*. Only let the error be disinterested – let it wear *not the mask*, but the *mark* of principle, and 'tis pardonable. It is on this large and liberal ground, that we distinguish between men and their tenets, and generously preserve our friendship for the one, while we combat with every prejudice the other" (CW II, 61). In this passage Paine cites one of the fundamental concerns for all participants in the arena of public debate: "how were they to continue to debate"' as Goodman has put it, "and disagree in person and still remain collaborators and friends?" (96). The trick for Paine, then, was to devise a strategy that would allow him to make the personal, or the private, relevant without sliding into insult.

As with the introductory remarks to *Common Sense*, however, Paine's appeal to disinterested political debate in "Forester I" seems to contain the seeds of doubt about the validity of that practice. In the opening sentence he provides an avenue for escape from this impersonal mode of debate by suggesting that character, in this case identified as manliness, plays a significant role in the nature of the debate. By the end of the letter, though, Paine's patience seems to have worn thin:

For the present, Sir, farewell. I have seen thy soliloquy and despise it. Remember thou has thrown me the glove, Cato, and either thee or I must tire. I fear not the field of fair debate, but thou hast stepped aside and made it personal. Thou hast tauntingly called on me by name; and if I cease to hunt thee from every lane and lurking hole of mischief, and bring thee not a trembling culprit before the public bar, then brand me with reproach, by naming me in the list of your confederates. (CW II, 65)

Paine has forsworn the impersonal in favor of a deeply personalized discourse where individuals can be held responsible for their words and punished bodily for them. Curiously, Paine's language changes in this last paragraph into a much more performative mode, referring to Cato as thee and thou. Adopting the informal tones of this Quaker father's idiom, Paine's language calls attention to and enacts his desire to narrow the distance between author and individual.

It seems only fitting, given the ending of "Forester I," that Paine opens the second installment with an argument in favor of including the personal in political debates. After restating his commitment to the notion that "measures and not men are the thing in question," Paine, in apparent contradiction, observes:

But the political, characters, political dependencies, and political connections of men, being of a public nature, differ exceedingly from the circumstances of private life: and are in many instances so nearly related to the measures they propose, that to prevent our being deceived by the last, we must be acquainted with the first. A total ignorance of men lays us under the danger of mistaking plausibility for principle. Could the wolf bleat like the lamb the flock would soon be enticed into ruin; wherefore to prevent the mischief, he ought to be *seen* as well as *heard*. There never was nor ever will be, nor ever ought to be, any important political debate carried on, in which a total separation in all cases between men and measures could be admitted with sufficient safety. When hypocrisy shall be banished from the earth, the knowledge of men will be unnecessary, because their measures cannot then be fraudulent; but until that time come (which never will come) they ought, under proper limitations, to go together. (CW II, 66)

Here, Paine effectively denies the validity of the maxim that he had upheld earlier in the same paragraph. In the second half of this passage Paine offers a powerful rationale for including a consideration of the individual advocating a particular course of action in the evaluation of that measure. However, the apparent contradiction in the long and contorted first sentence of the quotation suggests the difficulty he had in articulating this point. In the clause preceding the colon Paine appears to endorse the separation of public and private, but after the colon he reintroduces at least a partial consideration of the "man" into public political debates. The distinction Paine makes is worth noting because although he accepts the differentiation between public and private, he is asserting a space for taking the individual into account. Essentially, Paine is attempting to redefine what ought to be included under the rubric of the public.

Uncharacteristically, Paine struggles to articulate his point. He struggles not only because the distinction between public and private is, as it continues to be, slippery, but because the ideology he is combating, republicanism, is equally elusive and difficult to counteract. The crucial point Paine seeks to communicate in this passage, however, is the notion of disinterestedness that lies at the heart of republicanism. By asserting that "the political characters, political dependencies, and political connections of men" ought properly to be included in a consideration of the measures they propose, Paine undermines the notion that anyone is capable of disinterestedness. Paine would not have been able to reach this conclusion had he subscribed to the republican notion of disinterestedness. His commitment to Lockean liberal ideology and its emphasis on individual rights and self-interest, however, made him an ideal critic of the republican public sphere because it enabled him to perceive the underlying class assumptions buttressing it. Most scholarship on the eighteenth century public sphere has attempted to merge republicanism and Lockean liberalism.

However, Paine, following in Locke's footsteps, illustrates that the two cannot be reconciled because the republican public sphere is founded upon the very class assumptions that he, following Locke, is dedicated to destroying.

Paradoxically, Paine presents his argument for the need to consider the individual proposing measures in an anonymous text at a time when his identity as the author of *Common Sense* was known only to a small cadre of the Philadelphia elite. This need not imply that Paine's criticism of one of the fundamental courtesies of the public sphere was misplaced, only that for the moment, at least, he recognized the benefit of anonymity and took advantage of it. Just as he recognized that anonymity served the interests of the author, Paine clearly also understood that it could pose a real danger in the public arena. Nonetheless, by disavowing the impersonality of political discourse, Paine almost invites personal criticism. As we shall see below, instead of maintaining the focus on the strength of his arguments, Paine's perceptive analysis of the intimate relationship between the public and the private served to draw attention to him personally.

LOSING CREDIT, OR THE EFFECT OF THE DEANE AFFAIR

A few lines before commenting on Paine's declining reputation in 1781, Sarah Franklin Bache informed her father of their cooling friendship: "I hear Mr. Payne is gone to France with Mr. Lawrence, he did not call on us. I had a little dispute with him more than a year ago about Mr. Deane, since which time he has never even moved his hat to me." Although she does not explicitly link the two events in her letter – her dispute with Paine regarding Silas Deane, and Paine's loss of "credit" with the American public – Bache's observation suggests that she was aware of the degree to which Paine's credibility had suffered as a result of his role in the Deane Affair. More generally, as Paine became more and more involved in the affairs of the new United States government he distanced himself from his audience and soon began to alienate the very "people" whose rights he had worked so hard to secure. Indeed, Paine's penchant for engaging in very public vitriolic personal disputes with his political foes, regardless of their popularity or public stature, probably did more to distance him from "the people" than did any of the policies he advocated.[17]

---

[17] Although scholars have often emphasized the detrimental effects that *The Age of Reason* had on Paine's popularity (see, for example Hawke), it is important to note that

To a large extent, Paine's dispute with Silas Deane over Deane's conduct in France on behalf of the United States, which would be played out publicly in the Philadelphia newspapers in December 1778 and January 1779, and his subsequent public assault on then President George Washington on July 30, 1796, cost Paine his role as the voice of the people. To be sure, the publication of *The Age of Reason* outraged a large segment of the population and probably had a greater long-term effect on his reputation, but his two ill-advised public personal confrontations, with Silas Deane and George Washington respectively, probably attracted the greatest attention in terms of his own "public character." In both cases, Paine's attacks backfired and served only to raise questions about his fitness for public office and allegiance to the principles of republicanism and democracy.

Originally, Paine was not at all involved in the Continental Congress' investigation of Deane's transactions with the French, although he was probably well aware of it in his capacity as secretary of the Committee of Foreign Affairs. Deane had been recalled by Congress from his post as American commissioner to France due to questions about financial improprieties in negotiations and purchases of arms and other supplies for the United States' war effort. On December 5, 1778, Deane, who had grown impatient after waiting for almost four months to address Congress, published an open letter "*To the Free and Virtuous* CITIZENS of AMERICA" in which the matter was made public for the first time. In his letter Deane, however, did not limit his address to an account of the facts of the case or to exonerating himself from any wrongdoing; he also leveled a serious assault on the Lee family of Virginia, aiming his attack mostly at Arthur Lee and William Lee, but also questioning Richard Henry Lee's character and devotion to the American cause. Paine, who had not been implicated in Deane's letter and had no personal stake in the matter, decided to respond partly out of friendship for the Lees, but also because he knew Deane was lying.

The controversy began because of allegations that various shipments of supplies, provided gratis by the French crown prior to the official Franco-American alliance of 1778, had been billed to the United States

Paine's religious tract sold in great numbers and was generally well received among the artisan and laboring classes in England and America (see Keane, 389–400). In light of its popularity, it seems facile to argue that it was solely responsible for Paine's public downfall.

government. In essence, Deane and Caron de Beaumarchais, the French king's agent, had conspired to bilk the United States government by representing the transaction as a commercial arrangement between the two countries, thereby profiting from the sale of supplies that had cost them nothing. However, for fear of British retaliation against France for giving the colonies supplies, the details of the investigation were secret and Paine had to be careful about what he said. Unfortunately (and characteristically), he was not careful enough; he failed to abide by one of the fundamental rules governing the statements of "public men" that he accused Deane of violating: "He mentions names without restraint, and stops at no discovery of persons. A public man, in Mr. Deane's former character, ought to be as silent as the grave; for who would trust a person with a secret who showed such a talent for revealing? Under the pretence of doing good he is doing mischief, and in a tumult of his own creating will expose and distress himself" (*Packet*, December 15, 1778). Paine's indiscretion cost him his position as secretary of foreign affairs. Because of the secret nature of the crucial evidence implicating Deane in Beaumarchais' embezzlement scheme, the debate became entirely personal.

In fact, in his letter of December 5, which ignited the controversy, Deane's aim was to transform the Continental Congress' investigation of his actions from a policy matter into a personal dispute. He begins his address with an attempt to set the terms of any future debate about his role: "The happiness or misfortunes, the benefits or injuries, of an individual, have generally no claim to public attention. I do not therefore address you on my own account, but on yours" (*Packet*, December 5, 1778). With this awkward and contradictory statement – the nation is not an individual, so it cannot be on account of the nation's reputation that he writes – Deane deflects attention from himself by suggesting that he is the protector of American virtue. Deane projects his anxiety about his own reputation, which is the true subject at issue, onto the nation, and the apparent contradiction in his statement accentuates Deane's sense of urgency respecting his own fate. Continuing this pattern of deflection, Deane then proceeds as promised, not to defend his own actions, but to question the motives and actions of others, specifically those of William and Arthur Lee, who were also serving as United States commissioners in Europe at the time when Deane was in France.

Only after he has spent the largest portion of his article generating suspicion about the Lee brothers by insinuating that they are at best incompetent for their positions and at worst traitors, does Deane state his own case. After explaining his situation, which occupies less than a quarter of the entire piece, Deane returns to his attack on the Lees, now directing his efforts at Richard Henry Lee, whom he accuses of aiding a known British spy, Dr. Berkenhout.[18] Once he has concluded his remarks on Richard Henry Lee's purported relationship with Dr. Berkenhout, Deane, perhaps sensing that he has overstepped the bounds of proper public discourse, attempts to justify his personal attacks even as he continues assaulting the Lees: "I do not speak from any pique against them, for altho' they are my personal and lately my avowed enemies, yet their conduct on many occasions hath been such, that to honor them with the emotions of anger, would be degrading to that character, which I hope always to maintain. My object is, merely to rescue your reputation." In other words, Deane, recalling his opening statement, attempts to mitigate his decision to engage in a personal assault by suggesting that it is borne out of a reasonable concern for the United States' image abroad. Thus far, the dispute remained a personal quarrel between Deane and the Lee family; that would change ten days later with Paine's open letter to Deane.

Implementing the policy he had espoused in "Forester's Letters," of taking the characters of men into account in matters of public debate – something he had done to great effect in *The American Crisis* – Paine attempted to subject Deane to the same treatment he had used on Lord Howe. On December 15, Paine entered the fray with an open letter addressed to Deane in the *Pennsylvania Packet*, and Silas Deane's case with the Continental Congress became a full-blown public controversy. At the beginning of his piece Paine stresses his disinterestedness: "Mr. Deane must very well know that I have no interest in, so likewise am I no stranger to, his negotiations and contracts in France, his difference with his colleagues, the reason of his return to America, and the matters which have occurred since." Continuing the debate on the terms Deane had established in his piece, Paine focuses his article on Deane's character and credibility, repeatedly questioning his status as a "gentleman":

There is a certain and necessary association of dignity between the person and the employment which perhaps did not appear when Mr. Deane was considered the ambassador. His address to the public confirms the justness of this remark. The spirit and language of it differ exceedingly from that cool penetrating judgment and refinement of manners and expression which fits, and is absolutely necessary in, the plenipotentiary." (*Packet*, December 15, 1778)

---

[18] Deane dedicates eight paragraphs to William and Arthur Lee, and only three to his own affairs with the Continental Congress.

Later, echoing Deane's claims that the public interest, not "pique," motivated his attack on the Lees, Paine appeals to Deane's status as a gentleman to validate his own disinterestedness: "Mr. Deane cannot have the least right to think that I am moved by any party difference or personal antipathy. He is a gentleman with whom I never had a syllable of dispute, nor with any other person upon his account." But then, returning to his defense of Richard Henry Lee, Paine suggests that Deane lacks the qualities of a gentleman: "Mr. Deane has involved a gentleman in his unlimited censure, whose fidelity and personal qualities I have been well acquainted with for three years past; and in respect to an absent injured friend, Colonel Richard Henry Lee, I will venture to tell Mr. Deane, that in any style of character in which a gentleman may be spoken of, Mr. Deane would suffer by comparison."

It seems surprising that Paine, who had been among the most vocal advocates of democracy a few years earlier, would now invoke the language of elitist politics, which had served to exclude "the people" from political participation. Paine's equation of gentility with a certain set of qualifications that make one fit for public office corresponds with an earlier rhetoric whose logic had made politics the exclusive domain of the landed gentry in England. Steven Shapin documents the close relationship between truth and gentility in the seventeenth century when "Gentility was a massively powerful instrument in the recognition, constitution, and protection of truth" (42). So much so, that "the definition of gentility implied a conception of truth, just as the location of truth in [early modern culture] might invoke a notion of gentility" (42).

The political implications of this conjunction of truth and gentility only reinforced the authority of the landed classes, for, as Shapin goes on to say,

Just as the ideal gentleman's integrity and independence were used to account for and enjoin his truthfulness, so the unreliable truthfulness of others was pervasively referred to their constrained circumstances. Those whose placement in society rendered them dependent upon others, whose actions were at others bidding, or who were so placed as to need relative advantage were *for these reasons* deemed liable to misrepresent real states of affairs-what they were actually thinking, what their intentions were with respect to future actions, how matters stood in the world. (86)

This equation of social class and/or wealth with a particular set of superior values is precisely the kind of nonsense that Paine decries in the second part of *Common Sense*, "Of Monarchy and Hereditary Succession," where he notes that "Male and female are the distinctions of nature, good and bad the distinctions of heaven; but how a race of men came into the world so exalted above the rest, and distinguished like some new species, is worth inquiring into, and whether they are the means of happiness or of misery to mankind" (CW I, 9). While Paine's remark is directed specifically at monarchs and the practice of hereditary succession, in practice it also applies to the aristocracy and gentry in general who set themselves above the common people by virtue of their ownership of the land. Paradoxically, then, in his attack on Deane, Paine resorts to the very rhetoric of political exclusion that he was working so diligently to undermine in other places. Thus, even as Paine sought to change the political landscape of the late eighteenth-century Anglo-American world, he could not avoid appealing to the fundamental assumptions that buttressed the institutions whose authority he was attempting to overthrow.[19]

Deane did not answer Paine directly; instead, on December 21, William Smith, who as "Cato" had previously responded to Paine's *Common Sense*, adopted the persona of "Plain Truth," to attack his old enemy in a piece entitled "Strictures of the Address of Common Sense to Mr. Deane, published in Mr. Dunlap's Paper of the 15th of December." "Plain Truth" wastes no time in using Paine's arguments respecting Deane's character to question Paine's integrity and credibility:

Others, who possessed themselves better acquainted with the circumstances and motives of your coming to this country, of the manner in which you had by the violence of the storm and the puffs of your friends been elevated to an important office, averred that the object of your address would be, if possible, to throw Mr. Deane under a cloud, and to cast a gloss of the character and conduct of those whose connections and adherents you deemed yourself indebted to, not only for the acquisition of your office, but for your future enjoyment of it; and that the language you would use would be worthy of the possession you have been brought up in, and the nature of the contest you meant to adopt.... As this matter is of some importance, not only as it respects the present subject, but the degree of

---

[19] Warner has argued that "an emerging political language – republicanism – and a new set of ground rules for discourse – the public sphere – jointly made each other intelligible" (xiii). The foundation of that public sphere, which Warner characterizes as an arena in which "political discourse could be separated both from the state and from civil society, the realm of private life (including economic life)" (x), was the practice of limiting oneself to criticizing measures instead of their advocates. For one thing, this policy appeared to minimize the powerful role that class distinctions played in establishing the legitimacy of the speaker. As Paine had noted several years earlier, in his "Forester's Letters," however, this policy also allowed the political and social elites to conceal their true motives when participating in public political debates. In this instance, Paine and his opponents show that while they were aware of the general guidelines regulating participation in the public sphere, they simply chose to disregard them when it was convenient to do so.

credibility which you are intitled to in future, I shall take the liberty to make some strictures upon your studied address, in order to enable the honest and reflecting part of the community to form a judgement. (*Packet*, December 21, 1778)

Besides abusing Paine personally – insinuating that he gained his position because of his connections, not his merit – "Plain Truth" cleverly sets himself apart from Paine by suggesting that the object of his attention is not Paine himself but rather the content of Paine's text. Moreover, to emphasize the difference between himself and Paine, "Plain Truth" notes that those unaware of the specific details of Paine's career – "such as only knew you by your *nom de guerre*, or travelling name" – probably expected that Paine "would have expressed [his] sentiments on this matter with the honest zeal of a patriot, who makes measures, not men, the objects of his discussion." Of course, "Plain Truth's" attack is also personal, insofar as his contrast between what those ignorant of "Common Sense's" real identity would have expected and those aware of his true character knew would be the case establishes a direct link between Paine's character and his opinions. "Plain Truth" remarks on the general connection between men and measures when he observes that the public is "often too credulous in believing whatever comes from a person in office, without considering his character and views." But "Plain Truth" disguises his attack on Paine's character by making Paine's article on Deane the subject of this contrast between expectation and realization.

Instead of focusing on Paine's character directly, "Plain Truth" always raises questions about Paine within the context of a critique of some aspect of his piece addressed to Deane. Smith's strategy is consistent with Thomas Gustafson's observation that "the colonists shared . . . a sophisticated awareness about how the struggle for interests and power was conducted through verbal means and how people could be governed, manipulated – indeed tyrannized over – by words as well as by the rule of force and about how politics thus had to be conducted in part as literary criticism or even as a language game that could be won by those most skilled in opposing the abuse of words" (138). While Paine epitomized this rhetorical strategy in texts such as *Common Sense* and the *The Age of Reason*, his antagonists also employed it with varying degrees of skill when responding to him. The fact that Paine was a professional writer, and not simply an ordinary citizen choosing to participate in a political controversy, made him even more vulnerable to such literary, critical-based attacks on his political opinions. In his "Strictures," "Plain Truth" employs this strategy to great effect.

Just after announcing his intention to "make some strictures on" Paine's text, "Plain Truth" attributes the difference between their respective skills as writers to larger differences between them as individuals: "Should I in doing this avoid those flowers of rhetoric, those *coarse and vehement expressions* which yourself (with what justice the public can easily determine) censure in Mr. Deane, and yet adopt, you will not, I flatter myself, impute it to a contempt of the great talents you possess in this line, but to a difference of education and profession in the present writer, and to the motives which call forth his pen. . . . My path shall be different; and I will take for my guides plain truth and purity of intentions." Throughout his article "Plain Truth" succeeds in his effort to connect each of his various insinuations about the fundamental flaws in Paine's character to a specific criticism of Paine's address to Deane, finally concluding with the lamentation,

Common Sense! for shame! How great is the triumph of truth and virtue, when a writer who justly acquired fame, when his talents were exercised on public principles, sinks in understanding, genius and composition, almost below the level of hireling writers, when he draws his pen with a view of deceiving, not informing the public mind, and of advocating measures, not because they are right, but because he may deem it expedient for a temporary system of politics.[20]

Thus, by abiding by the policy to attack measures and not men, "Plain Truth" indicts Paine's character through a close reading of his article. By avoiding any direct jibes at Paine's character, "Plain Truth" endows his article with a sense of dignity and forthright political discussion, while concurrently implying that these very qualities were absent from Paine's address to Deane.

Smith registers much the same ambivalence about the inclusion of the personal in public debates as Paine had in "The Forester." He struggles to define a middle ground where he can legitimately attack both Paine's character and his ideas. Rather than a stable set of rules of engagement, the idea of this distinction between men and measures functions as a rhetorical tactic that is almost always deployed to discredit one's opponent rather than as a policy to be genuinely embraced or scrupulously followed. In a wonderful twist of irony, accusing their opponents of

---

[20] Smith's cynicism in remarks like this one is worth noting, for as one of the most prominent Tory writers of the revolutionary period Smith certainly did not feel Paine's original arguments in *Common Sense* or his subsequent fame were due to an adherence to "public principles." Quite the contrary, in "Cato's Letters" he set out to counter the impact of Paine's pamphlet.

violating this putative norm becomes an excuse that allows Smith and Paine to employ *ad hominem* attacks but appear reluctant to engage in such untoward but necessary form of argumentation. In the end, neither Paine nor Smith truly believes in the validity of this foundational trope of the public sphere, but Smith is not prepared to overtly disown a concept that allows him to speak for the many in spite of his elite status.

"Plain Truth's" "Strictures" evidently had a significant impact on Paine, for before actually undertaking to defend himself from his old nemesis' critique, Paine announced "To the Public" that he intended to vindicate himself in the near future. Aware of Deane's thievery, Paine set the stakes high, asserting that "I desire to stand or fall in the opinion of every man in America, in proportion as I am in this *affair* of Mr. Deane right or wrong, faithful, or unfaithful" (*Packet*, December 29, 1778). Two days later, on December 31, 1778, Paine delivered on his promise, and published the first part of a letter that he continued in the January 2, 5, 7, and 9, editions of the *Packet*. Paine begins his letter with a direct response to "Plain Truth's" charges about his language, asserting that, "As it is my design to make those that can scarcely read understand, I shall therefore avoid every literary ornament, and put it in language as plain as the alphabet."[21] Immediately thereafter he answers a second major charge: "I desire the public to understand that this is not a personal dispute between Mr. Deane and me, but is a matter of business in which they are more interested than they seemed at first to be apprised of." Thus, Paine returned the dispute to a matter of measures and not men. Unfortunately for Paine, the moment he revealed the crucial fact that proved that Deane had in fact embezzled thousands of dollars from the United States government, he also betrayed his trust as secretary of foreign affairs. This was one fight Paine could not win. The French minister, Conrad Alexandre Gerard, demanded a formal retraction, and that Paine be punished for his indiscretion. On January 12, 1779, the Continental Congress published a statement in the *Packet* asserting that "they are convinced by indisputable evidence, that the supplies shipped in the *Amphitrite, Seine,* and *Mercury* were not a present" and four days later Paine resigned his post

---

[21] Two years earlier Paine had emphasized the forthrightness of his contentions in the first number of the *Crisis* series in similar fashion: "I dwell not upon the vapors of imagination; I bring reason to your ears, and in language as plain as A, B, C, hold up truth to your eyes" (CW II, 56). For Paine the alphabet seems to have symbolized the combination of orderliness and simplicity with which he sought to imbue all of his writing so as to make it readily accessible to all readers.

as secretary of foreign affairs to avoid the humiliation of being dismissed (Hawke, 85–91).

After his dismissal, Paine continued his lonely dispute with Deane and his allies in a volley of charges and countercharges that continued to appear in the *Packet* through September 1779. Losing his post, however, wasn't Paine's chief concern. In a letter he wrote to Benjamin Franklin in the aftermath of the Deane Affair, Paine discussed the impact it had on his reputation: "I have lately met with a turn, which, sooner or later, happens to all men in popular life, that is, I fell, all at once, from high credit to disgrace, and the worst word was thought too good for me" (CW II, 1167–1168). Humiliated, Paine endeavored to salvage his reputation. He eagerly petitioned Congress on various occasions, asking that they clarify their statements regarding his articles and his dismissal: "It is my design to furnish the United States with a History of the Revolution, and it is necessary that my character should stand fair as that of any member of this honorable House. Neither can I suffer a blemish to be thrown on me which I am conscious I do not deserve, or desire a defection to be concealed which I am proved guilty of (1172)."[22] Because he was barred from the session when his involvement in the Deane controversy was discussed, Paine wanted to see the evidence that had forced his resignation. Knowing that Deane had stolen from the government, Paine was confident that the evidence would clear his name, if not restore his *official* position. However, not until 1781 was Paine vindicated by a set of letters stolen by the British and published in New York; there Deane advocated reconciliation with England. It would not be until 150 years later that the full extent of Deane's deception became known (Hawke, 94–95).

MAKING IT PERSONAL: "THE LETTER TO GEORGE WASHINGTON"

After the personal and political disaster precipitated by his dispute with Deane, one would think that Paine would have avoided future confrontations with prominent figures in the United States government. But, nearly two decades later Paine publicly attacked the foremost figure of the founding era, George Washington. The consequences proved disastrous for Paine. A series of events beginning in 1791 led up to his miscalculation.

---

[22] Paine first asked for the details regarding the hearing against him on March 30, 1779, and repeated his request on April 3, April 21, April 23, May 20, May 25, and June 17, 1779.

Despite his sagging popularity in the United States, by 1792, Paine had become so identified with the young republic and the principles of freedom and independence that the United States had come to symbolize that he was made an honorary citizen of France and elected to the National Assembly as a representative of Calais. On his way to Paris to accept his seat at the Convention, Paine received a hero's welcome in Calais when he arrived in mid-September of 1792 (Hawke, 256–257). And, less than a month later, on October 11, 1792, Paine was selected as one of the eight representatives charged with writing a constitution for the new French republic. Yet, little more than a year later, on December 28, 1793, Paine, whose opposition to the execution of Louis XVI had irritated Robespierre, was imprisoned for not being radical enough and for being a foreigner.[23] Two other Americans imprisoned by the Committee of General Security were promptly released after members of the American community in France had petitioned the Convention. When they asked that Paine be released too, however, they were rebuffed. In order not to alienate crucial American support for the Revolution, President Marc Vadier asserted that Paine was an Englishman by virtue of his birth, and the American representatives did not pursue their case further.

Paine remained in prison for the next ten months, during which time he suffered a severe illness, revised *The Rights of Man*, and wrote the first part of *The Age of Reason*. In 1796 another significant, but often overlooked, text resulted from Paine's imprisonment, *The Letter to George Washington, President of the United States of America, on Affairs Public and Private*. In the short term, Paine's scathing attack on Washington, whom he blamed for the length of his imprisonment, may have had as great a negative impact on his career and credibility in America as *The Age of Reason*. In the *Letter* Paine, who to the French had once represented the "principles of America," which had "opened the Bastille," indicts America's highest elected official for failing to act out those very principles.[24] Although much of the *Letter* concerns Washington's administration and the

---

[23] Robespierre, who was extremely suspicious of foreigners, ordered an investigation of all foreign members of the Convention: "I demand that a purifying scrutiny be held at the tribune, to detect and drive out all the agents of foreign powers who under their auspices have introduced themselves into this society" (qtd. in Hawke, 291). Moreover, "Robespierre detested Englishmen and suspected them especially of working to undermine the Revolution" (Hawke, 291).

[24] After receiving the key to the Bastille on Washington's behalf Paine wrote to Washington, "That the principles of America opened the Bastille is not to be doubted; and therefore the key comes to the right place" (CW II, 1303).

problems its policies were creating for the United States – the rise of mo-
nopolies and the precarious diplomatic state of affairs with England and
France caused by the Jay Treaty – Paine was motivated primarily by a
sense of personal betrayal.[25] He considered Washington his friend, and
therefore Washington's failure to act on his behalf constituted not only
a betrayal of his duty to Paine as an American citizen, but more importantly a betrayal of their friendship: "Mr. Washington owed it to me on
every score of private acquaintance, I will not now say, friendship; for
it has some time been known by those who know him, that he has no
friendships; that he is incapable of forming any; he can serve or desert
a man, or a cause, with constitutional indifference" (698). Echoing his
earlier critique of his opponents in the debates over *Common Sense*,
Paine here, through the strategic placement of the word constitutional,
implicitly links Washington's private failings to his actions in the political
arena.

Ironically, it was Paine's decision to dedicate *Rights of Man* (1791) to
Washington five years earlier that had caused a considerable cooling of
their friendship.[26] Paine aimed to transplant the work of the American
Revolution to Europe first as a member of the French National Assembly
and then to extend it to England by challenging Edmund Burke's monarchical vision with *The Rights of Man*. Now, however, Paine identified
Washington as one of the parties subverting fundamental principles of
freedom in America. Despite its personal undertones, Paine's *Letter to
Washington* illustrates the polarizing divisions surrounding the question
of who constitutes "the People" that had arisen in the early years of the
republic. While Paine realized that the definition of what America might
represent was at stake in this debate, he also realized that his identity as
an American was in question. Was Paine really an American? What did it
mean to be an American? And, who was more representative of the principles of "America," Paine or Washington? These are some of the questions
that Paine's *Letter to Washington* raises, questions that would haunt Paine
for the rest of his life. For Paine the questions about his nationality were
intertwined with notions of public and private identity that were, in turn,
ultimately linked to his participation in the public sphere. Likewise, the
circumstances of his imprisonment finally made it impossible for him to

---

[25] More than half of the pamphlet is dedicated to a discussion of the Jay Treaty.
[26] "Paine's attempt to use Washington to protect himself from George III so soured relations
with the president that nearly a year passed before he responded to Paine's dedication
and gift of fifty copies of *Rights of Man*" (Keane, 309).

accept the distinction between measures and men that formed the basis for the Republic of Letters.

Paine begins *The Letter to Washington*, in typical fashion, with a broad statement intended to pique the reader's curiosity: "As censure is but awkwardly softened by apology, I shall offer you no apology for this letter. The eventful crisis to which your double politics have conducted the affairs of your country, requires an investigation uncramped by ceremony" (CW II, 691). In this short opening paragraph Paine sets the tone for his pamphlet, and focuses on the Washington administration's "double politics" as the source of his displeasure. For the moment he avoids any sort of personal attack on the president's character, but his refusal to justify, to offer apology for promised "censure," does not bode well for a focus on measures and not men. In the very next paragraph, where he contrasts the international status of America prior to Washington's administration to the country's current situation, Paine begins to weave an attack on Washington's character into his criticism of the administration's political measures:

> There was a time when the fame of America, moral and political, stood fair and high in the world. The lustre of her Revolution extended itself to every individual; and to be a citizen of America gave a title to respect in Europe. Neither meanness nor ingratitude had been mingled in the composition of her character. Her resistance to the attempted tyranny of England left her unsuspected of the one, and her open acknowledgement of the aid she received from France precluded all suspicion of the other. The Washington of politics had not then appeared. (CW II, 691)

With the last sentence of this paragraph, Paine implicates the president's character in the shortcomings of his policies. It is not Washington's politics that he blames for America's injured character; instead, it is "the Washington of politics" who has tainted America's reputation. By inserting the preposition, "of," Paine specifically singles out Washington the man as the responsible party. The focus is no longer on Washington's politics but on Washington's person, who by implication has infected America with "meanness and ingratitude."

If there was any doubt about the personal nature of Paine's dispute with Washington, he erases it when he comments on his motives for writing the *Letter*:

> It will be supposed by those into whose hands this letter may fall that I have some personal resentment against you; I will therefore settle this point before I proceed further.

If I have any resentment you must acknowledge that I have not been hasty in declaring it; neither would it now be declared (for what are private resentments to the public) if the cause of it did not unite itself as well with your public as well as your private character, and with the motives of your political conduct. (CW II, 695)

At the same time as he admits a personal grudge with Washington, Paine justifies its validity as the subject of public discussion on the basis that Washington's private or personal misconduct has larger political implications for the nation's conduct. Paine's position here is consistent with his earlier argument from "The Forester's Letters." Washington's private character, therefore, is fair game because of the consequences it has for his public role.

Once Paine has established the connection between the private Washington and the public Washington, he can justifiably air his personal complaints about the president's behavior toward him in a public forum, because those actions are now understood as representative of Washington's public character. Thus, it is not accidental that Paine raises the matter of his imprisonment in France only after he has thoroughly implicated Washington's personal character in his administration's supposed wrong-doings. Paine reiterates that crucial connection at the moment when he first mentions the matter of his imprisonment:

Could I have known to what degree of corruption and perfidy the administrative part of the Government of America had descended, I could have been at no loss to have understood the reservedness of Mr. Washington toward me, during my imprisonment in the Luxembourg. There are cases in which silence is a loud language. I will here explain the cause of that imprisonment, and return to Mr. Washington afterwards. (CW II, 696)

Paine blamed Washington for the length of his imprisonment, when in fact, Gouverneur Morris, whom Washington had chosen as American minister to France, was largely responsible for the U.S. government's inaction. Morris, who disliked Paine and had sought to rescue the monarchy in France, created the impression of active advocacy, when in fact he had merely inquired after the reasons for Paine's imprisonment. Unbeknownst to Washington, Morris's passivity kept Paine in prison.[27]

It would not be until July 1793, when James Monroe arrived to supersede Gouverneur Morris as the U.S. minister to France, that any action was taken on Paine's behalf. Upon hearing of Monroe's arrival Paine

---

[27] As Hawke notes, "Morris believed that Paine could not legally claim American citizenship after sitting in the [French] Convention" (298).

promptly wrote to him, and Monroe immediately set out to gain Paine's release. In a letter to Paine, which Paine includes in the text of the *Letter to Washington*, Monroe asserts his conviction of Paine's American citizenship and assures Paine that his well-being concerns all Americans. Four months later, on November 4, 1793, thanks to Monroe's efforts Paine was freed by the French government, and shortly thereafter he was invited to return to his seat in the Convention.

As in the dispute over Silas Deane, Paine's *Letter to Washington* failed to generate a sympathetic response for his personal plight made public. Even many of his supporters were displeased. Washington, although not as popular as he once was, was still widely admired and Paine's attacks were too personal. As Keane notes, the "furious Federalist counterblasts" attacking him for the *Letter* "may have done more to damage Paine's reputation in America than any other circumstance of his life – more even than the Silas Deane affair or the publication of *The Age of Reason*" (432). More than anything, the *Letter* made it difficult for Paine's allies to publicly defend him against the Federalists' attacks. The Federalist *Gazette of the United States*, for example, raised the question of Paine's citizenship and cited the *Letter to Washington* as evidence that Paine was not truly an American:

Our government have so long permitted foreign convicts and renegades to go on, with impunity, in insulting the nation and dictating public measures, that they now seem to consider this country as the natural right and common property of all those who have shewn themselves pre-eminent in baseness and impiety, of whatever nation they may be. The [Philadelphia] Aurora now talks of the services of Tom Paine to *his country!* and pretends to justify the President for making him the offer of a public vessel to convey him *home.* He says, "in offering him a passage, it was offering no more than Thomas Paine had an equal claim to with any OTHER AMERICAN CITIZEN" . . . If Tom is an American citizen and *this* country *is his* country, we would fain be informed whether his letter to *"George Washington, Esquire,"* published at the office of the Aurora, was a letter to *his* President. It will not be pretended, that at *that time,* this was Paine's country, for then law and religion prevailed and were respected; and his motto is "where religion or law dwells there is *not my country.*" (August 13, 1801)

Much of the rhetoric of this letter while directed at Paine, is actually aimed at Jefferson and the Republicans. Once again, Paine had managed to become a lightning rod. As Jerry W. Knudson has noted, "Paine's esteem had fallen so low that his return triggered the first all-out attack upon the administration of Thomas Jefferson, an attack unparalleled in its searing viciousness" (34). The attacks on Paine actually began months before his arrival when the Federalist press learned that President Jefferson had offered to provide a ship for Paine's return. And yet, once he actually arrived, he was greeted with muted praise. Even Federalist newspapers gave him credit for his contributions to the American cause. The *Baltimore Republican; or Anti-Democrat*, for example, grudgingly observed: "It is but justice to observe that this man [Paine] has some claims on our gratitude for his work entitled 'Common Sense'; for, though the motives that induced him to collect together and publish the general arguments of the day, at that time, were, as might easily be proved, those of a hireling, yet that little work was of essential service in our revolution." Of course, Paine felt he deserved acclaim for his contributions to the American Revolution but his assaults on Christianity and on George Washington had made that impossible. Its one thing to polarize people, quite another to become so controversial that even your friends can't risk supporting you too strongly in public.

DISCOVERING THE LIMITS OF THE PUBLIC SPHERE

Doubtless, Paine's rhetorical strategy of combining *ad hominem* attacks with his reasoned arguments worked to great effect throughout his writing career. However well Paine's writings served to strengthen the various causes he supported, they did not secure their author's popularity. Like few others, Franklin understood the problem embedded in Paine's rhetorical style. Late in *The Autobiography* Franklin tells an anecdote of his meeting Robert Hunter Morris, the new governor of New York. Like Paine, Morris loved arguing and provided Franklin with the opportunity to comment on the pitfalls of a contentious attitude: "He had some Reason for loving to dispute, being eloquent, an acute Sophister, and therefore generally successful in argumentative Conversation. . . . in the Course of my Observation, these disputing, contradicting & confuting People are generally unfortunate in their Affairs. They get Victory sometimes, but they never get Good Will, which would be of more use to them" (1432). Franklin's astute observation about the power of good will in political affairs, served him well over the course of his career and, in the long run, insured a positive public image for him, whereas Paine's approach, while productive of greater book sales and attention, did little for his popularity.

In large measure, the problem for Paine was that he lacked prudence, a virtue in public life that he regarded as an evil. In fact, he indicts Washington for his prudence: "The character which Mr. Washington has attempted to act in the world is a sort of indescribable, chameleon-colored thing called *prudence*. It is in many cases, a substitute for principle, and is so nearly allied to hypocrisy that it easily slides into it" (CW II, 710). In this case Paine would have done well to follow the advice of his friend James Monroe to suppress his *Letter to George Washington*, but Paine, who throughout his career repeatedly stigmatized silence as cowardly submission, felt an obligation to voice his grievance. Angry with his former friend Washington for failing to rescue him, Paine was blind to the folly of his actions. But, if it is true that Paine failed to grasp the benefits of distinguishing between men and the measures they advocate, it is also true that in France that distinction would have been untenable, for his public opinions and actions had landed him in jail, where insofar as his public and private identities are unified in their confinement, any distinction between measures and men becomes meaningless. For Paine, prison only confirmed his conviction that any distinction between men and measures was simply impossible to maintain.

Moreover, to blame Paine's lack of discretion, his willful public disclosure of "secret" and "personal" matters, for his downfall is to fail to discern the larger causes of his troubles. Ultimately, in his attempt to reform the public sphere, Paine was struggling to overcome too many obstacles at once. The moment he advocated the consideration of private character in any evaluation of public measures, he invited, albeit unintentionally and unwillingly, his political enemies to reassert their control over the public sphere. Paine, the son of a staymaker and an artisan in his own right, repeatedly rejected any connection between status and merit (if anything, he suggested that the "quality" were tainted by their social and economic interests). The historical, social, and cultural forces marshaled against him were not easily overcome. Paine was confronting a complex web of interdependent ideas and assumptions that worked to maintain power in the hands of the elites while appearing to expand access to power. As Nancy Fraser has put it:

The official bourgeois public sphere is the institutional vehicle for a major historical transformation in the nature of political domination. This is the shift from a repressive mode of domination to a hegemonic one, from rule primarily on acquiescence to superior force to rule based primarily on consent supplemented with some measure of repression. The important point is that this new mode of political domination, like the older one, secures the ability of one stratum of society to rule the rest. (117)

Paine's aim throughout his career was to undermine the authority of any particular institution or stratum of society and to open political participation to "the people." One of the solutions for Paine was to attempt to educate the people in texts such as *Rights of Man* and *The Age of Reason*, thus enabling them to identify themselves and their oppressors so they can study to be informed citizens. Such citizens could participate in the public sphere and, de facto, reform it by asserting their right to shape "public opinion." In any case, Paine's concern over the public sphere had a profound effect on his writing as he continually struggled to find ways to create a language of politics that would enfranchise the people.

Perhaps understandably, those who maintained a tenuous hold on the reins of government and a new public sphere relied partly on the assertion that measures, and not men, ought to be the sole basis of discussion in the public arena. At the same time, access to the public sphere was structurally limited to propertied men because, as Fraser, points out, "a network of clubs and associations – philanthropic, civic, professional, and cultural – was anything but accessible to everyone. Paradoxically, it was this arena, this training ground, that eventually nurtured the power base of a stratum of prosperous men who were coming to see themselves as a 'universal class' and prepared to assert their fitness to govern" (114).[28] When Paine pointed out such strategies of exclusion, he was making the private (in this case an individual's wealth and social status) a relevant subject for public discussion and simultaneously threatening the aristocracy's control of the public sphere. Ironically, once Paine reasserts the need to consider men as well as measures, he also makes himself vulnerable to personal attacks, which were often based on historical prejudices about his economic and social background that served to marginalize or exclude his voice in the public sphere, for, unlike Franklin, Paine had not reinvented himself as a member of the political and cultural aristocracy.

Paine continued to write until 1807, when his failing health made it impossible for him to continue to participate in the political debates of the era. Despite his abilities, his pen no longer carried the weight it once had. He had lost the credibility that *Common Sense* and the *Rights of Man* had earned him with the American public. Unfortunately for Paine, he had never acquired the goodwill that would have been so useful to him in the years after the conclusion of the War of Independence. As Franklin had suggested about such contentious people, Paine had earned victory for his causes sometimes, but he had never gained goodwill for himself. In fact, Paine's refusal to adopt an impersonal mode of discourse made

---

[28] See also Eley, 296–297. Along similar lines, Richard D. Brown has recently noted that in the early republic "advocates of an informed citizenry who were themselves leading men often favored some form of elite nationalism" (*Strength*, 96).

it practically impossible for him to gain that elusive goodwill: Because he would not separate his public and private personae, neither would his readers. Paine wanted his writing to be taken personally, but that also meant he would be held accountable by his readers. On the other hand, his refusal to adopt the impersonal mode invigorated his prose and made him one of the most effective polemical writers of the period. Thus, to a certain extent Paine's downfall was inevitable, because unlike Franklin, for one, Paine was a writer by profession, and as a writer he abhorred silence as much as he feared it. As I have shown previously, in his "Strictures on the Address of Common Sense to Mr. Deane" Plain Truth (William Smith) repeatedly insinuates that the chief consequence of Paine's skill as a writer is his ability to mislead the public. Ironically, but not surprisingly, it was precisely Paine's status as a professional writer that elicited the suspicions of his rivals.

3

Writing Revolutionary History

In the summer of 1783, shortly after the conclusion of the War of Independence, Paine attempted to secure a congressional pension in recompense for services rendered during the previous seven years. Rather than grant him a pension or other form of direct remuneration, the committee reviewing his petition proposed that Paine be appointed to the salaried position of historiographer to the United States. The committee suggested that "a just and impartial account of our interest for public Freedom and happiness should be handed down to posterity," and noted that "a History of the American revolution compiled by Mr. Paine is certainly to be desired" (qtd. in Keane, 245). In his recent biography of Paine, John Keane argues that "The report annoyed and depressed Paine" because "It smacked of America's 'cold conduct' toward its own writers, and it failed to understand that as a political writer, Paine needed material support now, not in the future" (245). But Keane, like Paine before him, misreads the situation. It wasn't so much because of his professional status as a political writer, but because of the Congress' desperate financial straits that Paine was denied compensation.[1] Given the state of the Congress' finances at the time, and their inability to pay many soldiers for back pay, it would have been a serious political blunder to grant Paine a pension at this moment.[2]

---

[1] Paine, who had not profited from any of his immensely successful writings on behalf of the American cause, had been reduced to depending on the goodwill of friends and political allies for his subsistence. As we shall see, Paine's professional occupation as a political writer made accepting money from anyone a delicate matter.

[2] Just two weeks after Paine's initial request for a financial reward, the Continental Congress was laid siege to by Pennsylvania troops who claimed they were owed back pay.

Four years earlier, in the wake of the Deane Affair and his subsequent dismissal from the post of secretary of foreign affairs, Paine had written to Congress requesting a hearing so that he might defend his course of action. Among his reasons for such a hearing he cited his intention to write a history of the Revolution as the primary rationale for their allowing him to clear his name: "It is my design to furnish the United States with a History of the Revolution, and it is necessary that my character should stand fair as that of any member of this honorable House" (1172). Paine would repeat this point for emphasis at the end of his letter: "I have generally stated my reasons for this request, viz., the reputation of an historian" (1173). Thus, in 1783 the committee reviewing Paine's plea for financial remuneration would have been well aware of his intention to write a history of the Revolution and was only trying to find a way to reward him for something they thought he was going to do anyway. This way they could both recognize Paine's past contributions and avoid a public relations disaster, by rewarding him for future work. He, however, was not satisfied with the Congress' action on his behalf. In typical fashion, Paine, generally obtuse about such delicate matters of political expediency, failed to recognize this subtle attempt to assist him without seeming to be paying him for past service.

Nevertheless, this episode reflects Paine's profound concern over the writing of the history of the Revolution, a task he had been contemplating for about six years. As early as 1777 he had shared his plan to write a history of the American Revolution with his friend and patron Benjamin Franklin,[3] whose assistance he sought in compiling the necessary documents for such a history: "I intend next winter to begin on the first volume of the Revolution of America, when I mentioned it to you the winter before last you was so kind as to offer me such materials in your possession as might be necessary for that purpose" (CW II, 1133). This letter suggests that he may have conceived of the plan as early as December of 1776. A month later, in another letter to Franklin, Paine would reiterate his desire to write a history of the recent events in America, but this time Paine seeks Franklin's "approbation of the plan on which I intend to conduct the History of this Revolution" (1136). Less than a year later Paine would once again express a desire to consult with Franklin about his proposed history. For Paine, who had drawn heavily upon historical arguments in

---

[3] In a May 16, 1778 letter to Franklin, Paine asserts that "among other pleasures I feel in having uniformly done my duty, I feel that of not having discredited your friendship and patronage" (1151).

Common Sense to justify his position in favor of declaring independence, this project was a natural extension of his role in the American cause, a cause that for him transcended the local dispute over colonial sovereignty and included, as we shall see, larger questions about the true nature of government and the future course of governments throughout the world. In this chapter I will explore Paine's attitudes regarding the writing of the history of the Revolution. I will argue that, although it has not been recognized as such, Paine actually wrote a version of a history of the Revolution that proved to be a pivotal text for him. In the process I will examine Paine's theory of history and his frequent attempts to incorporate historical arguments into his seminal texts, from *Common Sense* to *The Age of Reason.*

ORIGINS, HISTORY, AND POLITICS

Although we remember *Common Sense* mainly for its last two sections, where Paine specifically addresses the colonies' situation at the time, he prefaced his arguments for independence with two largely historical sections that laid the groundwork for his account of the political options remaining for the colonists in 1776. These first two sections, "On the Origin and Design of Government in General, With Concise Remarks on the English Constitution," and "Of Monarchy and Hereditary Succession," bear titles that suggest an eighteenth-century work of political philosophy or philosophical history in the mode of Rousseau's "Discourse on the Origin of Inequality" or Adam Ferguson's more recent "Origins of Civil Society." In these two opening sections Paine makes his political points by investigating the history of the subject at issue. Like Rousseau and Ferguson, Paine is particularly concerned with the origins of the various practices and forms of government under investigation. In fact, the opening line of the main body of *Common Sense* involves a question of origins: "Some writers have so confounded society with government, as to leave little or no distinction between them; whereas they are not only different, but have different origins" (4). Paine might have added that they are different precisely because they have different origins. Naturally, the way to resolve this confusion is to investigate the origins of government and of society.

Once he has established the basic distinction between society and government, Paine presents his own narrative of origins. In a brilliant stroke Paine constructs a narrative that parallels, at least in its broad outlines, the settling of British North America[4]:

> In order to gain a clear and just idea of the design and end of government, let us suppose a small number of persons settled in some sequestered part of the earth, unconnected with the rest; they will then represent the first peopling of any country, or of the world. . . .
>
>   Thus necessity, like a gravitating power, would soon form our newly arrived emigrants into society, the reciprocal blessings of which would supercede, and render the obligations of law and government unnecessary while they remained perfectly just to each other; but as nothing but Heaven is impregnable to vice, it will unavoidably happen that in proportion as they surmount the first difficulties of emigration, which bound them together in a common cause, they will begin to relax in their duty and attachment to each other: and this remissness will point out the necessity of establishing some form of government to supply the defect of moral virtue. (5)

As he slides from an imaginary or mythical account of the origins of government into a retelling of the founding of the British colonies in North America, it becomes clear that Paine's political philosophy is not grounded in some ahistorical mythical tale of origins, but, instead, is based on the specific historical past of the colonies. Rhetorically this narrative slippage serves two related purposes. On the one hand, it provides a readily accessible account of the origins of society and government that serves to support a larger theoretical argument Paine wishes to make about the proper role of government. On the other hand, by presenting a narrative that his readers would immediately identify as their own, he was also preparing the reader for his subsequent claims about the colonies' right to declare independence by making this debate about the true nature of government their story. Furthermore, by providing the colonists with their own narrative of origins, Paine lays the foundation for a distinct American identity. At a time when most of the colonists saw themselves as British subjects, this was a crucial move. By giving Americans a history of their own, separate from English history, Paine implicitly severs one of the key forces connecting the colonists to England. Paine understands that the most effective way to counter the force of history, and of historical ties, it seems, is through a counterhistory. Thus, the issues at stake in political theory here do not involve some mysterious or impossibly complicated force, but rather are immediately available to his readers, who are now

---

[4] For Rousseau in the *Discourse on the Origin of Inequality*, America is also the crucial historical referent. The American Indians, or at least Rousseau's version of them, serve as the model for natural man upon which he builds his theory of the origin of inequality.

enfranchised as actors in a larger historical narrative. Paine thus renders, at least rhetorically, both the theory and the practice of politics accessible to his readers.

Although the first section of the pamphlet emphasizes the history of the questions being raised, perhaps the most explicitly historiographical argument in *Common Sense* is the account of the origins of monarchy in the second section of the pamphlet. Rather than simply attack the British monarchy for its recent conduct, Paine indicts the institution of monarchy by calling into question both its origins and its religious sanction: "All antimonarchical parts of scripture, have been very smoothly glossed over in monarchical governments, but they undoubtedly merit the attention of countries which have their governments yet to form" (CW I, 10). Hence the relevance of this discussion to an American audience, for the colonies had yet to form a government. They were, therefore, in the midst of an originary moment. Paine takes this as his cue to investigate the historical origins of monarchy.

He traces the advent of monarchy to the biblical account, from 1 Samuel, of Samuel's anointing of Saul, and then David, to the role of King of the Israelites: "Government by kings was first introduced into the world by the heathens, from whom the children of Israel copied the custom. It was the most prosperous invention the devil ever set on foot for the promotion of idolatry. The heathens paid divine honors to their deceased kings, and the Christian world has improved on the plan by doing the same to their living ones" (CW I, 10). Paine thus not only undercuts the religious sanction for monarchy, but also impugns the institution by associating it with antireligious origins. He even goes so far as to assert that "Monarchy is ranked in scripture as one of the sins of the Jews, for which a curse in reserve is denounced against them" (10). "The history of that transaction," Paine cleverly notes, "is worth attending to" (10). Paine has now moved from an investigation of the origins of government to an investigation of the origins of a particular form of government.

He proceeds to summarize in some detail the story from 1 Samuel of the Israelites "hankering" for a king, and Samuel's warnings about the dangers of monarchical government. He makes the case for the incompatibility of Christianity with monarchy most explicitly when he cites passages from 1 Samuel where God speaks out against kings.

But the thing displeased Samuel when they said, give us a king to judge us; and Samuel prayed unto the Lord, and the Lord said unto Samuel, hearken unto the voice of the people in all that they say unto thee, for they have not rejected thee, but they have rejected me, THAT I SHOULD NOT REIGN OVER THEM. *According to all the works which they have done since the day that I brought them up out of Egypt even unto this day, wherewhith they have forsaken me, and served other Gods: so do they also unto thee.* (11)[5]

Not only does the Christian God disapprove of monarchy, but monarchy itself is fundamentally antithetical to Christianity.[6] Paine admits *a priori* that the Bible could be used to reinforce the claims of a monarch, but he also recognizes that it can be used to attack it. The question, as usual, is which parts of the Bible you choose to read. However, by focusing on the moment when monarchy is first introduced as the form of government for God's chosen people, Paine could emphasize the condemnation of monarchy in the text. At this point he is also relying on the historical content of the Bible to support his position, rather than on the philosophical or moral precepts contained in it.

As had been the case with his argument regarding the origins of government, however, Paine is not satisfied with making a general case. He feels the need to complement the general with specific examples that are more immediately available to his audience. In this instance, instead of addressing the misdeeds of George III, a potentially dangerous tack,[7] Paine turns to the matter of the origins of the British monarchy, observing that

England since the conquest hath known some few good monarchs, but groaned beneath a much larger number of bad ones; yet no man in his senses can say that their claim under William the Conqueror is a very honorable one. A French bastard landing with an armed banditti and establishing himself king of England against the consent of the natives, is in plain terms a very paltry rascally original. (14)

Just as in his biblical argument, Paine is not providing his readers with any new information. Generally, they would be familiar with both the Bible and the history of the origins of the English monarchy. What has changed is the tone and the context within which these facts are presented. In other words, he does not rewrite or even offer a wholesale reinterpretation of a particular historical moment; instead, he uses the shared historical

---

[5] This account is from 1 Samuel 8: 1–9.

[6] Curiously, although Paine is using the Old Testament to make a point about the incompatibility of Christianity with monarchy and to show God's disapproval of monarchy, he blames the invention of monarchy on the Jews. So, while the God of the Old Testament is both the Jewish and the Christian God, for the purposes of his political history the Israelites are not both Jews and proto-Christians.

[7] At this early stage of affairs, Paine would be keen to avoid a charge of treason. It was one thing to make insinuations about the institution of monarchy, and another to directly attack the monarch.

knowledge of his readers and puts it in the service of a different set of goals. Moreover, by complementing his large historical points with specific and more immediate examples, Paine gives his arguments an air of simplicity and indisputability that his critics found impossible to contradict.

IMPARTIALITY, HISTORIOGRAPHY, AND THE LESSONS OF THE PAST

In the two examples from *Common Sense* we can begin to discern a larger systematic sense of history in Paine. A few years later, in the third number of the *American Crisis* he clearly states his theory of the usefulness of history:

Were a man to be totally deprived of memory, he would be incapable of forming any just opinion; every thing about him would seem a chaos: he would have even his own history to ask from every one; and by not knowing how the world went in his absence, he would be at a loss to know how it *ought* to go on when he recovered, or rather, returned to it again. In like manner, though in a less degree, a too great inattention to past occurrences retards and bewilders our judgment in everything; while, on the contrary, by comparing what is past with what is present, we frequently hit on the true character of both, and become wise with very little trouble. It is a kind of counter-march, by which we get into the rear of time, and mark the movements and meanings of things as we make our return. (74)

History here serves to order the present and direct the future, and in so doing it also provides the fundamental basis for all criticism. In this respect, history becomes the crucial form of knowledge for human society because without it we would be incapable of discerning the proper course of action in the present. Although Paine had a sense of the importance of history, it would not be until his *Letter to Raynal* that he would attempt to write a work of historiography, and he would not offer a theory of the role of historiography in shaping our understanding of the past and therefore of the present until a year later when he wrote to the Continental Congress to refuse the position of historiographer to the continent. The position had not been offered to him, or to anyone else for that matter, but Paine, who was still hoping to be compensated for his services during the previous seven years, nonetheless felt compelled to write a lengthy letter to the Congress detailing his reasons for not accepting the title.

In his 1783 "Letter to the Continental Congress" Paine articulated a coherent rationale for turning down the potentially lucrative position of historiographer to the continent. To Paine it was important that the money not be attached to the specific task of writing the history. Only two years earlier the French ambassador to the United States, Conrad Alexandre Gérard, had offered him a healthy reward should he be willing to publish articles in support of the alliance between France and the United States. Despite the fact that he already was in favor of the alliance against the British, he refused to accept Gérard's offer. As Keane has noted, "He was sure that the principle at stake – the freedom of political writers to express their views independently of any party or government – was inviolable, even if this meant personal pauperization" (187). After refusing Gérard's offer of one thousand dollars a year, how could he now accept Congress' offer of a salary in exchange for writing a history of the Revolution? Paine simply would not subject his political writings to the potential influence of money or to the suspicion of influence.

Paine was not comfortable with accepting patronage for the composition of his proposed history because, as he had been and would continue to be throughout his career, he was concerned with the problem of impartiality:

To leave the history of the Revolution to chance, to party, or partiality of any kind, or to be performed as a matter of profit, will subject the character of the present age to various and hazardous representations, and though it cannot be completed as it ought without the aid of, and a confidential communication with Congress, yet for Congress to reserve to themselves the least appearance of influence over an historian, by annexing thereto a yearly salary subject to their own control, will endanger the reputation of both the historian and the history. (CW II, 1240)

This was precisely the reason why Paine had refused to profit from his political writings during the Revolution: He insisted that principles take priority over more mundane issues that might cloud the real substance of his works. Moreover, he was deeply aware that preserving his reputation for independence and his integrity were crucial to his continuing success as a polemical writer in an age when writers were often perceived as mercenaries ready to employ their talents on behalf of the highest bidder. And yet, as the passage indicates, Paine felt strongly about the need for a history of the Revolution.

It was because of the crucial importance of the Revolution that he felt it would be best if its history were written for disinterested motives. His solution was for the title of historiographer to be simply that, a title that would afford the author access to the necessary documents, and that would also allow the author a measure of independence: "If after this I undertake a history of the revolution it will be perfectly voluntary and with freedom to myself, and if Congress pleases to give me the appointment of historiographer, as honorary, and without salary or conditions, it will facilitate the collection of materials and give the work the foundation of impartiality and clear it of all appearance or suspicion of influence"

(CW II, 1242). Keane takes Paine's statement to mean that he would not accept the position were it offered to him, and the fact that he never wrote such a history supports this interpretation. But Paine's rhetoric leaves the door open. He did not decline the position; he simply suggested that it should not carry a salary.

Paine, however, was never appointed historiographer and he never wrote a narrative history of the revolution. Had he received the appointment, on his terms, we might have a narrative history of the Revolution penned by Tom Paine. Nevertheless, this incident prompted him to articulate a clear vision of what such a history might look like. Indeed, nowhere does Paine express his sense of the broader significance of the Revolution better than in his 1783 "Letter to the Continental Congress" regarding the possibility of his appointment to the position of historiographer to the continent. While he touches on the subject at various moments in other texts, his emphasis on the larger implications of the Revolution is much more concentrated in the context of his discussion of the writing of the history of the Revolution. In this "Letter," Paine outlines a three-part plan for his history of the Revolution:

To give the present Revolution its full foundation and extent in the world, it seems necessary there should be three histories – one that should state fully all the leading principles, policy and facts of the revolution, so as not only to inform posterity but to confirm them in the true principles of freedom and civil government; a second, being rather an abstract of the first cast into easy and graceful language to be used as a standing school-book, and a third for Europe or the world. (CW II, 1240)

To Paine, then, the task of writing a history of the American Revolution was fundamentally a pedagogical project. While the second version, the schoolbook, represented the purest form of his vision of the history, each of his three histories was designed to teach a different audience about the true principles of the Revolution. Moreover, the histories would also serve to promote those principles throughout the world and thus, in effect, continue the Revolution. In other words, he assumed that by extending the knowledge of the Revolution to the rest of the world one would also extend its effects.

In his study of the early histories of the American Revolution, *The Revolutionary Histories*, Lester H. Cohen argues that "historical writing was for the historians [of the Revolution writing in the late eighteenth century] an ideological and ethical art. Writing history was for them not only a 'scholarly' enterprise concerned with instruction in history's lessons, but was, more importantly, a present- and future-oriented instrument of political and moral values and vision" (21–22). Ultimately, Cohen argues, they realized "that to write the history of the American Revolution was itself a revolutionary act" (22). Paine was no exception. This was why he felt it was so important that a thorough history of the Revolution be written and published not only in the United States, but also in Europe. Moreover, a year earlier he had published his *Letter to the Abbé Raynal, on the Affairs of North America: In which the Mistakes in the Abbés Account of the Revolution of America are Corrected and Cleared Up*, which, as he told his friend George Washington, was primarily aimed at a European audience: "I have begun some remarks on the Abbé Raynal's *History of the Revolution*. In several places he is mistaken, and in others injudicious and sometimes cynical. I believe I shall publish it in America, but my principal view is to republish it in Europe both in French and English" (CW II, 1204).

THE LETTER TO RAYNAL

Shortly after presenting his outline for a historical trilogy about the American Revolution in his 1783 "Letter to the Continental Congress," Paine identifies his *Letter to the Abbé Raynal*, published a year earlier, as the part targeted for a European audience.

This last is the plan on which my answer to the Abbé Raynal is conducted. There is nothing respecting forms of government in it, for as I intended it for the purpose of setting forth the affairs and advocating the cause of America in Europe I was careful in attending to this point, and by so doing it became eligible to be translated into the European languages, and has already been printed in French at Paris. (CW II, 1240)

Paine, thus, was in essence suggesting that he had already begun the work on this three-part history, although in inverted order. His evidence for the fact is that his *Letter to Raynal* had already been translated and published in France. Paradoxically, however, Paine, who had insisted on democracy as the key to overthrowing tyranny in his previous American writings, stresses the need to omit any recommendations pertaining to proper forms of government in the account of the Revolution intended for Europe. Although, he reiterates his point regarding the omission of any discussion of forms of government, he does not offer a rationale for this omission: "In this land [Europe] all partiality to forms of government or defence of any one in preference to another should be omitted, and the facts of the revolution only attended to, with such reflections on them as may serve to promote the general good and peace of mankind without disturbing their modes of government" (1240). These are hardly the words of a radical. How exactly did Paine expect reform to occur if monarchical governments were not to be changed? What, furthermore, were the principles that produced the American Revolution if they did not involve, as he seems to suggest in his letter to the Continental Congress, a sense of the proper forms of government?

Perhaps he was being mindful not to offend the sensibilities of his French audience. Or, he may have felt that the principles essentially argued for a radical reformation of modes of government and therefore any explicit discussion of the subject was unnecessary and would only serve to generate resistance to the principles. While he played down his desire to use such a history to promote revolution or reform in Europe in his "Letter to the Continental Congress," he shows no such reservations in the *Letter to Raynal* where he argues that "A total reformation is wanted in England. She wants an expanded mind – a heart which embraces the universe" (255). If this is not a recommendation of a specific mode of government, it is nevertheless a condemnation of a particular form of government. In any case, he never offers an explanation for his recommendation that only the principles of the Revolution, without mention of forms of government, be discussed in the history intended for Europe, but by the time of *Rights of Man* he would revert to his position in *Common Sense* that monarchical governments are antithetical to progress.

In the last chapter of Part II of *Rights on Man* Paine argues that changing forms of government is the fundamental aim of his text: "Having in all the preceding parts of this work endeavored to establish a system of principles as a basis on which governments ought to be erected, I shall proceed in this to the ways and means of rendering them into practise" (CW I, 398). Moreover, in *Rights of Man* Paine draws the connection between the "principles" and the "practice" of the American Revolution when he argues that it led directly to the French Revolution:

The French officers and soldiers who after this went to America, were eventually placed in the school of Freedom, and learned the practice as well as the principles of it by heart.

As it was impossible to separate the military events which took place from the principles of the American Revolution, the publication of those events in France necessarily connected themselves with the principles which produced them. (CW I, 299–300).

Surely, Paine did not think that his *Letter to Raynal* would serve any other purpose than promoting a reform in the oppressive modes of government prevalent in Europe.

As would always be the case with Paine, in the *Letter to Raynal* matters of principle and not matters of historical detail were the crucial issue. Only when they had a specific impact on a question of principle did Paine trouble himself with historical details.[8] Paine expresses his concern with the problem of principles in the second paragraph of the *Letter*:

> It is yet too soon to write the history of the Revolution, and whoever attempts it precipitately, will unavoidably mistake characters and circumstances, and involve himself in error and difficulty. Things, like men, are seldom understood rightly at first sight. But the Abbé is wrong even in the foundation of his work; that is, he has misconceived and mis-stated the causes which produced the rupture between England and her then colonies, and which led on, step by step, unstudied and uncontrived on the part of America, to a revolution, which has engaged the attention, and affected the interest of Europe. (CW II, 215)

In this paragraph Paine stakes out the ground for his *Letter* by emphasizing the need to properly understand the causes that led to the American Revolution, principles that he had helped articulate and would continue to shape. Paine understood that the successful conclusion of the war was only part of the work of the American Revolution. The other part was making sure that the lessons of the Revolution would be properly understood and learned by the rest of the world. As in the case with the distinction between historical details and principles, Paine was more interested in the general application of the larger lessons of the Revolution than in the details of its local manifestation. The details of history are only important insofar as they play a role in the larger political or philosophical questions at stake in any given era.

Curiously, though, the form he has chosen for his text, that of a response to a historical account, forces Paine to deal with details. While he emphasizes the principles at stake in the events in question, he must also attend to Raynal's account of the specific events in question. As he would note in his observations about the connections between the French Revolution and the American Revolution in *Rights of Man*, one cannot separate military events from ideological questions. In order to balance the competing demands of correcting Raynal and setting forth the principles and causes of the Revolution, Paine is forced to construct

---

[8] Among other things, this lack of interest in details might have been the reason why Paine would never write a narrative history of the Revolution.

his text on a different model. Just as Montesquieu, Rousseau, Ferguson, and Adam Smith had experimented with various forms of historical writing in their respective philosophical histories, so too would Paine. Pure narrative would not serve his purpose, but some narration would be required. Therefore, Paine improvises by constructing his text as a letter, which allows him to mix narrative, reflection, and criticism in one simple and straightforward text. Paine is conscious of this strategy and recognizes it as the formal aspect of his text that denies it the literary status of a history: "As it is not my design to extend these remarks to a history, I shall now take my leave of this passage of the Abbé" (CW II, 221). By "history" Paine does not mean that his text is not historical in nature, but rather that it is not a narrative history. While it was not the narrative history he had long planned, Paine considered this one of his most important works. As Philip S. Foner suggests, "How important Paine regarded this work is evidenced by the fact that he sometimes identified himself in his publications thereafter as the author of *Common Sense* and the *Letter to the Abbé Raynal*" (CW II, 212). Paine, then, chose not to write a narrative in response to Raynal, but instead employed a different form to write a counterhistory: he would write an epistolary history.

THE *LETTER TO RAYNAL* AS LETTER

If the *Letter to Raynal* is not a formal narrative history of the Revolution, in the mode of Gibbon's, Hume's, or Robertson's famous contemporary histories, it is nevertheless a kind of historical account. As the only part of this trilogy that Paine would write, the *Letter to Raynal* stands as Paine's history of the Revolution. Through it we can begin to understand Paine's sense of the role of historical writing in his revolutionary vision. As a result, the choices Paine made in writing his version of a history of the Revolution also become significant. Perhaps the most striking of those choices is that he wrote it in the first person as an epistle to another historiographer of the Revolution. To a certain extent the choice was overdetermined: Raynal had written an account of the Revolution that Paine found objectionable, so, as he had done many times before in his career, he decided to write a response to it in order to "prevent even accidental errors from intermixing with history, under the sanction of time and silence" (CW II, 212). However, Paine had been planning to write his own history of the Revolution so why not counter Raynal's account with a narrative of his own? Why write his history of the American Revolution for Europe as a letter? Why, in other words, did the formal structure and stylistic aspects of a letter make it a more attractive genre for writing history than the traditional narrative form? What did the letter make possible that would not have been possible in the context of a narrative history?

Lester H. Cohen opens his study of the eighteenth-century narrative histories of the Revolution with the statement that "In the Revolutionary histories we see a dramatic change not only in the categories of historical explanation, the theory of causation, and the understanding of chance, human character and will, *but in the literary conventions that govern historical narrative, in the language conventions, style, and form of historical presentation*" (15, emphasis mine). Drawing on Hayden White's theoretical work, Cohen proceeds to analyze the narrative histories written in the years immediately following the Revolution. Paradoxically, Cohen then limits his field of inquiry to "*formal* narratives" such as those written by David Ramsay, Mercy Otis Warren, and John Marshall, when his opening statement would seem to allow not only for changes within the genre of narrative history but for broader generic innovations (18). Cohen, in other words, fails to see that a revolution in form need not be limited to radical alteration within the structure and metaphorics of narrative, but might also entail a rejection of narrative history itself in favor of other discursive forms. Paine, for example, did not write a narrative history of the Revolution, but that does not mean he did not write a historical text.

Borrowing White's terms, then, I would like to suggest that Paine deliberately chose the letter as his "mode of emplotment." In his seminal essay, "Interpretation in History," White suggests that historians, more often unconsciously than consciously, construct their texts "as *a story of a particular kind*" (58). The type of story they tell, the mode of emplotment, White argues, tends to correspond with both a "mode of explanation," and a "mode of ideological implication" (70). In his essay, White focuses on narrative history and as a result he identifies four modes of emplotment that are fundamentally narrative: romance, tragedy, comedy, and satire. By writing his history as a letter Paine was able to escape narrative and serve the interest of his mode of explanation, which was fundamentally pedagogic. In this, the great age of epistolary literature, Paine's choice seems only fitting. In the eighteenth century the popular literary form most commonly associated with instruction was the letter. In texts as varied as Montesquieu's *Lettres Persanes*, Pope's *Moral Epistles*, Chesterfield's *Letter to His Son*, Madame de Genlis' *Adelaide and Theodore; or Letter on Education*, and Richardson's *Pamela* the letter had provided an ideal medium for authors to combine didacticism with entertainment in order to expand their readership. Furthermore, Paine's epistolary was not without precedents. Just a year earlier, in 1781, Peter Oliver had published his *Origin and Progress of the American Rebellion*, a letter with which Paine surely would have been acquainted.

For Paine writing his history as a letter both frees him from the linear constraints of writing a narrative and allows him to adopt the more personal tone that had served him so well in his previous writings. As a result, the text reads as a series of unrelated observations on Raynal's text and on the events of the Revolution that are connected only by Thomas Paine's voice. Paine uses his text's formal status as a letter to justify his limited response to Raynal: "But in these [Raynal's narrations], there is so much mistake, and so many omissions, that, to set them right, must be the business of a history and not of a letter" (CW II, 222). The ability to range freely over Raynal's text and address specific moments or reflections therein, afforded Paine the opportunity to emphasize what he saw as the key moments in the War and the crucial issues of the Revolution. Paine focuses on five central moments in Raynal's history: the causes of the Revolution, the account of the early battles in New York and New Jersey, the use of paper money, the state of the states in 1778, and the alliance with the French. In each case Paine does not simply correct Raynal's factual errors, he also correlates those errors to the mistaken conclusions they produce in his history.

Paine takes advantage of the freedom to be personal afforded him by the letter in the very opening paragraph of his text where he addresses Raynal directly:

To an author of such distinguished reputation as the Abbé Raynal, it might very well become me to apologize for the present undertaking; but as *to be right* is the first wish of philosophy, and the first principle of history, he will, I presume, accept from me a declaration of my motives, which are those of doing justice, in preference to any complimental apology I might otherwise make. (CW II, 215)

The casual tone of this sentence, combined with its apology for not apologizing to Raynal, sets the reader at ease by presenting the text as a friendly conversation. Paine also places himself in a subordinate position to Raynal, who is always addressed personally but respectfully. Instead of laying claim to his own reputation and stature to authorize his observations, Paine emphasizes the primacy of the motives and principles that have led him to publish this pamphlet. Thus he enfranchises the opinion of all readers by emphasizing the importance of the thought process over the social or intellectual status of the thinker.

Perhaps the most important aspect of the aforementioned sentence, however, is that it makes it clear that, in spite of its title, Paine's text is not really directed at Raynal. As would be the case throughout the text, when Paine uses a pronoun to identify Raynal in the text it is invariably the third person singular, "He," rather than the second person, "You." Paine thus never addresses Raynal directly in his text; instead, he addresses readers of Raynal's history. Paine's audience, therefore, is not the great man of letters, but the common reader. In order to reach that audience most effectively Paine employs the letter form to establish a personal connection with his reader. The letter allows him to avoid the authoritative voice of narrative history in favor of a more colloquial discussion. This is why instead of distinguishing himself from the reader, Paine chooses to distinguish himself from Raynal. In a rare instance of humility, even if it is faux humility, Paine comments on his intellectual stature in relation to Raynal's:

Hitherto my remarks have been confined to circumstance; the order in which they arose, and the events they produced. In these my information being better than the Abbé's, my task was easy. How I may succeed in controverting matters of sentiment and opinion, with one whom years, experience, and long established reputation have placed in a superior line, I am less confident in; but as they fall within the scope of my observations it would be improper to pass them over. (CW II, 236–237)

As in the excuse for not offering an apology for his text, Paine's remark is more strategic than heartfelt. There is no need to remind the reader of Raynal's intellectual stature or to apologize for his remarks on Raynal's text other than to establish his own subject position. Paine is more interested in establishing a relationship of equals with his readers than in deferring to Raynal's authority. Thus, he not only places Raynal at a distance physically, but also personally.

The difference between Paine's patient response to Raynal and his angry response to Silas Deane, both of which are published around the same time, again illustrates the ad hoc nature of his approach to public debate. Had he treated Deane with the diplomacy he displays in his critique of Raynal, he might not have found himself on the losing end of that debate. At the very least, he would have left himself a reasonable way out without compromising his personal integrity. However, that would imply a systematic, a la Franklin, and stable set of protocols shaping his approach to public debate. Of course, it is also true that Paine's response to Raynal was not a dialogue in the same sense that his letters about Deane were. Paine can afford Raynal such respect because there is virtually no possibility of a rebuttal. This immediately removes the personal from consideration. Generally, Paine only resorts to the personal when he feels that his authority might be in question. The irony of this is that in its more idealistic form the argument for the impersonal public sphere is precisely that an idea or argument should obtain power only because of its inherent value and not as a consequence of the status of its advocate. Throughout the *Letter to Raynal* Paine expresses great confidence in his authority, owing principally to his greater proximity to the events in question. But in his accusations regarding Deane and the ensuing debate, the validity of the claims is almost entirely, due to the complications with the evidence discussed in the previous chapter, based on the identity of the speaker. Thus at the very same time that Paine tragically misreads the situation with Deane, he masterfully navigates this reply to Raynal.

HISTORY OR LITERARY CRITICISM

Paine prefaces his critique of Raynal's text with a curious and seemingly tangential discussion of the publication history of Raynal's *On the Revolution of the English Colonies in North America*. He opens by emphasizing that Raynal's physical distance from the events in question may have been the cause of the errors in his account.[9] But he then promptly turns to the matter of the circumstances of the text's publication and the rumored theft of Raynal's manuscript. Paine takes advantage of this possibility to excuse Raynal: "There are declarations and sentiments in the Abbé's piece which, for my own part, I did not expect to find, and such as himself, on a revisal, might have seen occasion to change; but the anticipated piracy effectually prevented his having the opportunity, and precipitated him into difficulties, which, had it not been for such ungenerous fraud, might not have happened" (CW II, 214). Thus, before he has even begun to address any of the particular errors or problems in Raynal's text, Paine has already excused its author by suggesting that the writing process had been disrupted.

Paine's discussion of the theft of Raynal's work prepares the reader for one of his most pointed attacks on Raynal. The *Letter to Raynal* culminates in an accusation of plagiarism:

I observe the Abbé had made a sort of epitome of a considerable part of the pamphlet 'Common Sense,' and introduced it in that form into his publication. But

---

[9] Paine used this distance argument on several occasions. First in *Common Sense* he suggested that the distance separating England and the colonies made independence a natural conclusion.

there are other places where the Abbé has borrowed freely from the said pamphlet without acknowledging it. The difference between society and government, with which the pamphlet opens, is taken from it, and in some expressions almost literally, into the Abbé's work, as if originally his own; and through the whole of the Abbé's remarks on this head, the idea in 'Common Sense' is so closely copied and pursued, that the difference is only in the words, and in the arrangement of the thoughts, and not in the thoughts themselves. (CW II, 251)

Ironically, in the midst of disagreeing with Raynal's version of the Revolution, Paine finds himself accusing Raynal of stealing his theoretical observations on the nature of government. Paine even includes a note in which he presents various passages from *Common Sense* and from Raynal's *History* side by side for the reader to compare. No doubt, Raynal paraphrases several of Paine's theories. That Paine's critique of Raynal should culminate in this accusation of plagiarism is perhaps not surprising when we consider that he prefaces the *Letter* with an introduction that deals almost entirely with matters of literary property. Just as Raynal's text had been stolen by an unscrupulous printer, Paine feels his text has in some measure been stolen by Raynal.

Paine ends the "Introduction" with an assessment of the literary consequences of the theft of Raynal's manuscript, which leads him to describe the literary talents needed to write a proper history.

This mode of making an author appear before his time, will appear still more ungenerous, when we consider how very few men there are in any country, who can at once, and without the aid of reflection and revisal, combine warm passions with a cool temper, and the full expansion of the imagination with the natural and necessary gravity of judgment, so as to be rightly balanced within themselves, and to make a reader feel, fancy, and understand justly at the same time. To call three powers of the mind into action at once, in a manner that neither shall interrupt, and that each shall aid and invigorate the other, is a talent very rarely possessed. (CW II, 214)

In the context of excusing the errors in Raynal, which he attributes partly to the pirating of Raynal's manuscript, Paine outlines the task of the historian in terms that make it clear why he never got around to writing a formal history of the Revolution of his own. This delicate balancing act was, at least as he proposed it, a tall order indeed. Instead, by constructing his text as a response to Raynal's *History*, Paine allows himself free rein: He is simply correcting the mistakes of another writer and not undertaking the more burdensome task of creating a narrative history of the revolution.

Thus, Paine's brief introduction to the *Letter* frames his discussion in terms of a work of literary criticism. All of the issues he raises in the

"Introduction" regard authorship or literary ability rather than historiographical issues. The *Letter to Raynal* is fundamentally not so much a
work of history as a work of literary criticism. Correspondingly, Paine's
most persistent criticism of Raynal in the *Letter* concerns his lack of literary skill. Throughout the *Letter* Paine's strategy is that of a literary critic:
He first cites a passage from Raynal and then critiques it on the basis of its
writerly qualities. For example, he discusses Raynal's account of the early
battles of the Revolutionary War in the following terms: "The actions of
Trenton and Princeton, in New Jersey, in December 1776, and January
following, on which the fate of America stood for a while trembling on
the point of suspense, and from which the most important consequences
followed, are comprised within a single paragraph, faintly conceived, and
barren of character circumstance and description" (CW II, 222). He then
proceeds to quote the noted paragraph and critique its content, but only
after he has indicted it for a lack of style.

    While he begins the *Letter* by discussing a question of historical inter-
pretation in Raynal – the causes of the Revolution – Paine concludes this
discussion with an extended analysis of his rival's skills as a writer:

> Though the Abbé possesses and displays great powers of genius, and is a master
> of style and language, he seems not to pay equal attention to the office of the
> historian. His facts are coldly and carelessly stated. They neither inform the reader
> nor interest him. Many of them are erroneous, and most of them are defective
> and obscure. It is undoubtedly both an ornament and a useful addition to history,
> to accompany it with maxims and reflections. They afford likewise an agreeable
> change to the style, and more diversified manner of expression; but it is absolutely
> necessary that the root from whence they spring, or the foundation on which they
> are raised, should be well attended to, which in this work is not. The Abbé hastens
> through his narrations as if he was glad to get from them, that he may enter the
> more copious field of eloquence and imagination. (CW II, 221–222)

Paine's sharp critique of Raynal emphasizes his choices as a writer, and
resembles the work of a literary critic more than that of an historian.
What he identifies as the office of the historian are not Raynal's interpretive or descriptive skills, but rather his ability to tell a compelling story.
Raynal, instead, is too apt to philosophize, which is what Paine seems to
be referring to when he cites Raynal's propensity to indulge in "the more
copious field of eloquence and imagination." Ironically, Paine's tendency
as a writer is precisely the same; that is, he moves rather quickly to a
discussion of general principles. So, Paine's critique of Raynal once again
boils down to a question of emphasis and of writerly skill. In his view,

Raynal simply seems overly eager to make the transition from narration to general observation.

Initially, it seems as though Paine is drawing a distinction between literature and history when he juxtaposes eloquence and imagination to the "office of the historian." However, he defines the "office of the historian" in purely literary terms when he implies that those are precisely the qualities Raynal's narrations lack. This apparent contradiction mirrors Paine's strategy throughout the paragraph in which he first applauds Raynal and then follows that applause with a critique that undermines his initial praise. The opening two lines of the paragraph provide a good example of this tactic. Despite his professed admiration of Raynal's stylistic and narrative skills, Paine implicitly questions those aspects of Raynal's text when he calls his narrations cold and carelessly stated. Would a writer skilled in matters of style and language state his facts coldly or carelessly, never mind both? This is not a question of the accuracy of the facts, but rather of the manner in which they are presented. Ultimately, Paine emphasizes the need for a history to both entertain and inform the reader with a good story.

Paine would adopt a similar approach at several other key moments in the text. Of Raynal's account of the Americans' rejection of British offer of mediation in 1779, for example, Paine remarks:

> In this paragraph the conception is lofty and the expression elegant, but the coloring is too high for the original, and the likeness fails through excess of graces. To fit the powers of thinking and the turn of language to the subject, so as to bring out a clear conclusion that shall hit the point in question and nothing else, is the true criterion of writing. But the greater part of the Abbé's writings (if he will pardon me the remark) appear to me uncentral and burdened with variety. They represent the beautiful wilderness without paths; in which the eye is diverted by everything without being particularly directed to anything; and in which it is agreeable to be lost, and difficult to find the way out. (CW II, 246–247)

Only after he has criticized Raynal's prose for its lack of literary quality does Paine proceed to deal with its literal accuracy. He is first concerned with its "spirit and composition" (CW II, 247). To a certain extent, then, Paine's point is not so much that Raynal is mistaken in his facts, but that his literary choices have betrayed him by leading to a distorted picture of the events.

RIGHTS OF MAN, OR THE LETTER TO EDMUND BURKE?

In February of 1791, almost nine years after the appearance of his *Letter to Raynal*, Paine published another text on the same model. Just as the *Letter* to *Raynal* aimed to correct the mistakes in the Abbé Raynal's *Révolution d'Amérique*, *Rights of Man* aimed to correct those of Edmund Burke's *Reflections on the Revolution in France*. *Rights of Man*, however, would reach a much wider audience than his first effort in the format. Indeed, within three months of its publication over fifty thousand copies of *Rights of Man* were sold, at the time making it easily the best selling text ever published.[10] Paine, who had frequently directed his shorter articles at a specific individual, had gained invaluable experience in expanding the genre to pamphlet length with his *Letter to Raynal*.[11] And while he sheds the explicitly epistolary mode of The *Letter to Raynal* in *Rights of Man*, his text is essentially structured in the same way as the *Letter to Raynal*. The parallels between the two texts are striking and in the next few pages I will explore the connections between them.

Despite the fact that he does not present *Rights of Man* as a letter to Edmund Burke, Paine cannot resist incorporating into it a sense of an ongoing dialogue between himself and Burke. In the "Preface" to the English edition of the text, Paine refers to his prior correspondence with Burke, which, once private, has now become public. Not surprisingly, that correspondence centered on the recent course of events in France: "At the time Mr. Burke made his speech last winter in the English Parliament against the French Revolution and the National Assembly, I was in Paris, and had written to him but a short time before, to inform him how prosperously matters were going" (CW I, 244). Paine strategically emphasizes Burke's location in England and his own in France at the time of the events in question. As in the *Letter to Raynal*, Paine uses his opponent's distance from the site of the action to explain the inaccuracies in his text. This emphasis on their respective locations also allows Paine to incorporate a record of their past discussion on the subject of the French Revolution in order to position his present text. Paine thus subtly implies that *Rights of Man* constitutes a continuation of that correspondence.[12]

---

[10] See John Keane, 307. Paine comments on the sales of *Rights of Man Part I* in the "Preface" to *Rights of Man Part II*.

[11] For example, Paine had addressed his "Forester's Letters," "To Cato," and several numbers of the *American Crisis* were directed at various antagonists, including Lord Howe and his brother General William Howe (Nos. 2 and 5 respectively), Sir Guy Carleton ("A Supernumerary Crisis"), and the Earl of Shelburne (No. 12).

[12] It should be noted that Burke sets up the *Reflections* as a letter. The full title of the text is *Reflections on the Revolution in France, and on the Proceedings in Certain Societies in London Relative to that Event. In a Letter Intended to Have Been Sent to a Gentleman in Paris*, and he opens the text "Dear Sir."

Paine later returns to the matter of their correspondence to reinforce his claim that Burke has deliberately distorted the truth: "As I used sometimes to correspond with Mr. Burke, believing him then to be a man of sounder principles than his book shows him to be, I wrote him last winter from Paris and gave him an account of how prosperously matters were going on" (CW I, 297). This second allusion to his earlier letter to Burke solidifies the sense of a continuing discussion. It also serves to convey a sense of lost trust between them. In other words, the events in France have not only changed the public/political relations between Burke and himself, they have also brought about a change in their personal relationship. The kinship that came with political alliance has been lost, not because of Burke's difference of opinion, but because of his lack of principle, or so Paine would have us believe.

Paine thus personalizes the relationship between himself and Burke in much the same way he had constructed a personal relationship to Raynal in the *Letter*. This is not simply an instance of an ideological dispute between two thinkers, but it is a parting of the ways between two fellow travelers. To Paine, the American Revolution, which Burke had supported, was only the first step along a long path to the reformation of all nondemocratic forms of government.[13] Burke, once a friend to the American colonies, which Paine mistakenly equated with approval for democracy, had now become a defender of monarchy, which Paine saw as the most un-American of institutions. Paine uses that personal dimension of the relationship to further support his cause by suggesting that Burke's distortions are not the result of an innocent lack of information, but a deliberate effort to misrepresent the events in France. Paine goes so far as to suggest that Burke's reaction to the French Revolution is motivated by his general prejudice against the French: "When the French Revolution broke out, it certainly afforded to Mr. Burke an opportunity of doing some good, had he been disposed to it; instead of which, no sooner did he see the old prejudices wearing away than he immediately began sowing the seeds of a new inveteracy, as if he were afraid that England and France would cease to be enemies" (CW I, 246). Paine thus opens up this personal dispute to make it into a national one by personalizing the relationship between

---

[13] *Rights of Man Part I* ends with a vision of the impact of the American and French Revolutions: "What were formerly called revolutions, were little more than a change of persons, or an alteration of local circumstances. They rose and fell like things of course, and had nothing in their existence or fate that could influence beyond the spot that produced them. But what we now see in the world, from the revolutions of America and France, is a renovation of the natural order of things" (CW I, 341–342).

England and France. Paine believed letters played a crucial role in human relations:

Letters, the tongue of the world, have in some measure brought all mankind acquainted, and by an extension of their uses are every day promoting some new friendship. Through them distant nations became capable of conversation, and losing by degrees the awkwardness of strangers, and the moroseness of suspicion, they learn to know and understand each other. (CW II, 240)

By letters Paine, of course, refers to literature and writing in general, but no form of writing effected this operation more clearly than did personal letters. While Paine would attack Burke on a whole series of subjects, perhaps none infuriated Paine more than this one.

Since the conclusion of the American War of Independence, Paine's political goal was to bring about the end of animosity between nations. Paine first presents his vision at the end of the *Letter to Raynal*:

The true idea of a great nation, is that which extends and promotes the principles of universal society; whose mind rises above the atmosphere of local thoughts, and considers mankind, of whatever nation or profession they may be, as the work of one Creator. The rage for conquest has had its fashion, and its day. Why may not the amiable virtues have the same? . . .

Should the present revolution be distinguished by opening a new system of extended civilization, it will receive from heaven the highest evidence of approbation. (CW II, 256)

For this to occur, however, Paine felt that the old European enemies needed to find ways to reinvent their relationships, which would not be possible under the current monarchical governments. The key to this reinvention, therefore was democratic revolution. Once this was achieved he hoped for the formation of a league of nations in which disputes could be solved in a friendly manner, without recourse to the violence of war.

Paine ends the *Rights of Man* with this vision of a league of nations that would unite Europe:

From what we now see, nothing of reform on the political world ought to be held improbable. It is an age of revolutions, in which every thing may be looked for. The intrigue of courts, by which the system of war is kept up, may provoke a confederation of nations to abolish it: and an European congress, to patronize the progress of free government, and promote the civilization of nations with each other, is an event nearer in probability, than once were the revolutions and alliance of France and America. (CW I, 344)

This commitment to the renovation of relations between the warring nations of the world naturally leads Paine to make a distinction between the people and the government: "Every country in Europe considers the cause of the French people as identical with the cause of its own people, or rather, as embracing the interests of the entire world. But those who rule those countries do not entertain quite the same opinion. Now, this is a difference to which we are bound to give our deepest attention. The people are not to be confounded with their government; and this is especially the case when the relation of the English Government to its people is considered" (CW I, 247).[14] This also explains Paine's opening sentence to the body of *Rights of Man*: "Among the incivilities by which nations or individuals provoke and irritate each other, Mr. Burke's pamphlet on the French Revolution is an extraordinary instance" (249).[15] Paine thus recasts the *Reflections* as a personal insult to the French nation, but one not to be attributed to the English people but rather to one monarchical writer.

As in the *Letter to Raynal the* central aim of *Rights of Man* is to correct both the factual errors and the mistaken conclusions that the author of the text under examination reached on the basis of that misinformation. If Burke, unlike Raynal, never claims the status of a history for his *Reflections on the Revolution in France*, Paine manages to refocus the debate around matters of historical interpretation and representation. Rather than address Burke's *Reflections* as a work of political philosophy, Paine deals with it primarily as a work of history and only secondarily as a work of political theory. Once he has shifted the ground of the debate, Paine can take advantage of the factual errors in Burke's text to undermine the theoretical claims Burke makes on the basis of those facts. This strategy allows him to employ a counternarrative, not just a counterideology, to debunk Burke's claims: "As Mr. Burke has passed over the whole transaction of the Bastille (and his silence is nothing in his favor), and has entertained his readers with reflections on supposed facts distorted into real falsehoods, I will give, since he has not, some account of the circumstances which preceded the transaction" (260). In other words, Burke has not drawn his conclusions on the basis of the facts; he has allowed his imagination

---

[14] The first sentence of this paragraph, of course, paraphrases his famous statement from the "Introduction" to *Common Sense*: "The cause of America is in a great measure the cause of all mankind" (CW I, 3).

[15] In the *Letter to Raynal* Paine had also raised the matter of the English people's lack of civility: "It was equally as much from her manners as from her injustices that she [Britain] lost the colonies. By the latter she provoked their principles, by the former she wore out their temper; and it ought to be held out as an example to the world, to show how necessary it is to conduct the business of government with civility" (CW II, 220).

to twist the facts. Burke, like Raynal before him, Paine argues, is more interested in philosophizing than in attending to the truth of what happened. As he notes of Burke's account of the expedition to Versailles on October 6, 1789: "This is not the sober style of history, not the intention of it. It leaves everything to be guessed at, and mistaken" (269). For Paine, then, not only is the meaning of what happened in France at stake, but also what actually happened remains in question.

As a result, the core of the *Rights of Man* is a narrative retelling of the events leading up to the French Revolution. As in the *Letter to Raynal*, Paine emphasizes motives and principles. This retelling is necessitated by Burke's tendency to permit his imagination to blur the truth. Paine notes his motivation for writing the *Rights of Man* in his "Preface": "This [answering Burke] appeared to me the more necessary to be done, when I saw the flagrant misrepresentations which Mr. Burke's pamphlet contains; and that while it is an outrageous abuse on the French Revolution, and the principles of Liberty, it is an imposition on the rest of the world" (245). For Paine representation is indeed the key issue. He, more than anybody else, understood the power of the press to represent events in a way that would serve a particular political goal. After all, he was a master of this himself. Paine, then, also understood that the way a writer frames an event has a profound effect on its interpretation. Therefore, the best way to attack Burke was to question the way he had framed the events of the French Revolution. Accordingly, he accuses Burke of writing a play and trying to pass it off as a history: "I cannot consider Mr. Burke's book in scarcely any other light than a dramatic performance; and he must, I think, have considered it in the same light himself, by the poetical liberties he has taken of omitting some facts, distorting others, and making the machinery bend to produce a stage effect" (268). Burke, in other words, has failed to abide by the rules of the genre in which he writes.

According to Paine, the key source of misrepresentation in Burke's text stems from his choice of, to once again use Hayden White's term, emplotment. Paine argues that Burke has structured his text as a tragic drama, when, in fact, it ought to be structured as a heroic novel.

As to the tragic paintings by which Mr. Burke has outraged his own imagination, and seeks to work upon that of his readers, they are very well calculated for theatrical representation, where facts are manufactured for the sake of show, and accommodated to produce, through the weakness of sympathy, a weeping effect. But Mr. Burke should recollect that he is writing history, and not *plays*; and that his readers will expect truth, and not the spouting rant of high toned declamation. (CW I, 258–259)

The task of *Rights of Man*, then, is to recast the events leading to the French Revolution as such a tale.

Paine's critique of Burke is not limited, however, to an attack on the accuracy of his information or the tone of his narrations, but extends into the style of his philosophical meditations as well. "I have now to follow Mr. Burke through a pathless wilderness of rhapsodies, and a sort of descant upon governments, in which he asserts whatever he pleases, on the presumption of its being believed, without offering either evidence or reasons for doing so" (272). This passage echoes one of Paine's observations from the "Introduction" to the *Letter to Raynal*, where he notes: "But if either or both of the two former [passion and imagination] are raised too high, or heated too much, the judgement will be jostled from its seat, and the whole matter, however important in itself, will diminish into a pantomime of the mind, in which we create images and promote no other purpose than amusement" (214). In Burke's case, Paine might substitute outrage for amusement, but the effect is the same.

HISTORY AND/OR HISTORIOGRAPHY

The *Letter to Raynal* proved to be a pivotal text for Paine as it signaled both a new audience for him and a new approach to history. With the *Letter to Raynal* Paine would essentially reinvent himself for a European audience. He was still writing about an American subject, but now, for the first time, he was directing a text to a European readership. In this respect, it was the key text bridging the gap between his American and his European careers. Soon he would write *Rights of Man* where he would no longer rely directly on his knowledge of American affairs, and address the matter of democratic revolution in a European context. No doubt his own personal history as an advocate of democracy in America endowed his voice with authority and thus facilitated this career shift, but more importantly, this transition required a new approach to history. Whereas the American colonists felt they were in a unique situation that enabled them to invent their own history and culture, to the French and the English, history existed as a palpable force shaping their respective cultures. Aware of this difference in his audience's perception of history, Paine would adjust his treatment of the subject to better suit the needs of his new readers.

In *Common Sense, The American Crisis,* and his other early texts, texts aimed primarily at an American readership, Paine had relied on history as a stable source of evidence in a rather transparent and unselfconscious manner. With the *Letter to Raynal* he became much more concerned with the problems of historical evidence and with the function of history as a shaping force in society. In *Rights of Man*, and later in *The Age of Reason*, he would no longer simply draw on historical examples for evidence; instead he would interrogate the historical record and meditate on the force of history and the problems of historiography. History had become a much more complicated and mediated form of knowledge. Now, instead of dismissing history or reducing it to a convenient source of examples from the past, he would address its force directly by focusing on the problems of historiography and the constructedness of history.

All of this brings us to the question, What is a history?, or, more specifically, what makes a text a work of history? If a history is a text that offers an interpretation of past events, then surely Paine's *Letter to Raynal* and *Rights of Man* fit the category. Paine, although he seems to have recognized narrative as one of the qualities that make a text a history, stretched the boundaries of history by producing an account of the Revolution that is fundamentally not a narrative. The same can be said for Thomas Jefferson and John Adams in their famously self-conscious and semiprivate correspondence, as well as for Paine's rival Edmund Burke. All of these writers shared the conviction that our understanding of the past had a profound impact on the present and, consequently, they inferred that future historians' understanding of the Revolutionary era would have an impact on succeeding generations. In other words, they intuited that our understanding of the events of the past are always subject to the limitations and needs of our knowledge at a particular moment in time. As Michel De Certeau has put it:

The situation of the historiographer makes the study of the real appear in two quite different positions within the scientific process: the real insofar as it is the *known* (what the historian studies, understands, or "brings to life" from a past society), and the real insofar as it is entangled within the scientific operations (the present society, to which the historians' problematics, their procedures, modes of comprehension, and finally a practice of meaning are referable). On the one hand, the real is the result of analysis, while on the other, it is its postulate. Neither of these two forms of reality can be eliminated or reduced to the other. (35)

The blurring of the line between history and historiography is precisely what concerned Paine in the "Letter to Raynal": "the following tract therefore, is published with a view to rectify [the mistakes in Raynal], and prevent even accidental errors from intermixing with history, under the sanction of time and silence" (CW II, 212). As Paine so astutely observed, history is often a matter of interpretation.

Insisting that it was still much too early to write the history of the American Revolution, Paine nonetheless wrote the "Letter to Raynal" lest the errors in Raynal's text be taken for facts, which he felt would compromise future generations' ability to discern the true lesson of the Revolution. Or, in De Certeau's terms, Paine wished to insure that the postulates of Raynal's texts would not become the scientific truths, the reality, of future historians. The same reasoning applied to his decision to respond to Burke's account of the French Revolution. If didacticism was a key component to a history, then Paine's texts, as well as those by Jefferson and Adams, were more effective and overtly didactic than the narrative histories of the day. We have failed to see Paine's *Letter to Raynal* as a history, therefore, partly because of our formal definition of the genre as fundamentally narrative, but also because it foregrounds the place of interpretation in history and thus calls attention to its own status as an interpretation. But histories, as Hayden White and Michel De Certeau, among others, have noted, can take many forms and each of those forms, in turn, offers a different perspective on the past that other forms cannot replicate. Thus, although Paine evidently did not feel up to the task of writing a narrative history of either the American or the French Revolution, he sensed that he could affect the interpretation of these crucial events by creating a different kind of historical text on epistolary history.

4

The Science of Revolution

Technological Metaphors and Scientific Methodology in Rights of Man *and* The Age of Reason

Thomas Paine begins the Introduction to Part II of *Rights of Man* with an analogy comparing politics and mechanics:

> What Archimedes said of the mechanical powers may be applied to reason and liberty: *Had we*, said he, *a place to stand upon, we might raise the world.*
>
> The Revolution in America presented in politics what was only theory in mechanics. So deeply rooted were all the governments of the old world, and so effectually had the tyranny and the antiquity of the habit established itself over the mind, that no beginning could be made in Asia, Africa, or Europe to reform the political condition of man. (CW I, 354)

The American Revolution, according to the logic of Paine's mechanical analogy, provided the foundation necessary to reform the world's tyrannical governments. In America the theory had been sufficient because of the youth of the country, but the rest of the world had become so habituated to tyranny that other nations would require a more powerful form of persuasion if they were to reform their governments. Paine hoped *Rights of Man* would help promote those reforms by spreading the principles of freedom and democracy from the United States to the rest of the world. Using Archimedes's theory of leverage, Paine argues that the United States constitutes a fulcrum that can be used to bring about change elsewhere. What is needed now is a long enough lever, the missing part of Archimedes's formulation as presented by Paine. That lever, in political terms, is *Rights of Man*.

Paine takes for granted the applicability of Archimedes' mechanical theory when, in fact, there is no necessary reason why it should describe political activity. More significantly, his use of the analogy shows that he believes he can assume that his readers will accept the validity of the analogy. Paine could safely employ this strategy because, as I. Bernard Cohen has observed, during the Enlightenment scientific metaphors were often used to legitimize political discourse. The language of science could lend an argument an air of authority, because in the Enlightenment "science was esteemed as the highest expression of human rationality" (Cohen, 20). In Paine's case, however, using a mechanical analogy was not simply a discursive strategy meant to endow his text with the aura of scientific authority. After years of dedication to technological pursuits science had not only become an integral part of Paine's life, it had gained a central role in his political imagination.

Paine had spent the previous seven years of his life principally devoted to the task of designing a model for building cast iron bridges. At the conclusion of the American War of Independence Paine, as his most recent biographer has noted, found himself drifting. The Revolution had had a deeply personal impact on Paine for, as he acknowledges, "It was the cause of America that made me an author" (CW I, 235). He had become so identified with the American cause, which had radically changed his life, that once the goal of independence and democracy had been achieved he found himself at a loss:

> Now, in the face of victory and peace, his reputation threatened to slip beneath the horizon of public recognition. Thomas Paine, the writer made famous by the Revolution, was in danger of becoming a nobody. Victory might ruin him – or at least fling him into a pit of confusion about his role as a political writer. As it did. (Keane, 242)

In these years Paine turned his attention to various projects in an effort to create a new identity for himself. His attempt, discussed in the previous chapter, to gain a commission as "Historiographer to the Continent" in order to write his long proposed history of the revolution was Paine's original choice. When he failed to gain the support of Congress for such an appointment he turned his attention to designing bridges, to which he dedicated most of his energies for the following decade.

During this time, when Paine was fully engaged in the design and mechanics of his bridge, he would become so immersed in the practice and rhetoric of the new science that it came to shape his political thinking in fundamental ways. Although he had strategically employed scientific metaphors as part of his arguments in *Common Sense* and *The Crisis*, science was simply a source of useful and illustrative analogies that endowed his arguments with an aura of truthfulness and invoked the power of the natural to support his claims. In later works, like *Rights of Man Part II* and *The Age of Reason*, science becomes the foundation upon which he builds his political arguments. In his study of Paine's political thought, *Thomas Paine and the Religion of Nature*, Jack Fruchtman, Jr. argues that Paine's ultimate goal as a political writer was to promote the "religion of nature": "To follow nature as he understood it (as a creation of God and a vessel of God's immanence), was itself a religion, which Thomas Paine, the secular preacher, taught to all those who would listen, or at least read his work" (7). Moreover, Fruchtman asserts, "His adulation of nature, his infatuation with it, was the basis of his religious faith" (9). Extending Fruchtman's insight, I would argue that although it may be true that "Images and metaphors of nature abound throughout his writings," Paine's vision of nature, particularly in his later writings, is almost always mediated by his interest in science (*Nature*, 9). In the following pages, then, I will argue that science, and not nature, was the fundamental reference point for Paine's later political writings, particularly *Rights of Man* and *The Age of Reason*.

Late eighteenth-century science, and particularly mechanics, I will suggest, would become particularly important to Paine as it supplied yet another democratic framework for constructing his radical politics. Not only did it provide a systematic structure for organizing knowledge and certifying truths, but the systems of the new science also were, or at least appeared to be, open to all. This openness not only manifested itself in the increased dissemination and accessibility of information, but also would be seen in the expanded participation in scientific pursuits. As Jan Golinski has noted, for example, by the second half of the eighteenth century the scientific clubs and societies that were so important at the time "comprised both members of the traditionally recognized professions (clergy, doctors, and lawyers) and such new aspirants to their rank as artists, craftsmen, writers, and academics" (Culture, 12). This is precisely the kind of social leveling that Paine was seeking to institutionalize in politics. Hence, in order to truly understand the impact of science on Paine's writings we must first understand the state of scientific thinking in the latter half of the eighteenth century. The first part of this essay, therefore, traces the revolutionary developments taking place in the practice and dissemination of science during the period. Once I have established the context of Paine's understanding of science, I examine his commitment to the practice of science, primarily his attempt to design and build an iron bridge, and its ideological ramifications. Finally, the chapter explores Paine's attempts to import scientific metaphors and methodology into his political arguments.

BECOMING A MAN OF SCIENCE

By the 1770s science had evolved from a private endeavor practiced exclusively by gentlemen to a thoroughly public activity, with experiments being conducted for profit in coffeehouses and itinerant lecturers earning a living explaining Newtonian science.[1] During the eighteenth century, Larry Stewart has argued, Baconian experimentalism, and more particularly the fascination with Newton's physics, led to a transformation in the practice of science: "the rapid multiplication of the sites of science meant the emergence, in coffee houses and in county towns, of . . . public science" (xx). This "public science," based on Baconian experimentalism, in turn, played an integral part in the social, economic, and political changes that were taking place in the eighteenth century by "helping to redefine authority and legitimacy":

> It did so by establishing a forceful and credible experimentalism – but, far more importantly, by likewise creating a public science to which many might obtain entry. Readers, listeners, observers could prove as important as authors and orators. In these terms, it is less the creation of scientific facts that matters, rather than the manufacture of credibility. (Stewart, xvi)[2]

Stewart's account of the role of science in the transformation of the construction of authority in the eighteenth century not only echoes Cohen's account of the strategic use of science by political writers in the eighteenth century, but also intersects with Jay Fliegelman's account of the emergence of theatricality in eighteenth-century American political oratory. In *Declaring Independence: Jefferson, Natural Language and the Culture of Performance*, Fliegelman contends that when, with the emergence of republicanism, the "ability to secure consent" replaces coercion as the basis of effective government, the manufacture of credibility becomes fundamental to the governing process (35–36). Through an analysis of rhetoric manuals of the day Fliegelman concludes that: "Distinctions between 'sincere' and 'artful' to the contrary, 'the art of speaking' was always artful, the show of naturalness was still a show" (80). Ultimately, this emphasis on "natural theatricality" means that "The virtuosity of manipulating

---

[1] In *The Rise of Public Science* Larry Stewart traces the transformation of science from a gentlemanly pursuit to a public activity. According to Stewart, the political ramifications of this transformation in science are crucial because scientific methodology creates a new epistemology. See also Steven Shapin, *A Social History of Truth*.

[2] Stewart does not refer to Jürgen Habermas' work, but his assessment of the emergence and role of "public science" in the eighteenth century intersects with Habermas' account of the rise of the public sphere.

arguments gives way to the aural and moral spectacle of sincerity; the credibility of the speaker and not the credibility of the argument becomes paramount" (43). The credibility of the speaker, however, was no longer a function of his class – as it had been in the seventeenth century – but a function of his oratorical skill.[3]

While experimental science may have shifted the emphasis away from the credibility of the speaker, it did not necessarily reduce itself to the credibility of its arguments. On the contrary, the theatrical nature of public oratory is replicated in the performance of public experiments in local coffeehouses where entertainment takes precedence over science. Consequently, creating the illusion of a marvelous truth becomes more important than demonstrating the principles of physics or chemistry. In the arena of public performance, scientists, like orators, had to perfect the art of appearing. Paine believed that in the realm of politics, as in the world of science, the critical function of the public sphere would reveal the charlatans and insure that truth and virtue would be upheld. Indeed, the need for such a function is precisely what propelled Paine to enter the public arena on a regular basis.[4]

The political implications of this new public science, Stewart argues, were fundamental to its position at the center of public attention: "the unification of the rhetoric of science with the language of power was the means by which science emerged into public consciousness" (xxv). The larger cultural impact of the public science parallels the emergence of the bourgeois public sphere and its legitimation of public opinion by shifting the emphasis from the individual to the community: "the very fact that experiments could be repeated meant that acceptable knowledge was increasingly dependent on general consensus" (Stewart, 105). Thus, the epistemological consequences of the new science had specific political implications that mirrored Paine's democratic ideals. The "manufacture of credibility," which characterized the practice of the new science, was

---

[3] While it is surely true that class and oratorical skill would never be entirely unconnected from one another, in the seventeenth century class alone generally insured one's credibility. For a thorough analysis of the connections between class and credibility in seventeenth-century Britain see Steven Shapin, *A Social History of Truth*. Of course, there were also parallel developments in religion that culminated in the Great Awakening. For an analysis of the significance of oratory and performance see also Sandra Gustafson, *Eloquence is Power*. On the oral dimensions of the Revolution and early national period see Looby, *Voicing America*.

[4] This view of the scientific process also dovetails nicely with Paine's emphasis on the personal in his analysis of the public sphere. If part of the function of public debate is to expose charlatans, then the personal ought to be included in public debates.

crucial to Paine's democratic vision insofar as he was attempting, through his writings, to shift political authority from a small elite to a wider public by making public opinion, general consensus, the primary expression of the nation's political will. Thus, it was only natural for Paine to use the language of the new enlightenment science to reinforce his political ideas.

Paine had never had any formal scientific training, but he was not entirely ignorant of contemporary science and technology. He had benefited from the widespread dissemination of science taking place in the second half of the eighteenth century. As a young man living in London, he had developed a liaison with Benjamin Martin and James Ferguson, "two of England's most reputable itinerant lecturers, whose energies were poured into bringing Newtonian science to captivated audiences otherwise excluded by prejudice from advanced education" (Keane, 42). Paine regularly attended their lectures and even seems to have paid to attend some of their small-group lessons (Keane, 43). After about six months, however, he was forced to leave London in search of employment.[5] So, whatever he learned from Ferguson and Martin about mechanics and mathematics over the course of a six-month period in 1757 comprised the extent of Paine's knowledge of those subjects. He would not have the opportunity to dedicate himself to scientific pursuits until after the American Revolution, although he still demonstrated an occasional interest in matters of science.

Paine's renewed interest in science and technology coincided with his arrival in the colonies two decades later, when, as editor of the *Pennsylvania Magazine*, he wrote and published various pieces related to contemporary technological advances. Indeed, one of the first articles he published in the colonies, "Useful and Entertaining Hints," was an assessment of the general state of science in the colonies. In the essay Paine comments on the many benefits of scientific inquiry:

I have always considered these kinds of researches as productive of many advantages, and in a new country they are particularly so. As subjects for speculation, they afford entertainment to the curious; but as objects of utility they merit a close attention. The same materials which delight the fossilist, enrich the manufacturer and the merchant. While the one is scientifically examining their structure and composition, the others, by industry and commerce, are transmuting them to gold. Possessed of the power of pleasing, they gratify on both sides; the one contemplates their *natural* beauties in the cabinet, the others, their *re-created* ones in the coffer. (PM, February 1775)

---

5 Paine ran out of money after about six months in London, at which time he left for county Kent in search of employment (Keane, 45).

Curiously, Paine celebrates science not for the knowledge it provides, but for its value as both a form of entertainment and its commercial utility. Instead of celebrating the beauty of nature or the marvels of its internal logic, nature is valuable because of its practical benefit to humans.

The fossil promptly becomes the raw material for the manufacturer and the merchant. In either case the process of transforming natural objects into either entertainment or utility, preferably both simultaneously, effaces their connection to nature. Nature, it is implied, can be pleasurably contemplated only so long as it is contained in the "cabinet." At the same time, nature allows him to subvert the usual dichotomy of entertainment and utility by emphasizing the entertainment value of science. Controlling nature, in this case, translates into a form of entertainment that produces economic benefits. Ironically, Paine resorts to the metaphor of alchemy, the ultimate example of false science in the Enlightenment, to describe the economic value of science. Consequently, he legitimates antiscience, alchemy, by making it the real effect of natural science. In this vision, Enlightenment science ultimately seeks to understand nature in order to exploit it.

Sharing the attitude of many of his contemporaries, then, Paine sees science as both a commercial and an intellectual pursuit, and as editor of a magazine he seeks to take advantage of both of these approaches to science. Like the manufacturer and the merchant, Paine exploits the entertainment value of science by including in the magazine numerous articles and images of scientific and technological innovations of the period. The *Pennsylvania Magazine* would naturally benefit from the attractiveness to readers of articles on science, and readers, particularly artisans and mechanics, would benefit from the information contained therein. From the moment he adopted the bridge project in the 1780s, however, science and technology became for Paine more than simply a useful subject for attracting readers to a magazine. As he became more seriously engaged in his technological pursuits, science became less a type of entertainment and more an avenue into uncovering the basic truths ordering the universe. More importantly, though, Paine discovered that he could use science to complement his political aims.

TECHNOLOGY, COMMERCE, AND THE RIGHTS OF MAN

Paine never explained why he chose bridge building as the principal object of his technological interest. However, when he abandoned his iron bridge project in 1791 to return to political writing, he wrote to John Hall, his practical assistant on the bridge, about his new endeavor:

The Bridge has been put up, but being on wood butments they yielded, and it is now taken down... At present I am engaged on my political Bridge. I shall bring out a new work (Second part of *Rights of Man*) soon after New Year. It will produce something one way or other. I see the tide is yet the wrong way, but there is a change of sentiment beginning. (CW II, 1322)

With the reference to the tide in this last sentence, the language of rivers flows into his observation about the political climate in Britain. Curiously, though, Paine's acknowledgement of the relevance of the tide subverts his rhetoric of bridges since the tide only matters if you are in the water, or if there is no bridge to cross the river. A bridge might obviate the need for concern about the ebb and flow of the tide, but as Paine implies, the political bridge for democratic reform had yet to be erected in England. To Paine, then, the tasks of building a cast iron bridge and writing *Rights of Man* were not as dissimilar as they might at first seem. In each case he was trying to build a new structure that would overcome an ancient and powerful force. And while the British monarchy was man-made and the river was forged by nature, they are similar in that they exert a tyrannous rule over humankind.

Paine's use of the bridge as a metaphor for his political writing is particularly noteworthy when we consider that, according to the OED, the word was not used figuratively until 1853.[6] We might speculate that bridges and bridging could not serve as a metaphor until they had become a reliable form of communication, which would not occur until the third decade of the nineteenth century. In the eighteenth century bridges, especially long ones, were constantly vulnerable to the weather. Charles Willson Peale captures the sense of anxiety over the structural integrity of bridges in his 1797 pamphlet, promoting his design for building wooden bridges, *An Essay on Building Wooden Bridges*:

Easy and safe passages over the waters of the United States are much wanted – even our post roads are deficient; often the affrighted traveller stops, and surveys the turbulent torrent that hides an unknown bottom, – he hesitates doubts whether to risk passage or not; at last, by delay grown impatient, he with fear and trembling cautiously moves forward and perhaps arrives in safety on the opposite bank; but alas! too frequently the rash or fool-hardy driver, is carried down the stream and all is lost.

[6] Alfred, Lord Tennyson uses a bridge as a metaphor in 1853.

Legislatures, and you men of influence in the counties of each State! Turn your attention to this important object shorten the distance to market for the sale of the product of your lands. I offer you a cheap and easy mode of building Bridges. (n.p.)

Paradoxically, Peale's anecdote illustrates the degree to which bridges not only free one from the danger of nature, but also constitute a danger of their own. If it is true that in this anecdote Peale exaggerates for effect, it is also true that bridges were a common concern not only in the United States, but in France and England as well. Indeed, Peale and Paine were but two of many proposing new and improved methods of constructing bridges. For Paine, though, the bridge also became an important political metaphor.

What does it mean, then, that Paine thought of *Rights of Man* as a bridge? More specifically, in what ways is *Rights of Man* like a bridge? In order to understand the ways in which Paine's text functions as a bridge, we must first understand what bridges signified for Paine.

In the years just after the conclusion of the War of Independence Paine expressed great concern about the future of the federation of the American states. In fact, his last two *Crisis* papers, published in April and November 1783, respectively, primarily concentrate on the future of the states and urge a continuation of the union. In "Thoughts on the Peace, and the Probable Advantages Thereof," the thirteenth and penultimate article in the series, Paine warns of the importance of maintaining a strong union of the thirteen states:

But that which must more forcibly strike a thoughtful, penetrating mind, and which includes and renders easy all inferior concerns, is the UNION OF THE STATES. On this our great national character depends. It is this which must give us importance abroad and security at home. It is through this only that we are, or can be, nationally known in the world; it is the flag of the United States which renders our ships and commerce safe on the seas, or in a foreign port. Our Mediterranean passes must be obtained under the same style. All our treaties, whether of alliance, peace, or commerce, are formed under the sovereignty of the United States, and Europe knows us by no other name or title. (CW I, 233).

Paine had originally argued for the importance of a strong union among the colonies in *Common Sense*, where he had contended that "'Tis not in numbers but in unity that our great strength lies" (CW I, 31). Indeed, to reinforce his point Paine refers to this statement from *Common Sense* in a footnote to his *Crisis* article.[7]

7 See note 2 in CW I, 232–233.

If one of the central thrusts of *Common Sense* was to undermine the ties uniting Britain and America by demonstrating them to be unnatural, the *Crisis* argues for the naturalness of the connection between the colonies. In *Common Sense* he had argued that the distance between the colonies and the Mother Country reflected the unnaturalness of the connection: "Even the distance at which the Almighty hath placed England and America is a strong and natural proof that the authority of the one over the other, was never the design of heaven" (CW I, 21). Now, however, Paine advocates overcoming natural barriers, such as rivers, to unite the diverse colonies. Thus, Paine returns to the same fundamental issue that concerned him in *Common Sense*, only to advocate the opposite position.[8] Now that Great Britain, the common enemy that had unified the states, has been defeated, Paine is concerned that the individual states might deem confederation with other states an unnecessary burden. Ever aware of the power of economic arguments, Paine contends in his last piece in the series, "A Supernumerary Crisis," that a stronger union will benefit the commercial fortunes of the new nation: "But it is only by acting in union, that the usurpations of foreign nations on the freedom of trade can be counteracted, and security extended to the commerce of America" (CW I, 239). The protection of foreign commerce thus becomes the most important reason for maintaining the union of the states.

In the early national period, foreign commerce played a crucial role in the utopian vision of an agrarian-based economy in the new nation. Ironically, foreign commerce was seen by Jeffersonians as a way to promote agrarian interests while, at the same time, keeping local industry, which was associated with moral decay, from growing. In his study of early American political economy, *The Elusive Republic*, Drew McCoy notes:

The Revolutionaries almost unthinkingly absorbed into their republican outlook this logic of the importance of foreign markets and free trade to American agriculture. In so doing they embarked on a grand quest to achieve their vision of the good society – a society that would somehow reconcile their commitment to the cultivation of an active, industrious, enterprising, virtuous people with their

---

[8] Paine's optimism about bridges, however, overlooks the problem of distinguishing between desirable and undesirable connections, a problem that would surface most prominently in the nineteenth century when slavery would begin to strain relations between the states. Moreover, the difficulty of identifying proper and improper connections would become a frequent topic of nineteenth-century American literature. Whereas Whitman, one of Paine's most fervent admirers, would celebrate the merging of Americans, Thoreau was deeply anxious about his connections to the outside world and sought, at least imaginatively, to sever his connections to it.

commitment to the maintenance of a predominantly simple and agricultural social order. (85)

Paine shared his contemporaries' belief that "by encouraging the development of disciplined and energetic individuals, commerce had the capacity to promote, rather than to destroy, virtue (McCoy, 77–78). Commerce, then, not only strengthened the union by creating a common interest among the states, but also by improving the character of its citizens.

Paine had outlined his vision of the United States' commercial future in the last section of *Common Sense*, and he had later championed various political causes, such as the Bank of the United States, that he felt would work to strengthen commercial ties between the states.[9] According to Paine, the relationship between commerce and the states was mutually beneficial because while commercial relations served to strengthen the union, a strong union was necessary for a prosperous commerce. In his third "Letter to Rhode Island" Paine would argue that, in fact, commerce is primarily a national, and not a local, interest:

Commerce is not the local property of any State, anymore than it is the local property of any person, unless it can be proved, that such a State neither buys nor sells out of its own dominions. But as the commerce of every State is made up out of the produce and consumption of other States, as well as its own, therefore its regulation and protection can only be under the confederated patronage of all States. (CW II, 350)

Commerce is thus based on relations of interdependence that reinforce the union, and as such the construction of highways, canals, and bridges to facilitate trade represented one of the most important steps toward the solidification of this union. In order for the United States to build a successful foreign trade, though, it first needed to become more cohesive internally.

Internal improvements were a subject of great concern in the early republic as debates over the responsibility for funding such projects created controversy, often pitting local governing bodies against the federal government. In his *Report on Manufactures* Alexander Hamilton

---

[9] In his first letter on the Bank of North America, which appeared in the *Pennsylvania Packet* of March 25, 1786, Paine states his reason for supporting the bank: "As I have always considered the bank as one of the best institutions that could be devised to promote the commerce and agriculture of the country, and recover it from the ruined condition in which the war had left both the farmer and the merchant, as well as the most effective means to banish usury and establish credit among citizens, I have always been a friend to it" (CW II, 415).

notes the importance of internal improvements to the United States by citing their significance in Great Britain: "There is scarcely anything which has been better calculated to assist the manufacturers of Great Britain, than the amelioration of the public roads of that Kingdom, and the great progress which has been of late made in opening canals. Of the former, the United States stand much in need; for the latter they present uncommon facilities" (178). Hamilton then cites Adam Smith's *Wealth of Nations* at length on the crucial economic importance of internal improvements: "Good roads, canals, and navigable rivers, by diminishing the expense of carriage, put the *remote parts of a country* more nearly upon a level with those in the neighborhood of the town. They are *upon that account* the greatest of all improvements" (178). Although in Smith's formulation navigable rivers play an important role in connecting urban and rural areas, in the United States at the time, rivers literally divided many of the states, thus posing the greatest obstacle to easy communication within and between them.[10] In the case of Paine's favorite city, Philadelphia, the Schuylkill River and the Delaware River practically surround the city. Indeed, Paine hoped that his iron bridge design would be used in the plan to span the Schuylkill, a project that would occupy Philadelphia lawmakers for decades.[11] For Paine, then, the choice of bridge building would have been a natural one as it served both to facilitate communication and enhance the commercial ties between the states, thus contributing to his political goal of solidifying the union.

Paine saw this problem as a particularly American concern. In 1786 he would write to Benjamin Franklin about the suitability of his bridge plan: "The European method of Bridge architecture, by piers and arches, is not adapted to the condition of many of the rivers in America on account of the ice in winter. The construction of those I have the honor of presenting to you is designed to obviate that difficulty by leaving the whole passage of the river clear of the incumbrance of piers" (CW II, 1027). Almost twenty years later Paine continued to refer to the bridge model as his "American arch" (CW II, 1041), and would again note that it was the geographic

---

[10] In *Beautiful Machine* John Seelye examines the attempt to use rivers to unite the states by building canals and through the invention of the steamboat. This points to one of the paradoxes about rivers at the time: They could both connect and divide. Navigable rivers, of course, played an important role linking the states, but, at the same time, rivers posed formidable barriers for travelers seeking to cross them and, as Peale's account shows, in spring, rivers often overflowed and swept away bridges.

[11] A permanent bridge was finally built in 1805.

conditions of the United States that led him to attempt to design an iron bridge:

> As America abounds in rivers that interrupt the land communication, and as by violence of floods breaking up the ice in the spring, the bridges depending for support from the bottom of the river are frequently carried away, I turned my attention, after the Revolutionary War was over, to find a method of constructing an arch that might, without rendering the height inconvenient or the ascent difficult, extend at once from shore to shore, over rivers of three, four, and five hundred feet and probably more. (CW II, 1051–1052)

Echoing Peale's violent vision of nature, Paine presents his bridge as a means to overcome nature's fury. Paine's conceptualization of his bridge as an arch, however, emphasizes his structure's debt to nature. So, once again, by understanding nature and borrowing from it, science creates a substitute for nature that allows man to exert control over his natural surroundings.[12]

Paine's bridge design is, furthermore, significant in that he was specifically attempting to construct a bridge made of iron. Paine had been interested in iron from early on in his American career. In his initial scientific piece in the *Pennsylvania Magazine*, "Useful and Entertaining Hints," Paine had commented on the importance of iron: "Take away but the single article of iron, and half the felicities of life fall with it. Little as we may prize this common ore, the loss of it would cut deeper than the use of it. And by the way of laughing off misfortunes' 'tis easy to prove, by this method of investigation that, *an iron age is better than a golden one*" (CW II, 1023). Paine proposes a new ordering of the ages that will more

---

[12] Curiously, Paine, usually conscious of the metaphoric dimensions of his scientific endeavors, fails to see the political implications of his arch design, which would seem to contradict his democratic vision insofar as it does not depend for support from the bottom. The structure of democratic government, at least as Paine envisions it in his writings, is defined by its connection to the people. Figuratively, a democracy depends for support from the bottom. Paine's bridge design, on the other hand, attempts to eliminate the structural dependency on the bottom thereby replicating the form of a monarchical government. The monarchical nature of Paine's bridge design recalls his statement, in *Common Sense*, regarding the proper form of government: "I draw my idea of the form of government from a principle in nature which no art can overturn, viz. that the more simple any thing is, the less liable it is to be disordered, and the easier repaired when disordered" (CW I, 6). Paine concludes from this point, rather surprisingly, that "Absolute governments, (though the disgrace of human nature) have this advantage with them, they are simple" (CW I, 7). In order to triumph over nature, then, Paine has to build a structure that metaphorically replicates a monarchical form of government. Paine thus, paradoxically, employs a monarchical form in order to further the interests of a democratic nation.

accurately reflect the priorities of the day. In a commercial and industrial era, iron, not gold, is the most important material to his world. Unlike gold, iron is celebrated for its usefulness returning us, once again, to the preeminent position of science in the Enlightenment.

Paine's decision to use iron for his bridge also illustrates his broader commitment to American manufactures, for ironworks had become one of the United States' most significant industries. In his *Report on Manufactures* Hamilton singles out iron as an especially valuable natural resource in terms that echo Paine's remarks from "Useful and Entertaining Hints": "The manufactures of this article are entitled to preeminent rank. None are more essential in their kinds, nor so extensive in their uses. They constitute in whole or in part the implements or the materials or both of almost every useful occupation. Their instrumentality is almost everywhere conspicuous" (181). Hamilton's comments reflect the importance of the burgeoning iron industry to the young republic. In fact, "By the outbreak of the Revolution, the American colonies were producing almost 15 percent of the world's iron, more than England and Wales combined" (DAH, Vol. III, 472). Thus, Paine's choice of iron as the base material for his bridge becomes intertwined with his vision of the nation's future commercial success.

To the extent that it suggests an artisanal consciousness that permeates all of his endeavors, be they mechanical or literary, Paine's likening of his bridge building to his political writing reflects his continuing commitment to a less formal language of politics. As editor of the *Pennsylvania Magazine* he had sought to make science available to artisans because he understood how they could benefit from the latest innovations:

'Tis by the researches of the virtuoso that the hidden parts of the earth are brought to light, and from his discoveries of its qualities, the potter, the glassmaker, and numerous other artists, are enabled to furnish us with their productions. Artists considered *merely* as such, would have made but a slender progress, had they not been led on by the enterprising spirit of the curious. (CW II, 1021–1022)

As an artisan constructing a bridge – for Paine did not simply design a scheme on paper for others to execute, he actually erected a prototype of his bridge in Masborough, England with the assistance of several men – Paine benefited from the publication of the latest technological advances. Now, returning to his role as political essayist, Paine would draw on his scientific experience to appeal to that same broad-based audience of artisans and middling sorts whom he had always envisioned as the beneficiaries of his political writings. In this respect Paine's analogy to bridge building applies to all of his writings as he attempts to bridge the linguistic barriers that had served to limit access to politics by excluding those who were unable to communicate their ideas in a more refined language. Indeed, the bridge constitutes one of the fundamental metaphors for Paine, a metaphor that provides a natural sanction for his revolutionary aims.

While Paine's ideological commitments to commerce and manufactures made bridges a natural choice for his scientific/technological endeavors, Paine did not succeed in getting a commission for his bridge design to be built by any of the several cities that he attempted to persuade to adopt his model. He failed largely because, as one historian of science who has studied Paine's bridge has put it, "Even though the design was inspired by nature and in Paine's mind this insured its suitability, it was not a particularly efficient or useful solution to the problem of long span bridges" (Kemp, 36). Nevertheless, Paine played a significant role in the long-term development of iron bridges since many of his ideas were adopted and refined by more skilled engineers who then built iron bridges of their own.[13] As another, less sympathetic, critic has argued, Paine's "achievement [was] to advance progress by persuading investors to back practical projects rather than to improve technology *per se*" (James, 189).

Just as the political and philosophical arguments Paine employs to support his argument *for* independence in *Common Sense* had been culled from other sources, the main points of *Rights of Man* were not original to Paine.[14] In fact, he refashions the core ideas of *Rights of Man* out of the principal arguments of *Common Sense*. In the case of *Common Sense*, "What was brilliantly innovative," as Eric Foner has put it, "was the way Paine combined [the borrowed ideas] into a single comprehensive argument, and related them to the common experiences of Americans." Paine's originality lay both in his ability to synthesize and in the language in which he presented his political arguments. As Olivia Smith has argued, with *Common Sense* Paine became "the first pamphleteer to address a broadly-based audience with colloquial language and to articulate political ideas that had remained unexpressed" (41). Paine believed that simply articulating those ideas about democracy and equality in a language that

---

[13] See Kemp, 34–35.

[14] Paine's most notable source, James Burgh's *Political Disquisitions*, is also one of the few texts that he ever cites. In the *Political Disquisitions* Burgh constructs a coherent radical dissenting philosophy by borrowing from and critiquing major political theorists. Thus, Burgh's two volume work is itself essentially a synthesis of other political philosophers, from Plato to Locke, whom he puts in the service of his own ideological ends, ends that Paine shared. See Smith, 2–3.

would be accessible to middling and lower sorts was the first step on the road to revolution. He comments on the aristocracy's exclusionary strategies in *Rights of Man*: "In all cases they [courtiers] took care to represent government as a thing made up of mysteries, which only themselves understood, and they hid from the understanding of the nation, the only thing that was beneficial to know, namely, *That government is nothing more than a national association acting on the principles of society*" (CW I, 361). Paine's task in *Rights of Man*, then, is to enlighten the English people, the nation, about the rudimentary and accessible essence of government so that they could then assert their political will and force the government to promote their interests.

Paine was acutely aware of the radical nature of this proposition. Reflecting on the division of *Rights of Man* into two distinct parts, he comments on the novelty of his form of political discourse: "I wished to know the manner in which a work, written in a style of thinking and expression different to what had been customary in England, would be received before I ventured further" (349). He writes this somewhat disingenuous biographical note from the happy position of someone who has witnessed the astonishing popularity of *Rights of Man Part I*, thus reminding his readers of the success of his first book even as he revisits the subject in this sequel. Even as he is calling attention over his success, Paine points to the crucial source of both the radicalism of the text and its success: the correspondence between its content and its form.

If there had been any question about how that language and style would be received before the publication of *Rights of Man* in 1791, by the time he published the sequel a year later any such doubt would have been removed. The "Dedication" to the first part of *Rights of Man* reflects Paine's hope that the ideas promulgated in his new work would travel well:

Sir, I present you a small treatise in defense of those principles of freedom which your exemplary virtue hath so eminently contributed to establish. That the Rights of Man may become as universal as your benevolence can wish, and that you may enjoy the happiness of seeing the New World regenerate the Old. (CW I, 244)

From the time of the American Revolution Paine had hoped to help spread the principles of representative democracy from the United States to Great Britain. As had been the case in America, the key to furthering this transformation lay in providing the disenfranchised with a political language. Now, in the wake of the French Revolution and Burke's attack on it, Paine saw a new opportunity to accomplish this goal. Through his text he could both provide the language, and use it to transport the ideas that had led to the American Revolution from the United States to England.

Paine returns to the theme of "regenerating" the British political system later in "Part One" of *Rights of Man* when he addresses the question of the English Constitution: "The English Government is one of those which arose out of a conquest, and not out of society, and consequently it arose over the people; and though it has been much modified from the opportunity of circumstances since the time of William the Conqueror, the country has never yet regenerated itself, and is therefore without a constitution" (CW I, 279). Paine implies that the only way to regenerate the government and produce a legitimate constitution is through a revolution. While he avoids openly calling for revolution in England, Paine ends the first part of *Rights of Man* with a prophecy of imminent revolution throughout Europe:

> From what we now see, nothing of reform in the political world ought to be held improbable. It is an age of revolutions, in which every thing may be looked for. The intrigue of courts, by which the system of war is kept up, may provoke a confederation of nations to abolish it: and an European Congress, to patronize the progress of free government, and promote civilization of nations with each other, is an event nearer in probability, than once were the revolutions and alliance of France and America. (CW I, 344)

Revolution in Europe, according to Paine, will not only lead to the replacement of monarchies with democracies, but will also involve the creation of a mutually beneficial alliance between the various new democratic nations. Just as his iron bridge would provide the connective tissue to unite the American States through commerce, revolution would lead to the creation of a "European Congress" which would bring together the European states. In Paine's utopian vision of the future, then, representative democracy, to continue the analogy, becomes the ideological internal improvement that unites Europe, and, as in his plan for the American states, commerce plays a crucial role in his hopes for a European union.

In the "Introduction" to the Second Part of *Rights of Man*, Paine attempts to establish what he sees as the fundamental connection between democracy and commercial prosperity: "If universal peace, civilization, and commerce, are ever to be the happy lot of man, it cannot be accomplished but by a revolution in the system of governments " (CW I, 355). In contrast to democratic governments, "All the monarchical governments are military. War is their trade, plunder and revenue their objects"

(CW I, 355). The complementary relationship among peace, commerce, and democracy forms the basis for Paine's utopian vision for the future in both the United States and Europe. Ironically, in 1776, Paine's theory of the pacifying influence of commerce had served to reinforce his argument that the colonists not delay declaring their independence from Great Britain. In *Common Sense* he advocates seeking independence immediately on the basis that over time an increase in commercial interests would lessen the colonists' enthusiasm for war: "The infant state of the colonies, as it is called, so far from being against, is an argument in favor of independence... for trade being the consequence of population, men become too much absorbed thereby to attend to any thing else. Commerce diminishes the spirit both of patriotism and military defence" (CW I, 36).

While democracy engenders commerce, commerce inevitably leads to a natural increase in peace, which further benefits commerce. In Paine's words: "In all my publications, where the matter would admit, I have been an advocate for commerce, because I am a friend to its effects. It is a pacific system, operating to unite mankind by rendering nations, as well as individuals, useful to each other" (CW I, 400). Paine's faith in the influence of commerce was not unique to him. As Drew McCoy has noted,

The [American] Revolutionaries' fundamental concern with sustaining their republican character was only part of their commitment to foreign commerce; they also believed that the expansion of American trade would have a missionary impact on the rest of the world.... A system of free trade would soften the brutal tendencies of primitive men by bringing them into contact with other nations and cultures. The natural result of this familiarity and interdependence was the promotion of peace; by gently cementing reciprocal ties of dependence among different countries, free trade would inevitably decrease the potential for war. (86)

But for Paine the targets of reform are Europe's primitive governments, and the path to reform is not simply commerce but democratic revolution. Democratic revolution would enable Europe's people to form the kinds of relationships of interdependence that its monarchical governments refuse to engage in. Moreover, democracy would also benefit science and technology: "In England the improvements in agriculture, useful arts, manufactures, and commerce have been made in opposition to the genius of its government, which is that of following precedents" (CW I, 387). In this optimistic view improvement in one facet of the society leads to improvement in all others. As Paine observes of the rest of the world: "From the rapid progress which America makes in every species of improvement it is rational to conclude, that if the governments of Asia,

Africa, and Europe, had begun of a principle similar to that of America, or had not been early corrupted therefrom, that those countries must, by this time, have been in a far superior condition to what they are" (CW I, 355). Thus the political innovation of democracy fosters innovation in all facets of society, including commerce and technology.

This returns us to the mechanics of Paine's bridge model, which also reflect his anxiety over the need to unify first the nation and then the world. In his application for a patent in England, Scotland, and Ireland, Paine attributes the effectiveness of his single arch model to its natural origin, asserting that it was inspired by the "spider's circular web ... from a conviction that when nature empowered this insect to make a web she also instructed her in the strongest mechanical method of constructing it" (CW II, 1032). The problem is that whereas spider's webs are tension structures, arches are compression structures. Paine did not understand the physical principle that makes arches possible – his desire that his bridge function on the same principle as the spider's web is revealing. The metaphorical consequences of these models suggest why Paine wanted his bridge to function as a tension structure: A compression structure works by placing pressure inward, but a tension structure relies on the capacity of the materials composing it to resist the force pulling it apart. If Paine saw his bridge as a means to unite the colonies at a time when they were being pulled apart by various political, social, and economic forces, then, naturally, what was required was a device that functioned on the model of a spider's web. To keep the union together, he needed something that would resist the force of the factors pulling it apart. For Paine that material was commerce. In Europe the binding material was also commerce, which would be made possible by the development of democratic politics.

Thus, in *Rights of Man* Paine was not simply drawing on the language of science to legitimate his political principles; instead, in Paine's mind, the relationship between his political writing and his bridge building was both analogical and causal. Just as his model bridge would build connections and enhance communication between the various regions and states in the United States, his political bridge would lead to better relations between Europe's traditional enemies. For Paine political writing and bridge building, therefore, share the same end: They both attempt to create the conditions that would enable the fulfillment of his utopian vision of a peaceful world where commercial democracies would flourish through open cooperation thanks to the elimination of all barriers to communication – be they physical or political, internal or international.

THE AGE OF REASON: SUBSTITUTING SCIENCE FOR RELIGION

While *Rights of Man* asserted the inherent civil and political rights of the people and sought to promote democratic revolution, Paine believed that government was not the only source of tyranny in the world. Echoing his previous attacks on monarchy, Paine next turned to what he saw as the other major source of tyranny, organized religion: "All national institutions of churches, whether Jewish, Christian or Turkish, appear to me no other than human inventions, set up to terrify and enslave mankind, and monopolize power and profit" (464).[15] He makes the connection between his earlier works and *The Age of Reason* near the end of the opening section of the text, "The Author's Profession of Faith,":

Soon after I had published the pamphlet "Common Sense," in America, I saw the exceeding probability that a revolution in the system of government would be followed by a revolution in the system of religion. The adulterous connection of church and state, wherever it has taken place, whether Jewish, Christian or Turkish, has so effectually prohibited by pains and penalties every discussion upon established creeds, and upon first principles of religion, that until – the system of government should be changed, those subjects could not be brought fairly and openly before the world; but that whenever this should be done, a revolution in the system of religion would follow. (CW I, 465)

Paine suggests that distinguishing between false connections and true connections has been one of the crucial themes of all his major writings, thus establishing a continuum unifying his career as a political writer from *Common Sense* to his present publication. Whereas the false connection that concerned him in *Common Sense* was that of the relationship between the American colonies with the British Crown, his concern here is with the connection between religion and government. In this context *The Age of Reason* complements his previous writings and represents a natural extension of Paine's revolutionary mission.[16]

The Age of Reason also represents a development in Paine's political writing as he continues to incorporate scientific discourse into his

---

[15] In both *Common Sense* and *Rights of Man* Paine insisted that monarchy was a human invention and not a divine creation. In fact, in *Common Sense* he further impugns monarchy when he asserts that "Government by kings was first introduced into the world by the heathens" (10). Much of the second section of *Common Sense*, entitled "Of Monarchy and Hereditary Succession," is dedicated to a history of the invention of monarchy and its eventual arrival in England.

[16] In their recent study of Paine's theological investigations, *Paine, Scripture, and Authority*, Edward Davidson and William Scheick refer to *The Age of Reason* as a "sequel to Paine's famous previous writings, especially *Rights of Man*" (18).

arguments. If scientific metaphors had played an important role in *Rights of Man*, scientific methodology would play the central role in *The Age of Reason*. In *The Age of Reason* he does not simply employ a scientific methodology to debunk Christianity's claims of truth, he literally replaces the Bible with science. Science, more than the ultimate manifestation of human reason, becomes the new word of God, and, consequently, Paine, as the advocate of that new gospel, becomes one of its prophets.

In *The Age of Reason* Paine structures the relationship between science and revealed religion as one of opposites. However, in the seventeenth and eighteenth centuries many believed these two areas of knowledge complemented one another. In *The Christian Philosopher* Cotton Mather, for example, sees no conflict between science and religion, instead calling them the Twofold Book of God: the Book of the Creatures, and the Book of the Scripture: God having taught first of all ... by his Works, did it afterwards ... by his words" (8). As Winton Solberg has shown, Mather was drawing on an earlier tradition and is just one example of the fairly common view that humans could attain a greater understanding of God through the empirical observation of the natural world.[17] Despite the common perception that religion and science were antithetical to one another, for many in the eighteenth century, as John Brooke has shown, "science was considered useful as a means of theological instruction" because "It gave content to arguments for God's power and foresight" (157). Thus the relationship between science and religion in the eighteenth century, as Brooke so insightfully suggests, was much more complex than a simple rivalry or partnership; it took a variety of different shapes. Paine's contemporary Joseph Priestly, for example, tries to employ his scientific theories to purify Christianity, thus using science not to undermine religion but, to use an eighteenth century term, to improve it.

More to the point of this study, Brooke points out that "religious disaffection commonly had political rather than scientific roots" (164). Perceiving the Church as a powerful ally to the monarchy and as an oppressor in its own right, Paine sees science as a means to displace religion altogether. He pushes the relationship to its extreme and strategically places these two systems of knowledge in opposition to one another. Traditional revealed religion is associated with superstition, whereas science becomes a

---

17 For a fuller account of Mather's view of the relationship between science and religion see Solberg's "Science and Religion in Early America: Cotton Mather's *Christian Philosopher,*" *Church History* 56 (1987): 73–92. I am indebted to Douglas Winiarski for pointing me to the Mather passages and to Solberg's analysis of them.

synonym for reason. Although Paine's polarization of science and religion oversimplifies matters, from a political theoretical perspective this opposition makes perfect sense, since one of the key effects of his emphasis on science is that it endows humans with a greater degree of agency. Although he does not specifically cite Paine, Brooke notes that one of the reasons science was so appealing was that "confidence had grown that solutions to human problems lay with human effort rather than through the protection of the Church" (155). A science of politics would necessarily imply that humans can comprehend and alter government in order to improve it or to solve problems. For Paine, of course, the Church was precisely the problem because it was using its authority to promote its own interests rather than to help the people. In *The Age of Reason* Paine sets out to undermine the Church's political power by using scientific methods to attack its claims to authority. Paine's ultimate goal, however, is not to dichotomize science and religion. Instead, he hopes to integrate them by proposing a new religion, based on deism, that fully incorporates scientific knowledge as its foundation. The first step in this process is to debunk the Bible.

Paine's "investigation of true and fabulous theology," which is how he defines the subject of *The Age of Reason* in its subtitle, focuses almost entirely on the validity of the evidence used to establish the central tenets of Christianity. He subjects that evidence, which Paine identifies as "revelation," to scientific scrutiny and contemporary scientific standards for evidence. After presenting his own "voluntary and individual profession of faith" in the opening section of the text, Paine raises the question of evidence in an example he gives to support his attack on the status of revelation:

When Moses told the children of Israel that he received the two tables of the commandments from the hands of God, they were not obliged to believe him, because they had no other authority for it than his telling them so; and I have no other authority for it than some historian telling me so. The commandments carry no internal evidence of divinity with them; they contain some good moral precepts, such as any man qualified to be a lawgiver, or a legislator, could produce himself, without having recourse to supernatural intervention. (466)

Paine's reference to the lawmakers and legislators is particularly noteworthy given the political implications of the commandments and because of the links he sees between politics and religion, but Paine's crucial point regarding the status of biblical moral injunctions stems from an understanding of what constitutes proper evidence for establishing "matters of fact."

Paine's attack on the validity of the Ten Commandments focuses on the account's excessive reliance on the character of Moses. Employing a scientific standard Paine emphasizes the need for the argument, internal evidence, to stand on its own. Paine illustrates his point by contrasting the Bible with an ancient scientific text:

I know however, but of one ancient book that authoritatively challenges universal consent and belief, and that is Euclid's "Elements of Geometry and the reason is, because it is a book of self-evident demonstration, entirely independent on its author, and of everything relating to time, place and circumstance. The matters contained in that book would have the same authority they now have, had they been written by any other person, or had the work been anonymous, or had the author never been known; for the identical certainty of who was the author makes no part of our belief of the matters contained in the book. (519)

Paine's assessment of the role of authorship and the force of Euclid's argument echoes his claim in the "Postscript to the Preface" of the third edition of *Common Sense:* "Who the author of this production is, is wholly unnecessary to the public, as the object for attention is the *doctrine itself*, not the *man*" (CW I, 4). This statement contrasts dramatically with the notion of political truth and its relationship to the author espoused by Paine in "The Forester Letters" and, most notably, in his various publications attacking Silas Deane in the 1780s and George Washington in 1796. Despite his professions to the contrary at the beginning of *Common Sense*, in political matters Paine almost always vigorously argued for the need to consider the author when one was evaluating the measures they propose. In this case, by effacing the author Paine analogizes himself to a scientist objectively investigating the true nature of politics.

Paine's argument rests upon a distinction between an old and outdated mode of evidence and the more recent standards of evidence that had emerged in the seventeenth century from Robert Boyle's experiments with the air pump and his subsequent debate with Thomas Hobbes, who was also an accomplished scientist and mechanical philosopher. Boyle and his supporters articulated protocols for authenticating scientific "matters of fact" that soon became the standard in scientific practice. As Steven Shapin and Simon Shaffer have noted:

In Boyle's view the capacity of experiments to yield matters of fact depended not only upon their actual performance but essentially upon the assurance of the relevant community that they had been so performed. . . . If knowledge was to be empirically based, as Boyle and the other experimentalists insisted it should, then its experimental foundations had to be *witnessed*. Experimental performances and their products had to be attested by the testimony of eye witnesses. (55–56)

In *The Age of Reason* Paine applies this standard of verification to the account of God and His place in history presented in the Bible. Demoting Moses from the status of a prophet to that of an historian, Paine suggests that his testimony alone is not sufficient to guarantee the authenticity of the events he describes, for no one else has witnessed the events in question.[18] This is crucial to Paine because the same sort of testimony used to authenticate the account of Moses in Exodus appears throughout both the Old and New Testaments and is used by the Church to justify its theological precepts. The Church then used those precepts to establish its authority to tax and control people's lives. This connection between religious and political or legal authority is precisely what Paine is attempting to dissolve in the text. Paine, in other words, wants to discredit the Bible not because he objects to its moral lessons, but because it is the best way to undercut the authority of the Church.

Consequently, much of *The Age of Reason* is dedicated to a close reading of the Bible in which Paine repeatedly demonstrates the inadmissibility of the evidence used to prove either the truthfulness of the prophet's accounts or the status of the prophets as divinely inspired (that more often than not, he points out, is used to guarantee the truthfulness of their narratives). Thus, not only does he systematically undermine the authority of the various "prophets" by questioning the authenticity of their authorship, he goes to the root and impugns their authority to speak for God. As Paine observes at the end of his analysis of Moses's authorship: "Take away from Genesis the belief that Moses was the author, on which only the strange belief that it is the Word of God has stood, and there remains nothing of Genesis but an anonymous book of stories, fables and traditionary or invented absurdities, or of downright lies" (CW I, 528). Paine was not alone in his suspicions about the authenticity of the Bible; Jefferson and Adams also engaged in intense exegetical exercises in which they questioned the validity of specific parts of the text.[19] In Jefferson's case he excised entire portions of the Gospels to create his "Life and Morals of Jesus." In the "Life and Morals of Jesus" Jefferson seems especially to object to the reference to the supernatural in the Gospels. For example, he generally excises any instances where miracles occur or angels appear. As

---

[18] In identifying Moses as a prophet I am using Paine's sense of Moses' Biblical status. While Moses is not generally considered one of the prophets, Paine sees him as occupying a similar authorial position in the Old Testament. From this perspective Moses is a prophet because he claims to speak for God.

[19] For an account of Adams' views of Christianity see C. Bradley Thompson, "Young John Adams and the New Philosophic Rationalism."

Edwin Gaustad has pointed out in his "religious biography of Jefferson," in the composition of "The Life and Morals" Jefferson generally rejected anything "which made of Jesus some sort of supernatural miracle-worker or street theatre healer" (126). Whereas Jefferson applies his empirical rationalism in an attempt to preserve some important moral lessons out of the Gospels, in *The Age of Reason* Paine feels a need to undermine the text's authority entirely because he sees its connection to the Church's exercise of power in the late eighteenth century. Naturally, Paine's approach reflects his goals, which, of course, are political more than moral or theological.

The case of Genesis is especially useful to Paine because his scientific training makes him particularly suspicious of any standards of evidence where a single individual's testimony or status serves as the foundation for establishing a truth. Paine articulates his conception of the proper standards of evidence in his assessment of the account of Jesus' resurrection:

A thing which everybody is required to believe requires that the proof and evidence of it should be equal to all, and universal; and as the public visibility of this last related act [Jesus' appearance before his disciples after his death] was the only evidence that could give sanction to the former part, the whole of it falls to the ground, because that evidence never was given. Instead of this, a small number of persons, not more than eight or nine, are introduced as proxies for the whole world to say they saw it, and all the rest of the world are called upon to believe it. (CW I, 468)

Although Paine invokes the ideals of the new science in this paragraph, the irony is that in actual practice science operated (and still operates today), more like the biblical case than his imaginary universal demonstration. As Golinski points out early in his study of public science, "Nonscientists typically do not experience the falsifiability of scientific knowledge or the supposedly democratic character of scientific decision-making. To them, rather, science often appears as a system of authority, the tool of powerful interests in society" (2). Nevertheless, in the context of the explosion of public science in the late eighteenth century Paine's point would resonate with readers, most of whom would have been exposed in some form or another to itinerant lecturers who would perform experiments to demonstrate the latest discoveries or simply to amuse and amaze.

Ironically, Paine's interpretation of the resurrection leads him to celebrate the apostle Thomas as the model for his own position: "But it appears that Thomas did not believe the resurrection, and, as they say, would not believe without having ocular and manual demonstration himself. So *neither will I*, and the reason is equally as good for me, and for every other person, as for Thomas" (CW I, 468). Paine's emphasis on the need for ocular proof and for the possibility of repeated demonstration practically reiterates Boyle's notion of the basis for establishing scientific truths. Thus, Paine's namesake, the Biblical "Doubting Thomas," also becomes a would-be hero of science. For Paine the essential point is that "Words, whether declarations or promises, that passed in private . . . even supposing them to have been spoken, could not be evidence in public" (CW I, 581). Truth, according to this standard, must always be public.

If truth must be public, then the act of publication becomes a crucial part of the scientific process. Indeed, one of Paine's chief concerns throughout *The Age of Reason* regards problems of publication. Paine seems deeply anxious about the difficulties inherent in the publishing process. This anxiety plays itself out in his new work, which he rightly anticipated would also meet with resistance from the authorities. Nature offers an ideal solution to the problem of censorship: "It is only in the CREATION that all our ideas and conceptions of a *Word of God* can unite. . . . It does not depend upon the will of man whether it shall be published or not; it publishes itself from one end of the earth to the other" (CW I, 482–483). Nature here not only eliminates the possibility of censorship, but it also enables full access to a total audience. It is an author's dream: a work that is accessible to all people and avoidable by no one.

Given the importance he ascribes to dissemination, it only seems natural that Paine would be deeply concerned with the reliable transmission of meaning through the written word. This anxiety informs his critique of the Bible as the word of God:

The continually progressive change to which the meaning of words is subject, the want of a universal language which renders translation necessary, the errors to which translations are again subject, the mistakes of copyists and printers, together with the possibility of willful alteration, are of themselves evidences that the human language, whether in speech or in print, cannot be the vehicle of the Word of God. (CW I, 477)

By suggesting that the natural world represents the true word of God, Paine attempts to obviate the potential for misrepresentation and misinterpretation that can obtain in a written text. The problems of publication and dissemination were even greater, Paine argues, prior to the invention of print: "At the time those books were written there was no printing, and consequently there could be no publication, otherwise than by written copies, which any man might make or alter at pleasure, and call them originals" (CW I, 585). In a footnote Paine uses the publication of *The Age of Reason* as an example of the problems that can result from publication. For Paine, who had struggled to find a publisher for several of his major political tracts, including *Common Sense* and *Rights of Man*, this concern was all too real. But Paine's concern here is as much a manifestation of his anxiety about the publication and reception of his own text as it is a critique of the authority of the Bible. Paine had even more reason for concern about *The Age of Reason*, not only because of its controversial treatment of religion, but also because of the circumstances of its publication: The text was originally published in French, which means that for its first version Paine, whose French was poor, had to entrust his work to a translator. Only later was it revised and published in English.[20]

THE TRUE REVELATION

"Doubting Thomas" may serve as the model for Paine's notion of scientific curiosity, but he aims much higher when he goes on to imply a parallel between himself and Jesus. At the end of his section on Jesus, "An Appreciation of the Character of Jesus Christ, and His History," Paine summarizes Jesus' fate in terms that resemble the reaction he expected, and got, to his latest works:

The accusation which those priests brought against him was that of sedition and conspiracy against the Roman government, to which the Jews were then subject and tributary; and it is not improbable that the Roman government might have some secret apprehensions of the effects of his doctrine, as well as the Jewish priests; neither is it improbable that Jesus Christ had in contemplation the delivery of the Jewish nation from the bondage of the Romans. Between the two, however, this virtuous reformer and revolutionist lost his life. (CW I, 469)

The parallels to Paine's own situation at the time are significant: After the publication of *Rights of Man Part II*, in 1792, he had been tried in absentia for seditious libel in England and he was found guilty. This meant that had he returned to England he would have been hanged for attempting, as he surely saw it, to deliver the English people from the bondage of the monarchy. Thus Paine transforms Jesus into an earlier version of Tom Paine. More importantly, though, like Jesus, Paine is advocating a radical new understanding of God and of man's relationship to God.

In an aside later in the text Paine observes that "It is somewhat curious that the three persons whose names are the most universally recorded, were of very obscure parentage. Moses was a foundling; Jesus Christ

[20] For a complete account of the publication of *Age of Reason* in France see Keane, 389–400.

was born in a stable; and Mahomet was a mule driver" (CW I, 478). Paine's odd and seemingly tangential observation about the connection between these three religious icons belies his aspirations of obtaining a similar stature for himself through the founding of a new sense of the divinity. For despite his assertion that "The first and last of these men were founders of different systems of religion; but Jesus Christ founded no new system" (CW I, 478), it is their respective roles in formulating a particular conceptualization of the divinity and of His relationship to man that connects the three figures he mentions. If Jesus did not found a new system, he certainly challenged an earlier understanding of God. With *The Age of Reason* Paine, who was also of obscure parentage, aspired to alter the sense of man's relationship to God in the same way that Moses, Mahomet, and Jesus had. It is not by accident, then, that Paine includes a fair amount of biographical material in text, much more than in any of his other works, since if he were to obtain the authority of those figures the history of his life would also become significant.

As had been the case with Jesus, this new understanding of God required a new scripture and a new language, in short, a new revelation. In order to pave the way for that new revelation, however, Paine had to demonstrate the limitations and flaws of the previous understanding of God. Hence the extended analysis and critique of the Bible. In its place Paine offers the natural world: "THE WORD OF GOD IS THE CREATION WE BEHOLD and it is in *this word*, which no human invention can counterfeit or alter, that God speaketh universally to man" (CW I, 482). If the natural world had become the word of God, then Paine deduces that "That which is now called natural philosophy, embracing the whole circle of science, of which astronomy occupies the chief place, is the study of the works of God, and of the power and wisdom of god in His works, and is the true theology" (CW I, 487). By transforming religion into science Paine effects the ultimate democratization of religion, for now religion is not subject to the control of any sort of institutional hierarchy or state affiliation. Each person can access God directly: "We can know God only through His works. . . . We can have no idea of His wisdom, but by knowing the order and manner in which it acts. The principles of science lead to this knowledge; for the Creator of man is the Creator of science, and it is through that medium that man can see God, as it were, face to face" (CW I, 601–602). In a bold and clever move Paine here even invokes one of the most famous passages of the Bible to support his proposition: "For now we see in a mirror dimly, but then face to face. Now I know in part;

then I shall understand fully."[21] Not only does Paine cite the passage but he takes advantage of its promise of a future revelation to implicate his project in a larger process of Enlightenment that, in his appropriation at least, seems to be endorsed by the Bible.

Whereas Jesus provided the model for Paine's role as reformer and revolutionary, God himself provides the model for Paine the scientist: "The Almighty is the great mechanic of the creation, the first philosopher and original teacher of all science" (CW I, 603). Earlier in the text Paine had observed, "The Almighty Lecturer, by displaying the principles of science in the structure of the universe, has invited man to study and to imitation" (CW I, 490). Paine singles out trigonometry as "the soul of science," because "it contains the *mathematical demonstration* of which man speaks, and the extent of its uses is unknown" (CW I, 488). Mechanics, as the product of trigonometry, represents one of the most important branches of science:

Since, then, man cannot make principles, from whence did he gain a knowledge of them, so as to be able to apply them, not only to things on earth, but to ascertain the motion of bodies so immensely distant from him as all the heavenly bodies are? From whence, I ask, could he gain that knowledge, but from the study of the true theology? It is the structure of the universe that has taught this knowledge to man. That structure is an ever-existing exhibition of every principle upon which every part of mathematical science is founded. The offspring of this science is mechanics; for mechanics is no other than the principles of science applied practically. (CW I, 489)

Paine's emphasis on the practicality of mechanics echoes his claim from *Rights of Man* that one of humankind's chief obligations is to improve upon God's creation. In *Rights of Man* political tyranny constitutes the chief obstacle to furthering the improvement of God's creation and democracy represents the ideal government for promoting improvement. Moreover, improvement, as Paine sees it, is fundamentally linked to the advancement of the sciences, hence his emphasis on the value of mechanics. With *Age of Reason*, then, Paine attempts to replace the other principal obstacle to improvement, religion, with science.[22]

Paine's celebration of mechanics once again reflects his commitment to popular politics. By associating mechanics directly with astronomy and mathematics Paine elevates what would be considered a rather low-grade

---

[21] *The New Oxford Annotated Bible*, 1 *Corinthians* 13 (12): 1392.
[22] This also explains why Paine cites various scientists who have been persecuted by the religious powers for their scientific undertakings (CW l, 493–494).

science from its menial status to one of significance, thus rendering knowledge of the universe available to a wider segment of the people. This is particularly apparent when we consider that according to the OED the word "mechanic" referred to "One who is employed in a manual occupation; a handicraftsman," and as an adjective it describes something "Belonging to or characteristic of the 'lower orders'; vulgar, low, base." Thus, as a science, mechanics was associated with the audience that Paine wanted to empower politically. Furthermore, choosing mechanics as the practical manifestation of science enables Paine to write about the potentially complex and difficult subject of theology that is at the core of *The Age of Reason* in the same simple and straightforward manner that characterized his earlier political writings. He could be certain that the metaphors and examples he used from the world of science would be clear to the general audience he was trying to reach. In this respect Paine is democratizing both science and religion simultaneously.

Although Paine had a troubled, at best, relationship to the Quakers, the analogies between the ideas about religion that he outlines in *The Age of Reason* and the fundamental tenets of the Society of Friends are striking and provocative. Democratic access, the refusal of hierarchy, revolution, simplicity, and a heightened concern with language are all central features of both Paine's deism and Quakerism. On the other hand, Paine's notion of an immanent God accessible via the contemplation of nature and the scientific laws of the universe, bears little relation to the doctrine of the inner light that forms the theological basis of the Quaker faith. Paine insistently locates his God outside the individual, not within. There is a fundamental materialism to Paine's "Almighty Lecturer" that violates the deeply spiritual conception of the divinity in Quakerism. Although with its belief that "a Measure of God or the eternal Christ dwelt within each man and could become a powerful presence involving the whole of his being in a new relationship," the inner light emphasizes a democratic relation to the divinity, Quakerism retained a strong sense of a need for a conversion experience (Endy, 63–64). Paine did not deny the potential for direct revelation in the mode of a conversion experience, but he refused to privilege these experiences of personal revelation. On the contrary, throughout both volumes of *The Age of Reason* he expresses great skepticism about these accounts of divine intervention largely because they have too often been put in the service of hierarchy, serving as the pretext for one individual or group of individuals to establish their authority over another (those who have not been privy to the revelation). So, his religion of science downplays ideas of conversion of direct revelation in favor of a more diffuse sense of God's presence in the world. Alas, one side effect of this denial of personal contact with the divinity is a loss of spirituality. Paine replaces those kinds of experiences with the observation of material phenomena such as the motion of the planets. The a-spirituality of Paine's deism is especially evident at the end of the second part of *The Age of Reason*: "It will perhaps be said, that if such a revolution in the system of religion take place, that every preacher ought to be a philosopher. *Most certainly*; and every house of devotion a school of science" (CW I, 604). This is why *The Age of Reason* both appealed to religious reformers who embraced its critique of religious institutions, but also proved inadequate to their religious and spiritual needs. Reformers such as Lorenzo Dow, William Miller, and Joseph Smith were attracted to Paine's religious ideas, but eventually disavowed them because *The Age of Reason* did not offer a spiritually satisfying alternative. They were seeking more personal experiences of the divinity, not ones mediated through nature and science. To Paine the rules of science offered a transparency that was simply not possible in the kinds of spiritual interiority that was so important to Quakers and other advocates of egalitarian religion. Paine may have abandoned the Quaker religion of his father, but he was also strongly influenced by its religious politics.

NATURE TAMED

If *Rights of Man* aims to overthrow the tyranny of government, and *The Age of Reason* aims to overthrow the tyranny of religion, both texts share a common desire to overthrow yet another tyrant, nature. Nature, rather than simply a benevolent source of knowledge, can also constitute a threatening force that needs to be understood so that it can be controlled. In their critical examination of the Enlightenment, Max Horkheimer and Theodor W. Adorno have observed more generally of the era, "What men want to learn from nature is how to use it in order wholly to dominate it and other men" (4). While Paine was not interested in dominating other people, his anxiety over nature's power bespeaks a desire to control and limit its power. Just as nature had the capacity to inspire awe (a positive version of fear), it also had the capacity to overwhelm and subjugate people to its power. Peale's anecdote concerning the fate of bridges in the spring conveys this very point. It is perhaps most famously articulated in Jefferson's account of the natural bridge in his *Notes on the State of Virginia*. The natural bridge, which Jefferson identifies as "the most sublime of nature's works" inspires such fear that it deprives people of their willpower:

Though the sides of this bridge are provided in some parts with a parapet of fixed rocks, yet few men have resolution to walk to them and look over into the abyss. You involuntarily fall on your hands and feet, creep to the parapet and peep over it. Looking down from this height about a minute, gave me a violent head ach [sic]. If the view from the top be painful and intolerable, that from below is delightful in an equal extreme. (148)

Like Peale's affrighted traveler, who is terrified by the awesome power of the overflowing river, Jefferson's viewer loses control of himself. Ultimately, nature is a tyrant because it is a coercive power: It forces people to behave in certain ways without first seeking their consent. It is no accident, therefore, that Paine's foremost political opponent, Edmund Burke, would celebrate this terror by renaming it the sublime. The sublime qualities of monarchical government were precisely its virtues in Burke's account.

The desire to rein in nature is implicit in Paine's articulation, in *The Age of Reason*, of the central tenet of deism: "The true Deist has but one Deity, and his religion consists in contemplating the power, wisdom and benignity of the Deity in His works, and in endeavoring to imitate Him in everything moral, scientifical and mechanical" (CW I, 498). Notably, Paine's religion does not end in contemplation; instead, contemplation has become a means to another more important end, action. Given that Paine saw unlimited power as the ultimate source of injustice and evil, we may conclude that he believed it was man's duty to learn from nature such that we might check the Deity's power, lest he too become a tyrant. But, to be sure, Paine is not arguing for the nonexistence of God; rather, he is replacing the Christian god with God the "Almighty Lecturer." Recognizing the centrality of religious discourse at the time, Paine presents his new system as an alternative religion. He would be well aware of the influence of religion among his target audience of middling and lower sorts, so it was essential that he present his ideas as a religion and not as an attempt to eradicate religion and faith from human society. Many critics have overlooked this aspect of *The Age of Reason*, instead focusing on his attacks on Christianity. A careful reading of the text shows that Paine is not just tearing down, he is simultaneously building an alternative. More to the point, being the skilled writer that he is, he uses the contrast between Christianity and his science-based religion to call attention to the advantages of his new system, which he sees as an improvement to Christianity that will better serve the needs of the modern state and its subjects.

In the end, science – and not nature – plays the decisive role in Paine's political philosophy and theology. Nature might be God's creation, but science allows us to understand that creation so that we may dominate it and improve upon it. In order to overthrow the tyranny of nature, then, we must learn to speak its language. In *The Age of Reason* Paine offers science, and particularly mechanics, as the solution to the problem of nature's tyranny.[23] The connection between science and politics in Paine is perhaps most clearly articulated in his observation in *The Age of Reason* regarding his approach to science in general: "It is an idea I have never lost sight of that all our knowledge of science is derived from the revolutions (exhibited to our eye and from thence to our understanding) which those several planets or worlds of which our system is composed make in their circuit round the Sun" (CW I, 503). Just as the revolutions of the planets literally provide us with knowledge of the physical world, the revolutions of societies and governments provide us with knowledge about the political world.[24] Paine's religion, thus, is not the religion of nature, but the religion of science, for it is science that allows us to overcome the tyranny of nature. Like the tyrants of Asia, Africa, and Europe, who, according to Paine, have hindered the improvement of their respective countries by interfering with commercial development, so too has nature impeded the progress of humankind. Thus, science itself becomes a version of an internal improvement as it constitutes a bridge between God and humankind enabling one to become like God. It is essential to Paine that this transformative power of science be available to everyone. He is cautious not to replace one arcane, mysterious, and inaccessible language with another, instead choosing mechanics because it offers a set of analogies that were broadly understood and/or easily learned in the late eighteenth century. Mechanics, in other words, will not only unlock the natural and political

[23] As had been the case in both America and France, Paine understood that the crucial weapon of revolution was language. As Christopher Looby has pointed out, "Paine's figuration of revolution as linguistic action was...a constant presence in his political writing" (66).

[24] In *Common Sense* Paine uses a different version of planetary relations to argue for American independence: "In no instance hath nature made the satellite larger than its primary planet; and as England and America, with respect to each other, reverse the common order of nature, it is evident that they belong to different systems. England to Europe: America to itself" (CW I, 24). In both instances, Paine takes for granted the applicability of astronomical phenomena to political philosophy.

mysteries of the universe, but it will do so in a language that is clear and accessible to a wide segment of the population.

Paine's science of politics, or politics of science as it were, like the radically democratic system of government he promotes in *Common Sense* and *Rights of Man*, is meant to enfranchise and empower lower and middling sorts by demystifying government and the operations of power. If power and government function as a series of levers and gears, for example, then why shouldn't people who actually work with levers and gears participate fully and equally in the nation's governance? Moreover, in this era of commercial expansion, mechanics and technological improvements had obtained great cultural currency. In the eighteenth century mechanical innovations were a crucial driver of commercial growth. In the wake of the Newtonian revolution, mechanics were producing myriad new and useful inventions that spurred commerce and were celebrated for improving the material conditions of peoples' lives. Taking it to the realm of political theory, Paine uses mechanics as a framework for imagining a better way to organize political relations and distribute political power. In a sense, Paine is just extending the developments in science and technology that had given radical dissenters in Britain so much success by putting them at the forefront of technological innovation and thus granting them access to power through economic means when they were legally denied it for religious reasons. Paine takes the logic of technological improvement and structures a new society around it, bringing together the commercial, religious, and political goals he finds embedded in mechanics to form a utopian vision of an egalitarian democratic commercial nation. Thus, mechanics in both its senses, as a branch of science and as individuals, is crucial to this vision: The former allows Paine to conjoin the commercial and the political, and the latter because, more than its beneficiaries, they are the foundation of this system.

By way of closing let me suggest that Paine's democratic mechanic is the urban analogue to Jefferson's republican farmer. If Jefferson's ideal democratic nation is predicated on a vision of the independent, educated farmer – illustrated so aptly by Crevecoeur's farmer James – then Paine's rests on a vision of equally idealized urban artisans and laborers. It should come as no surprise that both Jefferson and Paine essentially imagine their ideal subject for the democratic nation as versions of themselves. However, unlike Jefferson's palpable ambivalence toward his idealized farmers (clearly evident in *Notes on the State of Virginia*), Paine fully embraces the middling and lower sorts in whom he places so much faith in his science of politics. Perhaps this makes Paine the more naive of the two, but it also makes him the more truly democratic. This contrast in their judgment of the capabilities and limitations of the common people also explains why Paine was willing to publish his radical ideas about religion, whereas Jefferson largely chose to keep them to himself or to a close group of friends. Paine's faith in the middling and lower sorts meant that he was not afraid, as Jefferson, Adams, Washington, and other prominent deist politicians of the day were, that undermining the authority of Christianity would have a negative impact on their morals and therefore lead to social turmoil. To a much greater extent than his more celebrated fellow revolutionaries, Paine was committed to the idea that in order to create a government for the people and by the people, you had to have faith in the people and their ability to govern themselves. Human agency is at the heart of Paine's politics of science: By transforming religion and government into sciences he seeks to endow humans with greater control over their world. The scientific process is the foundation of this project because it not only organizes and systematizes the world, but it also strips away the illusions/false systems that were used by one set of people to dominate another. In *Rights of Man* and *The Age of Reason* Paine, thus, uses the language of science not only to strip away the mysteries of the state, the church, and the natural world, but also to enfranchise the people by giving them a language and a sense of agency that he hoped would allow them to assert their right to participate fully in the political process.

5

"Strong Friends and Violent Enemies"

The Historical Construction of Thomas Paine through the Nineteenth Century

Perhaps no Revolutionary American patriot figure has been as persistently maligned, misrepresented, and misunderstood as Tom Paine. The lack of reliable information on his life, combined with the controversial nature of his work, has made Paine's life story an open field for speculation on the part of admirers and detractors alike. A quick glance at the most recent biography of Paine, John Keane's *Tom Paine, A Political Life*, reveals that we still know very little about the first thirty seven years of his life, before he arrived in Philadelphia late in 1774.[1] Even after he became renowned for his role in the American Revolution, Paine remained an elusive character in both his public and private lives. This is not to say that there was a scarcity of images of Paine in the contemporary press, but rather that because of the profound impact he had on people, those images were generally exaggerated, and often contradictory. In this chapter I will not attempt to cast further light on the details of Paine's life; instead, I wish to explore what we might call his life in print: how his identity and ideas were constructed and appropriated by others from the publication of the first biography, authored by George Chalmers in 1791, to the first attempt at a comprehensive and nonpartisan biography in 1891. My hope is that exploring the vicissitudes of Paine's historical reputation will serve as an instructive lens through which to learn about the nuances and idiosyncrasies of the construction of an American literary and political history.

[1] Although Keane attempts to give "Paine's activities in England...their due weight," the scarcity of materials, reliable or otherwise, poses a serious obstacle to any such endeavor. Instead of the details of his life, therefore, Keane attempts to trace the "English roots of Paine's political identity" (xix), a task that David O. Wilson and Isaac Kramnick have each undertaken with interesting results.

Paine was acutely aware of his effect on people, as is evident from a letter he wrote to George Washington shortly after the publication of *Rights of Man* in England: "The same fate follows me here as I at first experienced in America, strong friends and violent enemies, but as I have got the ear of the country, I shall go on" (CW II, 1319). Although his polarizing effect on the public may have assured brisk sales, it also led to a great deal of speculation about him on the part of his enemies. One thing is certain: Wherever he went from 1776 onward, Paine was always at the center of controversy. He would be loved and lionized by some, hated and maligned by others, but rarely ignored.

For his part, Paine generally refused to respond to the *ad hominem* attacks leveled at him by his political rivals. Unfortunately, his failure to exercise control over his public image opened him up to a series of vicious assaults on his character that would seriously damage his reputation. In one of the few places where he does include some account of himself in a text, the Preface to *The Age of Reason*, Paine explains why he has chosen not to defend himself from these personal attacks:

I have seen, since I have been at liberty, several publications written, some in America and some in England, as answers to the former part of 'The Age of Reason.' If the authors of these can amuse themselves by so doing, I shall not interrupt them. They may write against the work, and against me, as much as they please; they do me more service than they intend, and I can have no objection that they write on. They will find, however, by this second part, without its being written as an answer to them, that they must return to their work, and spin their cobweb over again. The first is brushed away by accident. (CW II, 517)

Refusing to contradict his enemies' allegations, Paine suggests that their attacks on him and his ideas are so insubstantial that they are not worthy of his attention. More importantly, he seems to have realized that the furor over his latest work would insure a large readership for it, and probably increase the audience for his next publication and thus insure that it would be read by even more people. If Paine's refusal to respond to the personal attacks leveled at him was an attempt to focus attention on the ideological and political issues at stake, his strategy backfired, for his character not his ideas became the subject of contention and the efficacy of his public advocacy was diminished in later years by questions about his character. He became, as we have seen in the aftermath of the publication of the "Letter to George Washington" and his return to the United States in 1802, too controversial to be associated with, even for an admirer and fellow traveler like Jefferson.

Paine's stubborn refusal to defend himself is astonishing not only in light of what was being said about him, but because in the "Forester's Letters" he had argued for the inclusion of the personal in the consideration of public matters. For someone who had argued that human hypocrisy necessitates a consideration of the person advocating certain political measures in order to evaluate the legitimacy of the proposed actions, Paine is remarkably careless about protecting his own public image. If Paine articulated a powerful argument for rejecting the rhetoric of depersonalization that would serve Franklin so well, he seems to have never fully considered the consequences that rejection might have for his long-term participation in the public sphere. On the one hand, Paine's failure to anticipate and deal with the personal attacks that his approach to polemical writing would elicit in his rivals once again attests to the unsettled nature of the public sphere in the late eighteenth century. On the other hand, we might say that Paine got what he asked for: His personality, private life, and intensely personal rhetorical voice were now up for grabs as objects of insinuation, ridicule, and satire. By insisting on personalizing his interventions in the public arena, Paine had made his own person a legitimate topic of discussion in the debates about the political, social, and economic policies he advocated.

Although the controversial nature of his writings and his refusal to contradict the allegations made about his personal behavior may have contributed to his negative public image, I would like to suggest that the primary reason for Paine's marginalization in American political, literary, and intellectual history was his status as a professional writer. If fiction writers were perceived as fundamentally untrustworthy, polemical writers such as Paine were even more suspect.[2] With no fixed constituency to represent or to whom he could be held accountable, political writers like Paine were widely perceived as potentially dangerous and irresponsible. Had he, for example, been elected or appointed to national political office, or participated in the Constitutional Convention, Paine probably would not have suffered the fate he did. Any of these positions would have immediately endowed him with a title of respect that would have insured better treatment.

Benjamin Franklin, once again, provides a useful contrast insofar as his participation in the Continental Congress and in the Constitutional

---

[2] In *Revolution and the Word*, Cathy N. Davidson discusses questions of authorship in the Early Republic and notes the generally low esteem in which the public held authors. Although she is principally concerned with fiction writers, political writers, if anything, would have been viewed with even greater skepticism.

Convention served to cleanse him of the stain of being a printer and writer by trade. Franklin's direct participation in these nation-forming political bodies established him as a "founding father" and thus secured his character as an heroic, and later iconic, American. Of course, Franklin also wrote a memoir that, although published well after his death, has contributed greatly to the cultural construction of Franklin as the prototype American. Paine, on the other hand, did neither: He did not write an autobiography and he never participated in a formal governmental body (and it seems he was never really interested in doing either). The first deprived him of a voice in his historical construction and the second insured that he would be viewed with suspicion in a culture where writers have been perceived as among the most suspect of public figures.[3]

THE DEATH OF A RADICAL

Considering his role as the most influential advocate of independence for the colonies, it seems remarkable that at the time of his death on June 8, 1809, Paine had already been largely forgotten as one of the heroes of the American Revolution. As Alfred F. Young has recently noted in his study of the collective memory of the Revolution in Boston during the early national period, however, from the 1780s to the 1820s the radical dimensions of the Revolution were more or less systematically repressed by Federalists who needed a "safe public memory of the Revolution," one that wouldn't threaten the legitimacy of their social status or economic and political power (124). This vision of the Revolution, Young suggests, was exemplified in their Fourth of July celebrations, which he characterizes as "more accurately a celebration of antirevolution": "Federalists – antidemocratic, Anglophile, and Francophobe – for the longest time would not even read the Declaration of Independence on the Fourth, fearful of the intense Anglophobia its list of grievances stirred and the democratic and equalitarian implications of its preamble, to say nothing of its justification of the right of revolution" (111). If the Declaration was deemed too radical, imagine *Common Sense* or *Rights of Man*, texts where Paine advocated unicameralism and annual elections, to name just two political ideas the Federalists would have found abhorrently democratic.

---

[3] For a more detailed analysis of attitudes toward political writers during the revolutionary and early national periods see Sandra Gustafson, *Eloquence is Power*, esp. Chapters 4 and 5.

By the time of his death Paine's contributions to the cause of American independence and his political radicalism had also been overshadowed by his highly visible contretemps with other American leaders (most notably George Washington), by allegations about his personal habits, and by his all too public religious beliefs. He died practically alone and still ostracized by the social and political community that had celebrated him four decades earlier. Only a few close friends and neighbors attended Paine's funeral.[4] But his death did not go completely unnoticed. Paine's demise was widely publicized and death notices appeared in all of the papers in the larger northeastern cities: New York, Boston, Salem, Hartford, Lancaster, and Philadelphia. In a few of the obituaries he was remembered as a heroic figure. The *New York Public Advertiser*, which seems to have printed the first notice of his death, identified Paine as a "distinguished Philanthropist, whose life was devoted to the cause of humanity" (June 9, 1809), and *The Democratic Press* of Philadelphia exhorted its readers, "Forgotten be his errors, and remembered eternally with gratitude, be his eminent services to the cause of Independence and Freedom" (June 12, 1809). More commonly, however, the death notices focused on Paine's religious ideas with comments such as the one in the *Connecticut Gazette*, which simply characterized him as, "notorious for his enmity to the gospel" (June 14, 1809).

Paine's deism was the principal subject of interest in the most commonly reprinted death notice, which first appeared in New York's *The American Citizen* on the morning of June 10, and was also reprinted in the *New York Evening Post* for June 10, 1809, the *Columbia Centinel* for June 10, the *New York Herald* for June 14, the *Connecticut Herald* for June 2, and the *Lancaster Journal* for June 30. The obituary read:

Died, on Thursday morning, the 8th inst. Thomas Paine, author of the Crisis, Rights of Man, &c, &c. Mr. Paine had a desire to be interred in the Quaker burying ground, and some days previous to his demise, had an interview with some Quaker gentlemen on the subject, but as he declined a renunciation of his deistical opinions, his anxious wishes were not complied with. He was yesterday interred at New-Rochelle, Westchester county, perhaps on his own farm. I am unacquainted with his age, but he had lived long, done some good, and much harm.

---

4 Hawke, 399. Although Paine received neither a procession nor a tribute, the parallel to Sam Adams is worth noting here, as Young points out, "When Adams died in 1803, a good number of Federalists were conveniently out of town for the funeral procession, and the legislature, as James Sullivan put it, 'whittled down' a tribute to him" (116).

The irony of this death notice is that the two works of Paine's that had the greatest impact on his American contemporaries and for which he has been most remembered, *Common Sense* and *The Age of Reason*, are not even mentioned by name.[5] In many respects these two works represented the bookends of Paine's tempestuous and celebrated career as a public figure. *Common Sense* established him as the preeminent radical voice in American politics during the founding era, and *The Age of Reason*, his last major work, completed his exodus from the mainstream political and social milieu. It was only because of the publication of *The Age of Reason* that most of the death notice is given over to speculation about Paine's final refusal to renounce his deism in favor of Christianity. The deathbed interview referred to in the obituary became the subject of intense speculation and several versions of it would be circulated during the years following Paine's death.

In a letter to his father, the Quaker merchant Jacob Harvey relates the events of the last days of Paine's life. Harvey seems to have been familiar with the apocryphal stories about Paine's demise. Before recounting his conversation with Willet Hicks, one of the Quakers who was present at Paine's bedside, Harvey remarks, "I spoke of the dreadful manner in which I had understood the celebrated Tom Paine died" (September 19, 1817). Hicks was one of the "Quaker gentlemen" that Paine had called upon in his desire to be buried in the Quaker burying ground. Harvey tells his father Hicks's account of the events of the days preceding Paine's death:

Just before WH's [Willet Hicks] arrival at P's lodgings, an ignorant, overbearing, Methodist preacher had been visiting the latter, & with the enthusiastic zeal that characterized that sect, had told P. in a tremendous voice, that unless he believed so & so he would be eternally damned! This mode of convincing so exasperated P. that with what little xxxxxxx remaining strength he had, he lifted himself up in the bed, seized his crutch, & swore he would beat the poor Methodist, unless he immediately quitted the apartment. (Jacob Harvey to Joseph Massey Harvey, September 19, 1817)[6]

When Hicks arrived, Paine requested that he ask the Quakers to allow him to be buried in the Quaker graveyard. Hicks returned with the Quakers' answer denying Paine's request, and "After this interview, WH found

---

[5] In England *Rights of Man* had enjoyed the greatest circulation of Paine's works and would continue to play an influential role in British constitutional political discussions well into the nineteenth century.

[6] A microfilm transcription of the Harvey papers is in the rare book collection of the American Philosophical Society. The manuscript belongs to Mr. and Mrs. Daniel Feins.

all religious conversation with him useless, & he died without making the least acknowledgement of his errors" (Harvey). According to Hicks's account, Paine wished to be buried among the Quakers because he felt their "society" to be "more clear of superstitions than any other," and because he "was once your [sic] way of thinking [him]self" (Harvey). Upon being denied his request by the Quakers, Paine "purchased a small plot of land at West Chester where he lies buried, & which by his will is to serve as a grave yard for all those who, like him, may be refused admittance into <u>Christian Grave Yards</u>" (Harvey).

The tale of Paine's refusal to retract his statements on religion, or as Harvey puts it, to "acknowledge his errors," nonetheless grew to almost mythical proportions. Nearly forty years after Paine's death, Grant Thorburn, who seems to have been the author of a sketch of Paine's life, retold yet another version of Paine's last days in a letter to a friend. Thorburn, who claims to have been Paine's friend, learned his account from another eyewitness, a Dr. James R. Manley, who tended to Paine during his last days. Unlike Hicks's more restrained and straightforward account, Manley's version transforms the moment of Paine's death into a spectacle:

In Mr Paine's last sickness, which was protracted, (perhaps over a twelve month) the Doctr was very attentive, and Mr Paine seemd very ^{sensible}, of his attentions, the Desease was very acute, brought on, by a Long and very <u>immoderate</u> use of Brandy, – about an hour before he died the Doctor told me he was at his bed-side, a severe spasm came on; and while it continued; Paine exclaimed alloud; Lord help, God help – Lord Jesus help, – the spasm ceased, says the Dr. – Mr Paine, before one hour you will be in eternity, we know your opinions as published to the world on what we term the Religion of the Bible; am I now to understand you as calling on God for help, – he made no answer, the spasms returned – again he exclaimed – Lord help, God help, Lord-Jesus-help – when the spasm ceased the Doctor resum'd, Mr. Paine before half an hour – you will be in eternity, I now ask you as a dieing man-am I to understand you as calling on the Lord-Jesus for help-he thought for a moment and reply'd, – <u>I dont wish-to-believe-on that-man</u>, – they were his Last words – in a few minutes thereafter, he ceased to breath, – you may rest assured – it was thus Paine died – the Doctor is a <u>man</u> of <u>truth</u> – I have often thought – the words – <u>I dont wish</u>-meant more than met the ear. (Grant Thorburn to John Orcutt, August 9, 1847)

Hicks' account neither denies nor confirms Manley's, for Hicks was not present for Paine's last moments. However, the overall impression given by each of their accounts differs markedly. Hicks' Paine remains soberly committed to the principles of deism, and is unwilling to compromise his beliefs. Thorburn, on the other hand, attempts to cast doubt on Paine's commitment to deism: He understands Paine's "I dont wish" as "I can't help but to" believe in Christianity. Ironically, however, in Thorburn's account Paine not only reasserts his deist beliefs, but is also forced to explain one of the central arguments of deism for one last time. Paine's statement "I dont wish-to-believe-on that-man," which Thorburn emphasizes by underlining it, in response to the question of whether he is asking "the Lord-Jesus for help," reiterates the crucial distinction between God and Jesus that Paine draws in *The Age of Reason.* Even to the end, in this version of his death, then, Paine was not fully understood.

The interest in Paine's death and in his failure to retract his deist principles suggests the extent to which in the public's eye Paine's religious opinions and beliefs eclipsed his radical political ideas, even to the point where his crucial role in the American cause of independence was nearly forgotten by many of his contemporaries. Nevertheless, the interest in the circumstances of Paine's death in 1809, almost thirteen years after the publication of his last major work, attests to his ability to capture the public's attention and imagination through his writings. Thus, to the extent that it insured that he would remain the subject of public discussion, Paine's notoriety continued to work to his advantage.

INVENTING A RADICAL'S LIFE

By the time Paine died in 1809, three different biographies, all intended to minimize his broad popular influence, had been published. The first biography, *The Life of Thomas Pain, The Author of Rights of Man, With a Defense of his Writings* appeared in London in 1791 and had been sponsored by the British ministry who were eager to counteract the unprecedented popularity of *Rights of Man.* George Chalmers, writing under the pseudonym Jonathan Oldys produced a propaganda piece with only a skeleton of factual information about Paine's life, which he fleshed out with scandalous allegations about Paine's life prior to his departure for the American colonies. The accusations ranged from petty insults regarding Paine's personal appearance and sexual potency to unfounded assertions of wife-beating and general dishonesty. Despite the sensational appeal of these personal insults, Chalmers's biography is mainly given over to an attempt to respond to the principles Paine had exposed in *Common Sense* and elaborated in *Rights of Man.*

Unlike future biographers of Paine, Chalmers realized that it would be in his best interest to cultivate an air of impartiality. His title might suggest that he is an admirer of Paine's ideals. He even remains noncommittal in his introductory passage on the responsibilities of the biographer:

It has been established by the reiterated suffrage of mankind, that the lives of those persons, who have either performed useful actions, or neglected essential duties, ought to be recounted, as much for an example to the present age, as for the instruction of future times.

Few men have more justly merited the honour of this notice, either as an example to be avoided at present, or as a lesson to be learned hereafter, than the personage whose actions we are now to recount, and whose writings we are about to defend. (3)

Chalmers's apparent neutrality serves him well for it does not immediately eliminate any particular group of readers. At the same time these opening sentences effectively pique the reader's curiosity: Will Paine represent an example to be followed or avoided? The careful reader might have noticed by now, however, the subtle hint offered by the intentional misspelling of Paine's last name in the title. Chalmers addresses the issue of the missing 'e' early in the biography asserting that "Our author's real name is *Pain*, his fictitious name is *Paine* with a final *e*: For his father's name was *Pain*" (3).[7] Chalmers cleverly avoids discussion of the punning possibilities in his famous subject's name, for he realizes that his point does not require elaboration.

Although Chalmers succumbs to the temptation to launch personal attacks on Paine's character at various moments in the text, on the whole Chalmers relies on a much more effective strategy to undermine his subject's accomplishments. Rather than indulge in juvenile insinuations about Paine's life, Chalmers cleverly constructs his biography as a mock-heroic tale in which Paine plays the role of the confused and misguided philosopher. In Chalmers's account Paine is not so much evil, as he would be depicted later, but wrong-headed. Of Paine's rapid ascent in colonial American politics, for example, Chalmers writes,

He who was born to illuminate the western hemisphere by his wisdom, was for some months engaged in retailing politics by the pennyworth, and carrying parcels by the dozen. It shews the strength of his character, and the vigor of his powers, that he should have speedily risen from the shopman to the statesman, from being the distributor of stationery, to be the dismemberer of provinces. (12)

The tone may seem overblown, but everything up to the last six words of the paragraph could easily have appeared in an admiring biography of Paine. Chalmers is effective because passages such as this one work to undermine Paine's achievements without reducing the text to a scurrilous hack job. Chalmers would prove to be the ablest of Paine's

---

7 It is true that Paine added the e to his surname.

antibiographers. His astutely placed sarcasm and subtle jibes would soon be replaced, in the hands of less skillful writers, by shrill and vulgar assaults on Paine's character and personal habits.

Although Chalmers's text had very little impact on the reception of *Rights of Man* in England, it would come to exert a great deal of influence on Paine's reputation. In the absence of a rebuttal by Paine or any of his supporters, Chalmers's account of Paine's life obtained a certain air of authenticity and thus became the foundation for future attacks on Paine. In fact, William Cobbett, popularly known as Peter Porcupine, advertised his debt to Chalmers in his biography of Paine: "His life was published in London in 1793; but like most other works calculated to stem the torrent of popular prejudice, it has never found admittance into the American press" (4). Cobbett would remedy that situation by publishing an abridged version of Chalmers in the September 1796 issue of *The Political Censor.* On the whole Cobbett's abridgement, interspersed with his own commentary, was unremarkable. More remarkable would be Cobbett's later transformation into one of Paine's foremost advocates in England.[8]

Chalmers' life and Cobbett's abridgement, both published more than fifteen years before Paine's death, would remain the only narratives of Paine's life published during their subject's lifetime. Paine refused to respond, and no one came to his defense. So, this distorted image of Paine went unchallenged. Eighteen years would pass before a new biography of Paine would be published on the year of his death. This one too would offer an unflattering portrayal. James Cheetham, whom Paine had been in the process of attempting to sue for libel, published his *The Life of Thomas Paine*, in which he attacks Paine's character as much as his political opinions. Cheetham depicts Paine as a depraved individual and a political hypocrite. In one particularly effective passage Cheetham combines the two: "He always, I afterwards found, in all companies, drunk or sober, would be listened to, but in this regard there were no *rights of men* with him, no equality, no reciprocal immunities and obligations, for he would listen to no one" (xxii). In this image Cheetham propagates the widespread rumor that Paine was an inebriate, but he also combines this suggestion of personal decadence with a larger political assault on Paine. Paine's alleged lack of civility in private has larger repercussions for Cheetham as it gives the lie to Paine's commitment to democratic

---

[8] For a fascinating account of the remarkable connections between Paine and Cobbett, see David Wilson, *Paine and Cobbett: The Transatlantic Connection.*

ideals. In other words, Cheetham would have us believe, that Paine was nothing more than a drunken tyrant whose political opinions applied to everyone but him. If Chalmers had established the precedent, Cheetham would create the masterpiece of anti-Paine propaganda. Cheetham, a former admirer and would-be friend of Paine's, was the source for the most pernicious and enduring accusations about Paine's private life.

From the outset, Cheetham's biography is framed in terms of the struggle between Federalists and democratic republicans that was at the center of contemporary politics. Cheetham dedicates his text to then Vice-President George Clinton and includes a pointed attack on Jefferson in the dedication. Cheetham's fear of the potential effects of democratic republicanism emerges in the subsequent Preface where he draws an apocalyptic picture of the publication of *Rights of Man* in England:

Never did the parched earth receive refreshing rain with more welcome than that with which the revolutionary people of England admitted amongst them the tumultuous writings of Paine. To that which was his object; to commotion, to the overthrow of the government, and to bloodshed in all its horrid forms, they were rapidly hastening. (xviii)

In a typically exaggerated image, Cheetham draws on the specter of the French Revolution to suggest that Paine's arguments for reform are merely a convenient disguise for his true destructive aims. Oddly, however, Cheetham's choice of metaphors seems to acknowledge a public eager for such a change, which, contrary to his claims elsewhere in the text, would indicate that something was not entirely right in England at the time.

Cheetham, however, quickly corrects this impression when he suggests that Paine owes his popularity not to any wide appeal inherent in his text, but to the machinations of a few well-organized and vocal agitators who successfully promoted Paine's works by taking advantage of the ignorant masses: "The clubs, zealous to a degree of frenzy; always vigilant, always alert, published a great edition of thirty thousand copies of the work, which was distributed among the poor, who could not afford to purchase it" (xviii). Thus, Cheetham deprives the reading public of any agency, instead rendering it a passive receptacle easily swayed by those who are skilled at manipulating public opinion. Cheetham does not limit his disdain for the public to such subtle passages. He is surprisingly blunt about his opinion of the common people:

Taking circumstances then as they are, I think that if England were made a republic like ours, England would be undone: she would be an adjunct to France in a few years; she could not avoid being so. France cannot indeed conquer her, but *universal suffrage* would. The people in whose hands the votes of the nation would be placed, and to whose blind direction the power of the nation would be confided, feel, but they do not think; they cannot, I mean, think as is necessary to save a nation. (151–152)

In passages such as this one, we can feel the rage and anxiety of the Federalists. The common people are openly the subject of disdain and Paine's desire to enfranchise them irritates, even angers, elites seeking to preserve deference and hierarchy in society. What are going to be the implications of democracy and the American Revolution? Would Paine and other likeminded reformers succeed in bearing out the more radical possibilities embedded in the Revolution or would the elites succeed in reasserting their authority? Would this Revolutionary fervor, moreover, spread to England? Paine and his fellow radicals, of course, lost this ideological contest. Cheetham, like Chalmers before him, perceived the threat that Paine's ideas posed to the social, political, and economic order in England. This passage makes it clear that to Cheetham the need to control the rabble, as he would surely call the common people, is a crucial motivating factor in his decision to attack Paine.

Shifting from passionate indignation to reasoned critique, Cheetham continues his "Preface" with a strategic distancing from Paine's previous two biographers, whom he accuses of partisanship. By relating the circumstances surrounding their publication and criticizing them for their *a priori* motives, one political and the other religious, Cheetham, in a clever rhetorical move, lends his own text an air of impartiality. He further emphasizes the sincerity of his text when he announces his sources, which generally consist of supposed friends and acquaintances of Paine's in England and America (xx). The most powerful source of authenticity for Cheetham's text is his own personal acquaintance with his subject:

My acquaintance with him continued, with very various views, two or three years. My intercourse with him was more frequent than agreeable, but what I suffered in feeling from his want in good manners, his dogmatism, the tyranny of his opinions, his peevishness, his intemperance, and the low company he kept, was perhaps compensated by acquiring a knowledge of the man. (xxiii)

Of course, if Paine was as obnoxious as Cheetham makes him out to be, the only sense in which acquiring knowledge of the man would be of any benefit was if he had been planning to write a biography. The compensation, Cheetham must have hoped, would come in the form of book sales. The irony is that Cheetham would be counting on Paine's "undeserved popularity," a popularity he was attempting to undercut, to insure the sale of his biography (xix).

Cheetham's text is as much a survey of Paine's seminal works as a recounting of the events of his life. The biographical material here serves to complement Cheetham's attempts to undermine the authority of Paine's arguments in *Common Sense, The Crisis, Rights of Man*, and *The Age of Reason*. For, in spite of his efforts to lend his text an air of impartiality, including statements such as "The object of my labor is neither to please nor displease any political party," Cheetham's biography remains nothing more than a scandalous, mudslinging assault on Paine's character (xxiii). At every turn Cheetham contrives to find a fault in Paine's character, such as when he questions Paine's appointment to the post of secretary of foreign affairs: "He had neither the soberness of habit, the reservedness of deportment, the urbanity of manners, the courteousness of language, the extent of reading, not the wide range of thought, which a station so distinguished required" (60). A classic eighteenth-century conservative, Cheetham implies that Paine was not fit to hold office because he wasn't a gentleman. Cheetham's critique of *Common Sense* extends the point to the question of Paine's qualification to write about political affairs:

As a literary work, Common Sense, energetically as it promoted the cause of independence, has no merit. Defective in arrangement, inelegant in diction, here and there a sentence excepted, with no profundity of argument, no felicity of remark, no extent of research, no classical allusion, nor comprehension of thought, it is fugitive in nature, and cannot be appealed to as authority on the subject of government. Its distinguishing characteristics are boldness and zeal; low sarcasm and deep-rooted malevolence. It owed its unprecedented popularity, on the one hand, to the British cabinet, which sought to triumph by bare-faced force instead of generous measures; and, on the other, to the manly spirit of the colonists, which though often depressed, could not be conquered. (47–48)

Cheetham, of course, has missed the very point of *Common Sense*. He judges it by the standards of a work of political philosophy aimed at the aristocracy in content as well as style, whereas Paine sought to write a text whose style and language would render it accessible to those to whom its message was intended. Research, allusion, and high diction are all strategies used by authors to earn the respect of the elite, establish their cultural authority, and exclude less-educated readers. Paine's rhetoric, as we have seen elsewhere in this study, was designed to subvert all of these traditional hallmarks of high culture.

According to Cheetham, *Common Sense* not only lacked literary merit, but its contribution to political philosophy was also negligible. In this instance Cheetham once again combines his political philosophical dismissal of Paine with a personal barb:

> Yet Paine, vain beyond any man I ever read of, or ever knew, was of opinion . . . that the revolution, of which he was in a great measure the parent, 'led to the *discovery* of the principles of government': The assertion was undoubtedly a dictate of gross ignorance. . . . He might have correctly said that it led, in some respects, to a new *practice*, but certainly no new *principle* was discovered. (48)

Here we find one of the earliest instances of the question of originality in Paine, a question that to this day is commonly used to reduce Paine to a secondary role in the intellectual history of the era. Ironically, in one of his attacks on Paine Cheetham identifies the crucial originality of Paine's work: his language. At a critical juncture in history, Paine recognized the need for a new language of politics that would be consistent with the theory it articulated. This is no small feat, for if we agree that nothing can be understood outside of language, then through his new language of politics, Paine not only made democracy and democratic revolution comprehensible, he made them possible. Cheetham, of course, cannot see this, because he refuses to accept democracy as a viable form of government.[9]

Denying the literary and philosophical value of Paine's work, however, is not enough for Cheetham. Although he acknowledges Paine as the "parent of the Revolution," or perhaps because he does so, Cheetham denies Paine's works any lasting or concrete effects on the state of affairs in the United States:

> For the liberty we enjoy in the United states, we are endebted to our ancestors. We have acquired nothing of it ourselves: not a jot of it is our own. All that we have done, is the effecting of a separation from the parent country: all that we have achieved, is independence. But we have no liberty but that which we have derived from England. We owe it all to our ancestors. (193)

At this point one wonders why Cheetham saw any need to write a biography of Paine. If Paine was so insignificant, then why bother to publish an account of his life? Paradoxically, biographers like Cheetham were drawing on the very fame they felt Paine did not deserve, while ultimately

---

[9] Unfortunately too many scholars have repeated Cheetham's error by judging Paine's thought on the basis of romantic notions of originality. This seems especially ironic when Paine's ideas about the educability of the common man and the language he crafted to pursue that end that constitute a major contribution to the development of English romanticism. On Paine's connections to British Romanticism see, for example, John Mee, *Dangerous Enthusiasm* and Jon P. Klancher, *The Making of English Reading Audiences, 1790–1832*.

contributing to that fame by keeping him in the public eye. In terms of the efficacy of Paine's writings, if nothing has changed, then surely Cheetham has nothing to worry about. But, of course, that was the problem for Cheetham; Paine had succeeded, at least in some degree, in promoting his political agenda. Rather than challenge Paine's ideas on their merits, Cheetham decided to deny that Paine had any ideas.

Cheetham concludes his biography of Paine with Dr. Manley's account of Paine's death, an account that perfectly corresponded with Cheetham's depiction of Paine as a hypocrite. He observes of the deathbed scene, "That he manifested symptoms of repentence, something like an inner willingness to believe in Jesus Christ, and yet an outward pride of obstinacy in denying that willingness in words, is certain from the testimony of Dr. Manley and Mrs. Hedden" (312). Fittingly, the image of Paine struggling to deny Jesus parallels Cheetham's efforts to deny Paine. How else do we explain Cheetham's need to publish an attack on Paine in which he admits to having sought out Paine's company? Although the profit motive would have been a potent incentive, Cheetham probably could not have been counting on a large audience given Paine's relative unpopularity at the time of his death.

ENGLISH RADICAL REFORMERS AND THE REHABILITATION OF PAINE

While Paine's public image plummeted in the United States during the Federalist era, he remained an important figure in England, and if anything, his popularity grew during these years. Although the recent events in France had cast suspicion, to put it mildly, on democratic revolution and popular politics – the bread and butter of *Rights of Man* – in the 1790s the emerging working-class movement in England, as E. P. Thompson has shown, embraced Paine as one of its foundational figures.[10] Not only did liberal-minded intellectuals in England such as William Godwin, Mary Wollstonecraft, and William Blake, to name just three, befriend and admire Paine, but artisans, laborers, and journalists also considered him one of their own. With such a wide constituency his rhetoric would permanently change English politics. As Thompson notes, "What he gave to English people was a new rhetoric of radical egalitarianism, which touched the deepest responses of the "free-born Englishman" and which

[10] For Thompson's analysis of Paine's influence on the "English working-class movement," see especially Chapter 4 of *The Making of the English Working Class*.

penetrated the subpolitical attitudes of the urban working people (94). Thompson goes on to point out that "the Paine tradition runs strongly through the popular journalism of the 19th century" and was "still present in the popular appeal of Lloyd George" (94). Although Paine's influence in England would wane significantly after the Terror and the growing fear of Jacobinism it occasioned, he would remain an important figure for English radicals and reformers. With the growing social unrest in England after the 1815 corn laws and subsequent controversies, Paine's ideas would reemerge as a major force in English politics. Hence, it is not surprising that the second wave of Paine biographies were published in Britain during this time of increasing agitation among the working classes.

In 1819 Thomas Clio Rickman, a close friend of Paine's, published his *The Life of Thomas Paine* in London, the first of three biographies of Paine to appear in 1819, a year that one scholar has called "one of the most troubled years of the nineteenth century" because of all the social and political turmoil in England that year (Briggs 208). John S. Harford and W. T. Sherwin also chose 1819 as the year to publish their respective biographies. Each of these biographies approached their subject from very different angles. While Rickman's aim was to rescue Paine's reputation from the accusations leveled in Cheetham's rendition, Harford followed in Cheetham's tradition by writing a biography in order to depict Paine as a despicable character whose works should be disregarded and condemned on the basis of their author's dissipated character. Sherwin's *Memoirs of the Life of Thomas Paine*, published by the famous London radical printer Richard Carlile, on the other hand, is the most interesting of the three insofar as he attempts to produce a narrative of Paine's life rather than the anecdote and opinion-riddled accounts offered by prior biographers. In the midst of the social unrest of 1819 these three authors clearly identified Paine as a crucial thinker whose ideas were central to the debates of the day. Hence, their respective biographies were each designed to promote a view of Paine's character that would further their political goals, be they radical reformers or conservatives.

Although it was not published until 1819, Rickman claims he wrote his biography eight years earlier. He does not offer an explanation as to why he had not published it until now, but the reemergence of Painite liberal thought in British politics almost certainly made this an opportune moment for Rickman to publish his long-dormant manuscript.[11] Rickman

---

[11] Rickman states that he did not make any alterations to the text between 1811 and 1819 (Preface, iii).

makes his agenda clear from the title page where he includes the following verses:

> To counteract foul SLANDER'S lies,
> And vindicate the good, and wise,
> Has been my only aim;
> If skilless I've performed my part,
> The error lies not with my HEART,
> My HEAD'S alone to blame.

Rickman's express target in publishing these recollections of Paine is his predecessor James Cheetham, who appears briefly in the Preface to this new life. If Cheetham was haunted by Paine's popularity, Rickman, it appears from the first two lines of the poem, was troubled by Paine's unpopularity. Rickman recalls Cheetham as a former admirer of Paine's: "Unhappily, Cheetham is the real name of a real apostate. He lived, when Mr. Paine was my inmate in 1792, at Manchester, and was a violent and furious idolater of his" (xiii). Given that eight years had passed since the publication of Cheetham's character assassination, Rickman's mission statement seems a bit out of date.

Moreover, although his intentions were good, the flaws in Rickman's account stem from his overindulgence in the "heart." As the poem suggests, Rickman was more concerned with responding to Paine's detractors than with producing a coherent and comprehensive biography of Paine's life. Rather than an account of Paine's life, Rickman's biography consists in a series of anecdotes and general meditations on Paine. One of the most remarkable such anecdotes is the tale of Paine's meeting with Napoleon:

When Mr. Buonaparte returned from Italy he called on Mr. Paine and invited him to dinner: in the course of his rapturous address to him he declared that a statue of gold ought to be erected to him in every city in the universe, assuring him that he always slept with his book 'Rights of Man' under his pillow, and conjured him to honor him with his correspondence and advice. (164)

Although the association with Napoleon is meant to establish the degree of Paine's influence and greatness, it also poses serious political problems. Did Rickman think that the association with Napoleon would heighten Paine's appeal? This image is particularly troubling because if Napoleon had read *Rights of Man* and admired its author, he certainly did not practice the principles of government propounded in it. One could just as easily see this episode employed by one of Paine's detractors, especially in England. The Napoleon stamp of approval would not carry much weight among British radicals.

Rickman's reluctance to provide a narrative of Paine's life becomes evident on the second page of the text when he remarks, " 'What manner of man' Mr. Paine was, his works will best exhibit, and from these his public, and much of his private character will be best ascertained. But, as solicitude about the life of a great man and an extraordinary writer is common to all, it is here attempted to be gratified" (2). This approach leaves the door open for Paine's critics whose strategy had been to draw connections between his works and his allegedly depraved character. While Paine's enemies often condemned his works on the basis of his character, many of them had inverted this operation and inferred a dissipated character from his works. This approach, for example, generally characterized the criticism of *The Age of Reason*. Instead of countering those readings, Rickman suggests that the texts provide a window into his character. Ironically, in his title page poem Rickman feels obligated to emphasize the good intentions of his own text, as if his work did not share the transparency of Paine's.

In spite of his eagerness to salvage Paine's reputation, Rickman does not deny some of the accusations about Paine's personal habits. Instead he blames Paine's demise on those who opposed him:

Shunned where he ought to have been caressed, coldly neglected where he ought to have been cherished, thrown into the back ground where he ought to have been prominent, and cruelly treated and calumniated by a host of ignorant and canting fanatics, it cannot be a subject of surprise, though it certainly must of regret, that he sometimes, toward the close of his life, gave into the too frequent indulgence of drinking, neglected his appearance, and retired, mortified and disgusted, from an ill judging, unkind, unjust world, into coarse obscurity, and the association of characters in inferior life. (10–11)

In passages such as this one Rickman transforms Paine into the tragic victim of a sentimental novel. Cheetham, by contrast, becomes the malicious villain who conspires to ruin the neglected and misunderstood hero of the age. Rickman also repeats the claim of ingratitude that Paine had expressed publicly on a number of occasions when he was struggling to secure a monetary reward for his services to the colonies during the Revolution, and repeated in the years after his incarceration in France. The suggestion that Paine's detractors were responsible for the deterioration of his character is probably Rickman's most effective strategy. Rickman, however, never attempts to explain why Paine's contributions failed to earn him the respect and admiration he deserved.

Although he was willing to concede some of his hero's personal mistakes, Rickman vigorously defends Paine's abilities as a writer. He goes

on at great length about Paine's skills, emphasizing both the content and
the style of Paine's works:

It has been a fashion among the enemies of Mr. Paine, when unable to cope with
his arguments, to attack his style, which they charge with inaccuracy and want
of elegance; and some even of those most friendly to his principles, have joined
in this captious criticism. It had not, perhaps, all the meretricious ornaments
and studied graces that glitter in the pages of Burke, which would have been so
many obscurities in the eyes of that part of the community for whose perusal
his writings were principally intended, but it is singularly nervous and pointed;
his arguments are always forcibly stated, nor does a languid line ever weary
the attention of the reader. It is true, he never studied variety of phrase at the
expence of perspicuity. His object was to enlighten, not to dazzle; and often, for
the sake of more forcibly impressing an idea on the mind of the reader, he had
made use of verbal repetitions which to a fastidious ear may perhaps sound unmu-
sical. But although, in the opinion of some, his pages may be deficient in elegance,
few will deny that they are copious in matter; and, if they sometimes fail to tickle
the ear, they will never fail to fill the mind. (31–32)

In an unusually attentive reading of Paine's style, Rickman neatly captures the essence of Paine's prose. He carefully dissects the logic of Paine's
approach to political writing and subtly includes several barbs aimed at
Paine's elitist critics. Rickman is one of the few people who understood
that Paine's style was a crucial part of his argument. The short sentences
and unadorned language are not merely accidental or peripheral aspects
of Paine's prose, they are deliberate features of a political language aimed
at a wide readership.

If Rickman was attempting to rescue the reputation of a friend, W. T.
Sherwin's aim was to defend an author whom he admired and whose
works he had recently published. Like Rickman, Sherwin, who two years
earlier had published the first new edition of Paine in thirty years, certainly had a vested interest in his subject. He makes no bones about the
fact that his primary goal is to recover Paine as a heroic historical figure:
"The principal motive which has induced me to undertake the Life of Mr.
PAINE, is the injustice which has been heaped upon his memory by those
who knew nothing either of the man or his principles. It may safely be
affirmed, that there never existed a public character whose reputation has
been assailed with more illiberality, or whose motives have been misrepresented with more virulence" (Preface, iii). Unlike Rickman, however,
he does not expend energy on responding to the specific character-based
smears articulated by Paine's detractors. Instead, Sherwin constructs a
positive narrative detailing the vicissitudes of Paine's life, "A life," Sherwin
notes, "more chequered, more eventful, more alternately distinguished by

honours and misfortunes, was perhaps never recorded" (viii). If Rickman had given us a sentimental novel, Sherwin seems to promise an epic.

One of the first orders of business for Sherwin is to clarify the matter of Paine's religious beliefs, which he rightly perceived to have become a significant liability for Paine in the public's eyes. In the Preface he addresses the most sensational story about Paine, the deathbed scene: "It will be some consolation to the conscientious unbeliever to know that Mr. Paine's death-bed recantation, about which we have heard so much, is an invented story, like those that were told about Voltaire, D'Alembert, and others who have held similar opinions" (vii). In this curious passage, Sherwin might succeed in countering the accusations of hypocrisy against Paine, but he will not win over the many skeptics. Oddly, he limits the revelation's significance to a particular audience, the "conscientious unbeliever," who would probably already be admirers of Paine. On the other hand, the comparison to Voltaire and D'Alembert places Paine in select intellectual company as if to suggest a direct line of descent linking these philosophical thinkers of the eighteenth century. The overall effect of the passage is to present Paine as a less isolated figure, thus making him seem less transgressive.

Sherwin returns to the subject of Paine's attitude toward religion in the early part of the biography. Approaching the matter with the idea of winning over a wider audience, Sherwin attempts to distance Paine's religious ideas from his political agenda by emphasizing the notion that Paine's ideas about religion were formed at an early age:

> It does not seem, or at least it is not known, that, during his boyhood, he exhibited any peculiar signs of that genius which was afterwards to exalt him to the very pinnacle of political fame. But from a passage in the *Age of Reason*, it is evident, that however matured in judgment he might be before he became a politician, his first impressions on the subject of religion were made at a very early period of his life. (4)[12]

Paine's rejection of organized religion is thus transformed from a revolutionary political act of rebellion into a natural and instinctive intuition formed at an apolitical moment in his life. Although this interpretation might not have rendered Paine's ideas less offensive to certain readers,

[12] The passage cited by Sherwin is from the "Comparing Christianism with Pantheism" section of Part I of *The Age of Reason* where Paine refers briefly to his own early education and intellectual stirrings. In reference to religion Paine recalls that "From the time I was capable of conceiving an idea and acting upon it by reflection, I either doubted the truth of the Christian system or thought it to be a strange affair" (CW I, 497).

it fundamentally challenged Paine's critics' assertion that in *The Age of Reason* Paine was simply transplanting his ideas about politics onto religion. Although Sherwin's is a valiant effort, it could not succeed in the face of the multiple statements by Paine linking his political and religious aims.[13]

Religion is not the only early influence on Paine's character that Sherwin emphasizes. In fact, Sherwin's account of Paine's early life is one of the most interesting to appear in any biography of Paine. In some respects it is more insightful than those offered by Paine's most recent biographers, who have tended to focus on recovering the facts of Paine's youth. Given the paucity of information and the unreliable nature of most of the sources, including Paine's own brief accounts of his youth, this would seem an impossible task. Sherwin is more interested in drawing connections between Paine's early education and the later development of his social and political ideas. Sherwin would be the first of Paine's biographers to explore the important role that science played in his subject's early development.

Although Sherwin might have used Paine's natural scientific interests to explain his religious skepticism, he is mostly concerned with the role science played in forming Paine's general approach to problem solving:

Indeed, as he himself expresses it, the natural bent of his mind appears to have been to science, and though from his disadvantageous situation in life he necessarily met with many obstacles, it is evident from several of his productions, that he attained a great proficiency in mechanics, mathematics, and astronomy. It was from his being well-grounded in the principles of science, during the earlier part of his life, that he afterwards became such a powerful adept in reasoning; it was from the mathematical principles which had been engrafted on his mind while it was yet tender enough to receive the impressions of instruction, that he was subsequently enabled to write with such precision upon almost any subject, that he was enabled to reduce abstruseness to simplicity, to understand difficult subjects himself, and to render them intelligible to others. (12)

Where Rickman had ascribed Paine's style to his political aims, and Cheetham to the coarseness of Paine's character and mind, Sherwin identifies Paine's direct style with a particular genre of writing, scientific discourse. Sherwin's account, of course, doesn't contradict or in any way disprove Rickman's. On the contrary, it reinforces the notion that Paine's

---

[13] For example, in the opening section of *The Age of Reason* Paine writes that "Soon after I had published the pamphlet 'Common Sense' in America, I saw the exceeding probability that a revolution in the system of government would be followed by a revolution in the system of religion" (CW, II 465).

style rather than accidental was the natural result of a particular way of thinking. Through Sherwin's eyes, Paine emerges as a political scientist in the most literal sense for the point is not only to develop a science of politics, but also to present politics in a scientific language.

For Sherwin, as had been the case with Cheetham and Rickman, *Rights of Man* was the defining text of Paine's career. Each of them acknowledges the importance of *Common Sense*, but the long-term contribution and influence of *Rights of Man* in England made it, to them, the most significant of Paine's texts. Whether it horrified or thrilled them, all agreed that *Rights of Man* had exerted an extraordinary power in England. In Sherwin's account *Rights of Man* fundamentally transformed British political thought:

> Perhaps there never was a period in which the people of this country were less disposed to attend to the discussion of politics, than at the time Mr. Paine's pamphlet made its appearance: they had been so often amused, and so often deceived by men who pretended to advocate their rights, that they were disgusted with the subject, and the apostacy of Mr. Burke was a confirmation of their sentiments. But the principles contained in the *Rights of Man* opened an entirely new field of argument and inquiry, and the thinking part of the people began to view the right of political reform, not as a boon to be expected or desired from the government, but as a power which the nation alone had the authority to exercise. (105)

Paine's success, in Sherwin's account, was remarkable because, unlike in the American colonies where he had entered an already charged political atmosphere, in England he had to first arouse the interest of the public. His task, therefore, was twofold: First, he had to instill a sense of urgency and a desire for change in a complacent public; and, second, he had to persuade them of the worthiness of his plan of action. Sherwin suggests that Paine was successful because he not only completely shifted the terms of the discussion, but he introduced a new set of participants into the political arena.

At this point it becomes clear that Sherwin's biography is not just about recuperating a working-class hero, but also aims to participate in the continuation of the process that Paine had initiated nearly three decades earlier. Sherwin's investment in Paine's revolutionary rhetoric can be seen in his description of the political effects of *Rights of Man*:

> The probability of a revolution now became a subject of general discussion. The nation was divided into two numerous and powerful classes, the one consisting of the ignorant and the majority of the wealthy, arranged under the banners of civil and religious tyranny, and declaring their attachment to all that was superstitious in the church, and all that was despotic in the state, – while the other,

more numerous and less dependent, more enlightened though less opulent, being convinced that the government in its existing state was the cause of the greater part of the misery with which the country was afflicted, were determined to let slip no opportunity of shaking off the load of oppression. (113)

Parroting Paine's clever inversion of traditional political notions, Sherwin equates the masses with political independence whereas republican ideology held that only the wealthy were capable of independent thinking because they were free of the private interests that affected the daily lives of the general public. Moreover, playing on the social status of Paine's readership, Sherwin cleverly lumps the wealthy with the ignorant, a category presumably defined by their unfamiliarity with Paine's writings.

Thus, for Sherwin, as had been the case for Rickman, *Rights of Man* occupies the central place in the Paine canon. However, when it comes to *The Age of Reason*, Sherwin, like Rickman, essentially sidesteps the issue. Even Cheetham seems to find Paine's controversial discussion of religion a less sensational and incriminating subject than the lurid details of Paine's personal habits. To John S. Harford, though, *The Age of Reason* seems to be precisely the issue. Indeed, he makes it clear that the reason he even bothered to write a biography of Paine is due to the continuing popularity of *Age of Reason*:

The cheap form in which the impious Carlile, subsequently to his conviction, has again printed the Age of Reason in the body of his trial, in outrageous defiance of public feeling, and the industry with which it has been circulated; united to the newspaper reports of the proceedings at the prosecution, have given, of late, an unusual currency to the name and the opinions of Paine. The Radical Reformers are also grown bold enough to acknowledge him as their Apostle and their Idol. It therefore becomes a duty to expose the wickedness of this man's principles, and the corresponding enormity of his life. (v–vi)

Upon closer inspection, however, it becomes clear that *Age of Reason* is not what bothers Harford, so much as Paine's influence upon a new generation of radicals. He properly perceives Paine's exposition of deism as only one part of a larger political agenda. Following in the tradition of Cheetham, then, Harford writes a biography to discredit Paine.

Although he admits to borrowing a great deal of information from Cheetham and Cobbett, stylistically Harford's text most closely resembles Rickman's. Just as Rickman had done in his account, Harford dispenses with the details of Paine's life to dwell instead on particular aspects of his character. For example, he reduces Paine's life in England to two central events: Paine's dismissal from the excise corps "under a charge of fraud and dishonesty," which leads him to determine that Paine's character is that of a "rogue" (1); and, Paine's relationship to his wives, the first of whom died in childbirth and the second of whom he treated "with such neglect and unkindness, that her life had been rendered truly miserable" (2). He concludes the page and a half dedicated to Paine's early life: "In this manner commenced the career of our pretended Reformer. His public character was blackened by dishonesty, his private conduct was marked by cruelty and dishonesty" (2).

In spite of passages like these Harford's disdain for Paine was not so much personal, as it had been for Cheetham, as the product of his antipathy for radical reform. Instead of dwelling on the lurid details of Paine's life, Harford deals with them in a perfunctory matter, as if he feels obligated to report them but takes no pleasure in their dissemination. The first indications that Harford may not be as eager as Cheetham to perpetuate various calumnies about Paine can be seen in his reflection on the nature of biography and the relationship of the writer to his subject in the Preface:

It has been observed, that to write Biography well the author should be proud of his hero. If the success of the present writer is to be measured by his admiration, he fears that his book will meet with a very discouraging reception. Certainly nothing would have tempted him to touch upon the history of a man whose very name is proverbial for infamy, had he not, in common with the great body of his countrymen, witnessed, with pain and wonder, the imprudent attempts lately made, in various ways, to confront the system of Paine with that of Christianity; in other words, to oppose the kingdom of darkness, sin and contention, to that of light, purity and love. (v)

For Harford this project isn't simply a matter of attacking Paine's character, it is part of a more important cause. Unlike Cheetham, therefore, Harford attempts to dismiss Paine's works by condemning their effects.

Nowhere is this strategy more evident than in his long account of the French Revolution, which occupies a greater portion of the text than the narration of Paine's life. Paine only appears very briefly in Harford's narrative of the French Revolution. Harford is much more interested in depicting the French Revolution as a horrible mistake that should have been avoided. Of course, the true concern for Harford is not the French Revolution either, but the resurgence of radicalism in 1819 and their leveling tendencies:

The whole system of 1793, and that of 1819, are equally founded on Thomas Paine's doctrine of the Rights of Man: that monstrous doctrine, the object of which is to seduce the weak and the ignorant, to unite with the violent and the wicked, in the object of overturning all religion, government, law, property, security, order, and of rendering, by these means, our happy country a naked waste, which the demons of anarchy, carnage, and confusion, may claim as their own.... But not only in their general system of proceeding, but in almost every minute particular, the Radicals of 1819 are copyists of the Revolutionists of 1793. (18)

In this case, Paine is found guilty by association as a general participant in reform. Paine's greatest sin, to Harford, appears to be that he became the symbol of democratic reform. In other words, it is no longer a question of who Paine was, what he did, or wrote, but of what he came to represent.

RECOVERING PAINE'S REPUTATION IN THE UNITED STATES

Relegated to a minor role in the Revolution in the principal biographies of the nineteenth century and misremembered mainly as an atheist, Paine would practically disappear from the American intellectual landscape until the end of the century. While Paine became the center of controversy in England during the 1820s, with two more short biographies published in 1821 and 1824, he essentially remained invisible in the United States until the last decade of the nineteenth century when a resurgence of interest in U.S. history led to renewed interest in the Revolution. As Michael Kammen has recently argued, after about a hundred years of resistance toward tradition and history "a hunger for tradition developed in Victorian America" (99). Whereas Antebellum Americans generally viewed interest in tradition and the past with suspicion, preferring to orient themselves toward the present and future, Postbellum Americans sought to find a common past upon which to rebuild the nation. Kammen suggests, in fact, that the Civil War taught Americans to see the value of commemorating the past (Chapter 4). More specifically, in the wake of the Centennial in 1876 the Revolution became a subject of particular interest. This last quarter of the nineteenth century would see the formation of a whole host of groups dedicated to preserving the memory of the Revolution including The Sons of the Revolution, the D.A.R., and the Colonial Dames of America (Kammen, 218).

In this context Paine would be championed by Moncure Daniel Conway, the distinguished abolitionist, reformer, and biographer, who published his comprehensive account of Paine's life in 1891.[14] With his two-volume *The Life of Thomas Paine, With a History of his Literary, Political*

---

[14] For an account of Conway's interesting life, see John d'Entremont, *Southern Emancipator: Moncure Conway, The American Years, 1832–1865*.

and Religious Career in America, France, and England, Conway would
inaugurate a new phase in the scholarship on Paine. Conway is the first
writer to approach Paine from a scholarly perspective. Although his excessive admiration, bordering on hero-worship, of Paine would seem to
place his text in the tradition of partisan writers that had begun with
Chalmers, unlike earlier biographers of Paine, Conway is interested in his
subject for historical reasons.[15]

Conway sets out to correct the historical record on Paine. He accurately describes Paine's fate in the historiography: "The meager references
to Paine by other than controversial writers are perfunctory; by most historians he is either wronged or ignored" (xviii). If prior biographers had
been obsessed with Paine the man, Conway attempts to recover Paine
the historical actor. Paine here is not put in the service of a particular
ideology or cause; if anything he is the cause. In this respect, Conway
is the intellectual heir to Rickman, who wrote not to support or con-
demn democracy, reform or deism, but to defend his dear friend. As we
have seen, however, Rickman's biography was openly partisan and controversial. Conway carefully avoids casting his work as a response to any
one particular rendition of Paine. As a consequence, Conway writes a
biography that is almost entirely devoid of speculation about Paine's character. Instead, he provides us with a very detailed account of the events
of Paine's life in what might have best been called the life and times of
Thomas Paine.

In place of a discussion of Paine's personal psychology, character, or
personality we are provided with vignettes illustrating the general atmosphere of the places Paine visited or lived. Often these vignettes are provided courtesy of a historian who has studied someone who knew Paine
or who lived in the same town as Paine. For example, we are provided
with a detailed description of Paine's birthplace by a historian who had
written a biography of the owner of the local newspaper (7–8), and later
we are treated to an account of the impression Paine made among the
iron workers in Rotherham by a professor who had visited the town and
inquired about Paine's brief residence there (244–245). By adding texture
to an otherwise dry narrative meticulously tracing Paine's life, these vignettes bring warmth to the biography, softening its empirical edge with
some emotional depth. This effect is particularly evident in Conway's

---

[15] This is not to suggest that Conway's interest in Paine wasn't motivated by political
considerations, but that those considerations do not become the thematic center of his
analysis.

description of Lewes, Sussex, one of the towns where Paine worked as an excise officer:

Not very unlike the old Norfolk borough in which Paine was born was Lewes, and with even literally an Ouse flowing through it. Here also marched the 'Heathen Men,' who have left only the legend of a wounded son of Harold nursed into health by a Christian maiden. The ruined castle commands a grander landscape than the height of Thetford, and much the same historic views. Seven centuries before Paine opened his office in Lewes came Harold's son, possibly to take charge of the excise as established by Edward the Confessor, just deceased. (21)

In passages such as this one, Conway seems to have displaced the discussion of Paine's character onto the landscape. Instead of going on about Paine's mannerisms or moral character, Conway brings to life the places Paine inhabited. After reading his biography, Conway's readers may not feel as though they have gotten to know Paine the man, although they have certainly been presented with an exhaustive account of his actions and have acquired a good sense of the world Paine inhabited.

This is not to say that Conway simply ignores the attacks on Paine. He addresses each of the major accusations, especially the questions about his drinking, but they do not structure his text the way they did Rickman's. Instead, this is a strictly chronological narrative that follows Paine from cradle to grave. A chapter on Paine's "Personal Traits" precedes the account of Paine's death, but by this point in the story Paine's life as a writer and political figure has ended. In "Personal Traits" Conway discredits Chalmers and Cheetham, upon whose depictions most of the subsequent malicious rumors about Paine were based. The primary charges he seeks to contradict are the ones alleging a lack of civility or manners in Paine, the supposed drunkenness, and the insinuations of "sexual immorality." To disprove these allegations, Conway both dissects Chalmers and Cheetham's sources and provides testimony about Paine's behavior from friends and acquaintances of Paine's. But the defense of Paine's personal habits remains secondary to the larger injustice Conway is attempting to correct – neglect. In Conway's words: "The educated ignorance concerning Paine is astounding" (xiv).

In his effort to correct the historical record and return Paine to his place as one of the crucial players in the American Enlightenment, Conway goes overboard and constructs Paine as a figure of mythological proportions. In this myth Paine embodies all of the best qualities of the American Revolution and as such he emerges as the prime mover behind every major event in the Revolution. Not only do his writings, from *Common Sense* and *The Crisis*, to his more obscure "Letters to Rhode Island," play a crucial role in insuring the success of the Revolution, but his diplomatic efforts also secure the American cause. Conway's account of Paine's contributions to the French Revolution is not quite as inflated, but through it all Paine remains the exemplum of Enlightenment reasonableness and morality. Conway, of course, could not hope single-handedly to redeem Paine's reputation and return him to the position of respect that he deserves, but he did herald a change in the treatment of Paine, particularly in terms of Paine's contributions to the American cause. He would also make it difficult for detractors to perpetuate the rumors about Paine's drinking.

POLITICAL WRITING AND AMERICAN LITERARY HISTORY

Although a variety of factors, including the early uncontroverted attacks on his character and the vicissitudes of historical recollection in the nineteenth century, contributed to Paine's marginalization in American literary and political history, the most important reason for his marginality was his status as a political writer. Without an institutional imprimatur to sanction his opinions, Paine would be taken less seriously by historians. While Franklin and Jefferson were both the victims of blistering *ad hominem* attacks by the opposition press at various times in their careers, their official roles in the Revolution as members of the Continental Congress, for example, secured their places in the historiography. Paine, however, remained nothing more and nothing less than a writer. Indeed, many of the accusations made by Paine's detractors about his private behavior were ones that were stereotypical of authors: excessive drinking, sexual licentiousness, and a lack of manners. Paine thus was overidentified as a writer and came to embody all the negative attitudes and popular myths about writers. Ironically, then, I would suggest that Paine has been victimized in literary and political history by the very thing that made him so successful in the late eighteenth century: his unbending commitment to popular political writing as a career in itself and not just a secondary activity or an instrument to promote a career in public politics. Evidently political writers have to engage in other types of public activities to obtain historical legitimacy.

Literary scholars, if anything, have paid even less attention than historians have to Paine and his ilk. Until quite recently the Revolutionary and Early National periods were virtually ignored in American literary history. Typically, the narrative would skip from the Puritans to Emerson and the American Renaissance. Over the last two decades or so scholars have been attempting to recover and reintegrate the literature of the Early Republic, but they have focused most intensively on either personal narrative or belles lettres. Although many literary scholars and cultural historians working in the last two decades have devoted significant attention to nonbelletristic writing – much more, arguably, than their colleagues studying nineteenth-century American literature and culture – more often than not these writings are studied for the light they shed on the novels or personal narratives of the era, the texts that form the principal object of their studies. Given the tendency to read the early novels and autobiographical writings of the time as allegories for democracy or the limits of democracy and freedom in the new nation, the subordination of the political and polemical writings to the fiction of the time seems especially ironic. Even if we exclude Paine's contributions, no form of writing was published more frequently or read as widely at the time as political polemics. Whether it was John Dickinson's *The Letters of an American Farmer*, Paine's *Common Sense*, or *The Federalist Papers*, political writing was the most popular form of American literature of the time. Moreover, the revolutionary and early national period produced probably the most important such writings in U.S. history.

Among the countless polemical pamphlets and works of political philosophy written in the last three decades of the eighteenth century Paine's, as I hope the earlier chapters of this study have shown, were exceptional in language, style, and persuasiveness. Paine's fate illustrates how we have continued to produce a version of the Revolution that dichotomizes literature and politics by separating writing into modern categories that do not adequately represent the complexity of eighteenth-century culture. Perhaps it is time we applied the same historicism that we apply to our textual analyses to our definition of literature. Expanding our parameters for what constitutes literature to make them better accommodate the sense it had in the eighteenth century will allow for a richer understanding of both the nature of writing in Early America and its relationship to political culture. Restoring Paine to his central role in U.S. political and literary history, in this sense, is just the first step toward recovering a whole body of American literature that has been understudied and underappreciated.

Epilogue

Paine and Nineteenth-Century American Literary History

> His Paine story amounted to a resurrection of Paine out of the horrible calumnies, infamies, under which orthodox hatred had buried him.
>
> Walt Whitman, 1789

In one of the most curious cameo roles in early American literature, Royall Tyler includes an encounter with Thomas Paine in his 1797 novel, *The Algerine Captive*. Updike Underhill, the hero of Tyler's bizarre but fascinating text, first meets Benjamin Franklin and then Thomas Paine during his travels in London. Given his strong Federalist politics, Tyler's representation of Paine is, not surprisingly, unflattering. However, Paine's inclusion reflects the extent to which he was still a voice to be reckoned with. Indeed, in the 1790s Paine was one of the most recognizable characters in the West, well known in the United States, Great Britain, and France. At the height of his fame in the last decade of the eighteenth century, Paine was frequently satirized by James Gillray and other cartoonists of the age for whom he served as a symbol of the twin evils of republican ideology and rational religion. Tyler disdains almost everything about Paine. When Underhill first meets Paine he is introduced as "the most singular curiosity, I saw in London," who is the author of several texts "whose tendency is to overturn ancient opinions of government and religion" (87). The strategy of Tyler's account of Paine, already evident in these passages, is to marvel at Paine's celebrity and, at the same time, wonder about its legitimacy. Paine is interesting to Underhill not only because he is famous, but also because he has managed to become famous in spite of his feeble intellect and the speciousness of his arguments.

Rather than simply insult Paine or engage in the kinds of petty personal attacks that so many of Paine's opponents had used, Tyler focuses on Paine's social interactions to suggest that his reasoning does not work when he is confronted by truly intelligent opponents. In the first chapter depicting Paine, Underhill observes that although normally reserved, "when a man of sense and elocution was present, and the company numerous, [Paine] delighted in advancing the most unaccountable, and often the most whimsical, paradoxes; which he defended in his own plausible manner" (88). Tyler subtly plays on the idea that there is no content to Paine's ideas, that he is all performance. Tyler suggests that Paine is more of a showman than an intellectual. This performative aspect is enhanced by the closing movement of the paragraph where Tyler comments: "If encouraged by success, or the applause of the company, his countenance was animated, with an expression of feature... but if interrupted by extraneous observation, by the inattention of his auditory, or in an irritable moment, even by the accidental fall of the poker, he would retire into himself, and no persuasions could induce him to proceed upon the most favourite topic" (88). So, instead of accusing Paine of being a drunk or a libertine, Tyler depicts him as a political mountebank who creates the illusion of sophistication but is incapable of genuine intellectual conversation. In the next chapter, he reproduces, almost in the mode of Bosworth's famous account of Johnson's meeting with Wilkes, a conversation between Paine and his political opponent Peter Pindar that reiterates the idea that Paine's argumentative skills are inadequate when challenged by a true intellectual. In this scene Pindar outwits the confusing and confused Paine in a debate over democracy and majority rule. The point of the chapter, in which Paine is made to argue that the minority should always rule, is not so much the substance of the debate, but the assertion of Pindar's rhetorical superiority to Paine. Paine, Tyler implies, is popular with the masses because they mistake his "paradoxes" for genius.

Although Tyler presents Paine only to dismiss him, in 1797 Paine was still perceived as a major political and literary figure whose influence needed to be contained. To Tyler, who like many of his Federalist compatriots was skeptical of popular democracy, Paine's appeal among common people and his potential ability to mobilize them politically was of great concern. The next fifty years in American literary history would prove that Tyler's fears were unfounded. Simply put, Thomas Paine virtually disappeared from the American literary landscape for much of the nineteenth century. The reasons for Paine's descent into obscurity are various. As I have suggested in this book, his style of personalizing political debates and his aggressive advocacy of deism had made him so controversial a figure in American culture that few people, even many who were sympathetic to his views, wanted their ideas or work associated with him. Tyler draws our attention to yet another factor that would contribute to Paine's marginalization: In the nineteenth century Paine's advocacy of a radically democratic political position would become a liability for him among the emergent class of cultural and political elites who rightly perceived his ideas as a threat to their attempts to consolidate power.

As the nation moved toward an increasingly conservative account of the Revolution, Paine became more and more marginal.[1] With this shift, Paine came to be seen as the voice of an extreme position rather than of the main thrust of the Revolution. To draw on Alfred Young's account of the relationship between commoners and elites in this transformative event, "The American Revolution was not a plebian revolution, but there was a powerful plebian current within it" (206). Paine spoke powerfully for that current, even embodied it at times. While he was widely read, if not always admired, by popular religious leaders and an emergent urban laboring class, he would be ignored by most of the major literary figures in the nineteenth century. To a certain extent this oversight was the product of shifting understandings of literature. By the middle of the nineteenth century a critical elite had established standards of literary taste that aligned the literary with belles lettres, and excluded forms such as political polemic. But we should not overlook the extent to which Paine's association with the cause of the common people and laboring classes, was also problematic for a literary marketplace that was increasingly designed to attract middle-class readers. Consequently, it seems only fitting that the two major nineteenth-century American writers who embraced Paine were Walt Whitman and Herman Melville, both of whom were not only outsiders to the literary establishment but were also profoundly concerned about the state of American democracy and were especially interested in the plight of the American laboring classes.[2]

Melville and Whitman both championed Paine, whom they saw as representative of an important lost dimension of the culture and ideas of

---

[1] On the gradual containment (or taming as he calls it) of the Revolution's more radical energies, see Alfred Young, *The Shoemaker and the Tea Party*, esp. 108–120.

[2] It is interesting in this context to consider that both Melville and Whitman were from New York and were never really accepted in Boston, the center of American publishing in the nineteenth century. Of the major nineteenth-century American writers they are also the most identified with urban writing. All of these factors make it seem all the more appropriate that they both looked to Paine as an important figure in American culture.

the late eighteenth century. He provided them with access to a different narrative of American origins, one that could be more inclusive and participatory but also one through which they could articulate a critique of what the United States had become by the second half of the nineteenth century. Never willing to go quietly into the night during his lifetime, Paine's ideas would show the same resilience as their author had shown during his relentless career as an advocate of democratic ideals. After a brief discussion of Whitman's admiration for Paine, in this epilogue I focus my analysis on the most obviously allegorical aspect of *Billy Budd*: its meditation on the nature of revolution. Oddly, although this aspect of the text is often acknowledged or registered by critics, it has not been explored in any depth (perhaps because of its very obviousness).[3] How does Melville cast the problem of revolution? What part does Paine play in Melville's understanding of what is at stake in a revolution? More specifically, what does the novella suggest about Melville's view of the American instance? These are important questions that reveal Melville returning to the abiding concerns with the nature of authority and its limits that preoccupy him in so much of his imaginative production. More importantly for my purposes, answering these questions will help us understand how Paine was recovered as an important cultural icon, political thinker, and writer at the end of the nineteenth century.

WHITMAN AND PAINE'S POPULAR IMAGE

In an 1877 address in Philadelphia, which he included in *Specimen Days*, Whitman comments on Paine's immeasurable service to the nation:

I dare not say how much of what our Union is owning and enjoying to-day – its independence – its ardent belief in, and substantial practice of, radical human rights – and the severance of its government from all ecclesiastical and superstitious dominion – I dare not say how much of all this is owing to Thomas Paine, but I am inclined to think a good portion of it decidedly is. (822)

Although somewhat vague, Whitman proposes a very different vision of Paine's role in American history. He emphasizes not only Paine's role in securing the colonies' independence, but also the extent to which his ideas about government, democracy, and human rights exerted a powerful influence on the early shaping of the nation. This is a Paine who is not

---

[3] For example, in a recent article one critic identifies *Billy Budd* as "his parable of revolution" (Berthold, 427), but he never explores how that parable operates specifically in the text.

limited to the role of pamphleteer or propagandist but who is credited with a crucial role in the creation of the nation and its values.[4]

In his conversations with Horace Traubel twelve years later, Whitman gives the impression that he not only admired Paine's political and cultural work, but that he intensely identified with him. When Traubel, a young socialist who had been attracted to Whitman's poetic descriptions of the laboring classes, suggests to Whitman that he should write about Paine, he replies passionately: "I don't think there's anybody living – anybody at all – (I don't think there ever was anybody, living or dead) – more able than I am to depict, to picture, Paine, in the right way" (23).[5] Whitman's fascination with Paine transcends an academic or cultural interest here and becomes deeply personal. He understood what had happened to Paine historically and resented it deeply:

Paine was old, alone, poor: its that, its what accrues from that, that his slanderers have made the most of: anything lower, meaner, more contemptible, I cannot imagine: to take an aged man – a man tired to death after a complicated life of toil, struggle, anxiety – weak, dragged down, at death's door: poor: with perhaps habits that might come with such distress: then to pull him into the mud, distort everything he does and says: oh! its infamous.... you start a prejudice against a man: it lasts, lasts: it seems impossible to break it down. (23–24)

Although later in the same conversation he attributes Paine's fate to his religious views, the emphasis on his poverty in these lines suggests the degree to which Whitman sensed that class played a crucial role in Paine's alienation from mainstream American culture. On several occasions in their conversations about Paine, Whitman attributes Paine's demise in the public eye to attacks leveled against him by elites who were threatened by Paine's more democratic vision of government and religion. To Whitman, Paine almost becomes a martyr who is victimized for his working-class origins and his advocacy of a participatory democracy that would more fully enfranchise ordinary citizens. In spite of his profound admiration for Paine, Whitman never published anything about or relating to Paine other than his short address in *Specimen Days*, nor did he invoke Paine in his major political essay *Democratic Vistas*. Instead, Paine remained a private fascination of his to be shared with sympathetic reformers like Traubel.

---

[4] In the same speech Whitman also attempts to rescue Paine's image by offering a rebuttal to the claims about Paine's drinking, manners, and personal habits. Whitman later observed to Moncure Conway, who had gone to interview him about the subject of his biography, that Paine was "doubly damn lied about" (423).

[5] David S. Reynolds provides a brief account of Traubel's politics and his relationship to Whitman in *Walt Whitman's America*. See especially, 556–558.

Melville, however, would invoke Paine's name to significant effect in his last unpublished text, *Billy Budd*.

BILLY BUDD AND THE INTERPRETATION OF THE REVOLUTION

Early in *Billy Budd* Melville offers an apparently marginal account of Billy's prior experience as a sailor in the merchant marine in which he invokes the famous dispute between Paine and Edmund Burke that resulted in the publication of Paine's political masterpiece, *Rights of Man*. Significantly, the reference to the Burke-Paine controversy appears when the narrator describes the moment Billy leaves his merchant marine ship to become a crew member on the naval vessel:

The transfer from chest to bag was made. And, after seeing his man into the cutter and then following him down, the lieutenant pushed off from the *Rights-of-Man*. That was the merchant ship's name, though by her master and crew abbreviated in sailor fashion into the *Rights*. The hardheaded Dundee owner was a staunch admirer of Thomas Paine, whose book in rejoinder to Burke's arraignment of the French Revolution had then been published for some time and had gone everywhere. In christening his vessel after the title of Paine's volume the man of Dundee was something like his contemporary shipowner, Stephen Girard, of Philadelphia, whose sympathies, alike with his native land and its liberal philosophers, he evinced by naming his ships after Voltaire, Diderot, and so forth. (48)

At the moment of Billy's impressment, a moment when his individual rights are superceded by the state's authority, Melville has placed a provocative reference to the eighteenth century's most widely read public debate over the role of government and the rights of individuals. Curiously, scholars have generally overlooked this passage or made very little of it.[6] Melville's invocation of Paine, however, illustrates the degree to

---

[6] The one significant exception is Ray B. Browne's "Billy Budd: Gospel of Democracy" where Browne places great emphasis on the references to Paine and Burke in the novella. Otherwise, taking a few of the more influential recent readings of the text as examples, the allusion to Paine, Burke, and the French Revolution has become virtually invisible in the text. In "Melville's Fist" Barbara Johnson sees the French Revolution as an important context for Vere's judgment of Billy and she briefly refers to Paine, but only for an analysis of the idea of "Nature" in the novella and not for his take on the Revolution. Neither Eve Kosofsky Sedgwick in *The Epistemology of the Closet*, Michael Paul Rogin in *Subversive Genealogy*, nor Nancy Ruttenburg in *Democratic Personality* attends to the invocation of the French Revolution at all. These authors are generally interested in other aspects of the novella – be they questions of Melville's representations of male sexuality, the way psychohistory shapes the narrative, or the problem of democratic authorship in America – so that the references to the Revolution become less important to their analyses.

which Paine had become synonymous with the more radically democratic possibilities of the late eighteenth century.

Building on Barbara Johnson's interpretation of the text as an allegory for reading, I argue that a careful reading of this passage and its bearing on the text suggests that in *Billy Budd* Melville explores the political choices implicit in the act of reading. Johnson emphasizes Vere's sophistication as a reader and his exercise of power through reading, manifested in the act of judgment, but Melville also draws a subtle, but clear, correspondence between Vere's interpretive strategies and the Burkean reading of the French Revolution. Here, the allusion to the *Rights of Man* obtains new significance. It establishes the context of debates over the nature of revolution by bringing the Paine-Burke controversy to the fore. In this context, Paine becomes the sign for a different interpretation of revolution, which, in turn, poses an alternative to Vere's Burkean approach to reading and, more generally, to the notions of judgment and justice that he deploys.

The passage establishes two competing political visions, Painite radicalism and Burkean conservatism, which provide a context for understanding Vere's approach to the situation, his internal conflict, and the larger philosophical implications of Billy's trial and execution. Melville also sets up several other key terms in this account of Billy's impressment. First, he invokes the French Revolution, and perhaps more to the point, the contentious public debate over the meaning and legitimacy of the Revolution. Second, he connects the French Revolution to the United States through the figure of Stephen Girard, a significant actor in the American Revolution and in early national Philadelphia politics. Finally, through these various figures he sets up the contest between commercial and military or national political goals. Girard, of course, stands in contrast to the Dundee owner in that he was able to bring the two together whereas the Dundee owner is finding that the military aspirations of his nation are interfering with his business interests.

The action of the novella really begins at this moment when Billy is asked to make the transition from a peaceful commercial ship to a naval vessel whose very name captures its purpose: the *Bellipotent*. Curiously, the ship's name could also be applied to the power that Billy's beauty exercises over his peers. On the *Rights* Billy had had a naturally pacifying effect on the crew: "Before I shipped that young fellow, my forecastle was a rat pit of quarrels. It was black times, I tell you, aboard the *Rights* here. I was worried to that degree my pipe had no comfort for me. But Billy came; and it was like a Catholic priest striking peace in an Irish shindy.

Not that he preached to them or said or did anything in particular; but a virtue went out of him, sugaring the sour ones" (46–47). Billy's impact on the crew is palpable and natural. His virtue readily wins the consent of the men who are incapable of opposing him. Billy, thus, constitutes an ideal image of the representative man. His authority, like the ideal of democratic governance, is secured by the consent of the people without force: Their consent is almost involuntarily given and yet they are in no way coerced.[7]

After introducing Billy and setting up the context for his impressment, Melville proceeds immediately to feminize him. Because his beauty is potent, Billy is recast in a feminine role: "As the Handsome Sailor, Billy Budd's position aboard the seventy-four was something analogous to that of a rustic beauty transplanted from the provinces and brought into competition with highborn dames of the court" (50–51). Billy's attractiveness makes him the object of jealousy for the other men of similar stature and makes him appealing to his superiors. In the homosocial world of the military ship, he is feminized by the power dynamics on the ship. Yet, this position reminds us of the connections of democracy to effeminacy in late eighteenth- and early nineteenth-century literature and politics. As a number of recent scholars have reminded us, it was no accident that the sentimental novel became so popular during the revolutionary era in the United States. The ideology of sympathy was what made democracy a viable political system in late eighteenth-century America. In Elizabeth Barnes's words, "For men to be *truly* American, that is, truly sympathetic, they must learn to be more like women: more suggestible, more seducible, more impressionable readers of both literature and human relations" (xi). Billy has mastered this transformation to the point where he can even sympathize with the man who condemns him to death.

Just as Billy sympathizes with Vere, Vere, in turn sympathizes with Billy, although not enough to spare his life. From the beginning Vere is described as someone who, while capable of sympathy, is also committed to the notion of a disinterested judgment. We can see this vividly in the

---

[7] I am borrowing from Jay Fliegelman's description, in *Declaring Independence*, of the shift in modes of authority during the American Revolutionary period: "No longer conceived of as the stigmatized power to coerce, political authority became redefined in a republican setting as the ability to secure consent, 'to command,' in Jefferson's phrase describing the Declaration, not individuals as subordinates, but 'their assent'" (35–36).

early account of his approach to politics where Vere is described as a classic Burkean conservative:

His settled convictions were as a dike against those invading waters of novel opinion social, political, and otherwise, which carried away as in a torrent no few minds in those days, minds by nature not inferior to his own. While other members of that aristocracy to which by birth he belonged were incensed at the innovators mainly because their theories were inimical to the privileged classes, Captain Vere disinterestedly opposed them not alone because they seemed to him insusceptible of embodiment in lasting institutions, but at war with the peace of the world and the true welfare of mankind. (62–63)

From this description it is clear that Vere is no ordinary conservative; he is a politically sophisticated and engaged conservative thinker, even philosopher. This passage bears striking similarities to Edmund Burke's reasoning for opposing the French Revolution. Burke, for example, expresses a similar discomfort with novelty throughout his text, at one point, dismissing all new thought: "A spirit of innovation is generally the result of a selfish temper and confined views" (29). Burke sets out in his *Reflections* to defend the institutions of the British Parliamentary Monarchy, which he argues can be modified (as it had been in 1688) to correct for its shortcomings without the need for revolution. By way of example, Burke comments on the nature of previous "revolutions" in England: "The two principles of conservation and correction operated strongly at the two critical periods of the Restoration and Revolution, when England found itself without a king. At both those periods the nation had lost the bond of union in their ancient edifice; they did not, however, dissolve the whole fabric. On the contrary, in both cases they regenerated the deficient part of the old constitution through the parts which were not impaired" (19). Thus, in essence, they preserved the institution by making important adjustments. Vere shares Burke's faith in institutions as the key structure ordering social and political relations for the good of the people.

Vere's philosophical conservatism is evident at several crucial moments in Billy's trial. The most telling instance comes toward the end of the proceedings when the sailing master, who is a member of the drumhead court, asks whether they might not "convict yet mitigate the penalty" (112). In his response, Vere invokes a traditional conservative view of class differences and their impact on power relations:

"Gentlemen, were that clearly lawful for us under the circumstances, consider the consequences of such clemency. The people" (meaning the ship's company) "have native sense; most of them are familiar with our naval usage and tradition; and how would they take it? Even could you explain to them – which our official position forbids – they, long molded by arbitrary discipline, have not that kind of **intelligent responsiveness** that might qualify them to comprehend and discriminate. No, to the people the foretopman's deed, however it be worded in the announcement, will be plain homicide committed in a flagrant act of mutiny." (112, bold mine)

Melville opens the passage with the key class identifier associated with Vere's notion of justice and governance: gentleman. Vere's substitution of "the people" for the crew calls attention to the analogy he envisions between the ordered ranks aboard the ship and the structure of civil society. His argument is predicated entirely on the need for the aristocracy, in this case constituted by the officers on the ship, to patronize and rule over an unsophisticated and ill-equipped "people." The people, Vere suggests in a passage that echoes the antidemocratic rhetoric of the late eighteenth century, are naturally inferior in intelligence and have not benefited from the education that makes it necessary for the aristocracy to rule them and thus curb their baser instincts. Vere's very term for the people's intellectual capacity, "native sense," contrasts sharply with the more democratic "common sense." The effect of the term native here is to imply that the people's sense amounts to no more than what they are born with. Common sense, on the other hand, generally implies a kind of intelligence derived in part from experience. More to the point, by using native sense as the term to describe the intellectual capacities of ordinary people, Vere implies that elites such as himself posses a different and higher form of (cultured?) intelligence.

Vere's speech also conceals the artificiality of the way the relationship between elites and commoners has been structured. He attributes the crew's lack of sophistication to the fact that they have been "long molded by arbitrary discipline," but, by using a passive construction he absolves himself of any responsibility for creating this condition in the people as a dispenser of arbitrary discipline. In a revealing tautology, the third sentence of the quotation simultaneously reports the need for arbitrary discipline (our official position forbids us from offering explanations) and then justifies it on the basis of its effect on the crew (they are not capable of understanding because they have been subject to arbitrary discipline for so long). Vere has disconnected the process from the product in order to render the product, in this case the uncomprehending people, a static or essentialized entity. Vere offers no alternative or vision of change. On the contrary, instead of considering how the navy's policies have shaped the crew in particular ways, Vere takes the policies at face value and objectifies the crew, which, in turn, makes it necessary for him to continue to reproduce the same behavior both in himself and in them. Hence, cause and effect relations have been vitiated and history itself has vanished in the relationship between the elites and the commoners. This was precisely Paine's quarrel with Burke.

Upon closer examination, however, it becomes evident that the people are lacking not simply in intellect, but in what Vere calls "intelligent responsiveness." Vere's intelligent responsiveness seems to serve as a more refined version of Adam Smith's sympathy. In Smith everyone is capable of sympathy: "The greatest ruffian, the most hardened violator of the laws of society, is not altogether without it" (*Theory*, 9). Here, as in his strategic reference to native rather than common sense, Vere employs a term that sets him apart from the people and makes him the possessor of a more sophisticated version of the same basic quality (native versus common sense; sympathy versus intelligent responsiveness). Ironically, the reason the people lack sympathy is that they have been subject to "arbitrary discipline" for their entire lives/careers. If the people are being fashioned into unsympathetic simpletons, then perhaps the problem is not with them but with the social and political structure. Thus, Vere unwittingly reiterates the logic of revolution, albeit with the intention of reasserting his power. In a further twist, Vere is the figure in whom sympathy appears to be most lacking in the text. Described from the outset as a cold rationalist (62), Vere's aim throughout Billy's trial is to obliterate the power of sympathy over both himself and the members of the drumhead court. This is not to suggests that Vere is unmoved by Billy's plight. On the contrary, the narrative makes it clear that Vere feels great compassion for the handsome sailor. Melville further complicates matters when he conceals from view the crucial interview when Vere informs Billy of his fate. The narrator offers only "conjecture," based on the characters of the two individuals, about what may have transpired in that meeting (115). Vere's internal struggle with his feelings for Billy, as this scene suggests, must always remain private. From the moment Billy strikes Claggart it is clear that, as a matter of philosophical conviction, Vere's sympathy has already lost out to his sense of duty and his paranoia about the need to maintain order. Thus, Vere's intelligent responsiveness serves the purpose of authorizing the suppression of sympathy where appropriate. That is, by adding the modifier intelligent, Vere strategically contains the power of his sympathetic response.

With the substitution of the people for the crew, Melville reminds his readers of the slippage between a mutiny and a revolution that informs his narrative. Melville had set up the context of mutiny and connected it to revolution early in the narrative: "Like some other events in every age befalling states everywhere, including America, the Great Mutiny was of such character that national pride along with views of policy would fain shade it off into the historical background. Such events cannot be ignored, but there is a considerate way of historically treating them" (55). At this moment Melville draws a direct parallel between a revolution and a mutiny. Melville, in fact, includes strategic references to revolution at various key moments in the text. In the second paragraph, well before introducing the Paine-Burke controversy, Melville alludes to the French Revolution through a reference to Anacharsis Cloots, who had joined Paine as one of the group of philosophers assigned to the committee charged with writing a new constitution for the French Republic (43–44). He invokes the radical Cloots to celebrate the diversity of races and ethnicities intermingling on the Liverpool docks, but is careful to associate Cloots with his role in the French Assembly where he identified himself first as "the voice of humanity" and later as "voice of the sans-culottes." In a sense, this represents another veiled reference to Paine, since the key document produced by the assembly, that echoes with this account of Cloots, is the "Déclaration des Droits de l'Homme," which, of course, was included in and served as a crucial touchstone for Paine's *Rights of Man.*[8]

Vere makes two crucial references to the French Revolution in the course of the narrative. The first appears in the middle of his urgent appeal to the drumhead court when he persuades them to execute Billy. In an attempt to anticipate the possible argument that Billy should be spared because he was impressed into service, Vere asks them to consider the impact the judgment might have on the other impressed men: "As regards the enemy's naval conscripts, some of whom may even share our own abhorrence of the regicidal French Directory, it is the same on our side" (112). There is no apparent reason for Vere to invoke the impressed sailors in the French navy, except that he has internalized the association between mutiny and revolution. This association becomes even more evident after Billy's execution when he seeks to justify his course of action by emphasizing the need to maintain the formal structure of social and political relations: " 'With mankind' he would say, 'forms, measured forms, are everything.' ... And this he once applied to the disruption of forms going on across the Channel and the consequences thereof" (128). Here, we see

---

[8] Paine was one of the three philosophers, along with Condorcet and Sieyès, who were assigned to the committee that drafted the first version of the French Déclaration.

Vere drawing an explicit connection between his approach to Billy's case and the political events in France.

In the case of the narrative of *Billy Budd* we should recall that Vere is profoundly concerned with the infectious nature of rumors and suggestions of mutiny. In much the same way, England, and Burke in particular, was anxious about the possibility of French revolutionary energies spreading to its shores. As I suggest earlier in this study, this extension of revolutionary fervor was precisely Paine's goal in *Rights of Man*. Just two paragraphs after the initial discussion of the Great Mutiny, Melville employs the language of infection that was so prevalent in political writing about the potential threat of revolution in the late eighteenth century, to describe the impact of the Nore Mutiny: "To some extent the Nore Mutiny may be regarded as analogous to the distempering irruption of contagious fever in a frame constitutionally sound, and which anon throws it off" (55). The parallels between mutiny and revolution are facilitated by the correspondences between the body and the state, which are captured by the dual meaning of "constitution" in this sentence.

Vere articulates the political rationale for maintaining the status quo by enforcing a system that is carefully designed to defend the interests of the aristocracy. Even though Vere never set out to defend or assist Claggart in his quest to destroy Billy, Claggart could not have succeeded without Vere's cooperation – intended or not. At this moment, they become allies, albeit reluctant ones, protecting the same territory. This institutional/systemic structure explains the sense of inevitability that pervades the novella. Melville has engineered a situation where a power perceives itself under threat and in the process manufactures a conflict in order to reassert its authority. In doing so, he returns us to the Paine-Burke debate, which begins when Burke perceives the English supporters of the French Revolution as a threat to order in England.[9] Ironically, that debate ends in a trial for treason and death sentence (in absentia) for Paine, which forced him to prolong his stay in France for several years for fear of being captured by a British ship. Had he been captured, Paine, like Billy, would have been hanged.

The Paine-Burke controversy is paralleled in the narrative by the contrast between the *Rights of Man* and the *Bellipotent*. Whereas Billy had

---

[9] In the first few pages of his *Reflections* Burke singles out the Society for Constitutional Information and the Revolution Society, both of which he believes are spreading dangerous misinformation about liberty, English history, and the English Constitution that could seriously undermine the state's ability to govern and perhaps even lead to the overthrow of the government.

served as a "peacemaker" on the merchant ship (47), he becomes a source of conflict and a murderer on the other. Melville thus sets up a contrast between the world of commerce and the state. In the commercial milieu Billy's natural merit (virtue) serves to bring peace and prosperity to the ship: The sailors get along better so the ship is more efficient and more profitable. In the military setting Billy's magnetic personality threatens the (artificial) hierarchical order of the ship, which leads to disorder, and threats of mutiny. Let us recall that Paine places great faith in the power of commerce to bring peace and democracy to the world. Melville, it seems, has not merely taken Paine's text to establish an allegorical context for his novella, but has constructed a tale that reinforces the fundamental mission of Paine's important work of political philosophy. In *Billy Budd*, Melville not only creates a situation where the system unjustly punishes an innocent man, but he also provides an alternative vision where this same innocent can shine as a leader and an example of virtue for others. The implication, ultimately, is that the institutional structure distorts Billy such that the system, not the individual, is what needs to be changed.[10]

Vere is too beholden to safeguard the institutional structure to respond to the sympathetic appeal of this particular individual. His capacity for sympathy – as he relates to Billy's plight – is limited by his refusal to act on Billy's behalf (if anything, his actions ensure Billy's death).[11] In spite of the fact that he sacrifices the convictions of his conscience in order to protect the institutions that endow him with authority, Vere becomes a sympathetic figure because of his very powerlessness to resist the hegemonic force of the institutions he embodies. In other words, the monarchical government in which Vere lives renders sympathy useless and transforms it into an obstacle instead of validating it as an essential human quality. Here, Melville mirrors the critique of government articulated by Paine in *Rights of Man*, where sympathy plays a central role in the creation of a good society: "[Nature] has not only forced man into society, by a

---

[10] This also coheres with Barbara Johnson's argument about Billy's complex strategy of repression. She points out that he preserves his innocence only through a process of strategic filtering where he represses experiences or events that do not conform to his literalist interpretation of the signs around him. I would suggest that this happens on the *Bellipotent* precisely in order to resist being corrupted by the ship's institutional structure, which is itself corrupt.

[11] Here Melville essentially anticipates Ann Douglas's argument in *The Feminization of American Culture*. What good is sympathy if it does not become a trigger for action?

diversity of wants, which the reciprocal aid of each other can supply, but she has implanted in him a system of social affections, which, though not necessary to his existence, are essential to his happiness" (CW I, 357). Consequently, Paine determines that the more government, or the state, interferes with the operation of this "system of social affections," the less happy the society. An ideal society, then, is one where sympathy rules. The problem, Paine notes is that too often governments serve their own interests instead of those of the people: "But how often is the natural propensity of society disturbed or destroyed by the operations of government. When the latter, instead of being ingrafted on the principles of the former, assumes to exist for itself, and acts by partialities of favor and oppression, it becomes the cause of the mischiefs it ought to prevent" (359). This, in a nutshell, is what dooms Billy, for Vere acts to ensure the survival of the power structure in spite of its human cost.

If Whitman's comments about Paine make it clear that he was always lurking beneath the surface of American literary history, Melville's invocation of Paine in *Billy Budd* brought him out into the open as the progenitor of an important but buried legacy of the revolutions of the late eighteenth century. Melville implies in *Billy Budd* that although Paine's critique of government had been targeted specifically at the British Monarchy in 1791–3, it has become an apt criticism of what the U.S. government has become in the nineteenth century. This is possible because as democracy became institutionalized in the United States in the nineteenth century, the structures of power it authorized had calcified and become hierarchical in many of the same ways that characterized the old British monarchical structures that Paine has sought to overthrow. Thus, the point is that Paine's critique, and Melville's by implication, isn't merely a critique of a particular form of government but of the organization and structure of power in any system of order that becomes hierarchical and institutionalized. In typical fashion, Melville recognizes this as an inevitable, if lamentable, problem inherent in government and human power relations, whereas Paine's optimism leads him to hope for and advocate measures that might produce a form of government that could escape these limitations.

The philosophical distance between Paine and Melville's respective views of the possibilities of government serves as an index of the degree to which the nation had gradually moved away from the radically egalitarian ideas that had sparked much of the early revolutionary energy and become a prisoner to the power of its own institutions. Serving as the crucial voice of that democratic optimism, Paine allows Melville and Whitman to recover those possibilities even if they are incapable of fully embracing them. Indeed, if the nation were to embrace the ideals that sparked the Revolution, as opposed to the ones that would contain and limit its impact in the Federalist era, then Thomas Paine would undoubtedly have become the crucial actor of the founding era.

Works Cited

Adams, John. *Thoughts on Government: Applicable to the Present State of the American Colonies: In a Letter from a Gentleman to his Friend.* Philadelphia: Dunlap, 1776.

Adams, John and Thomas Jefferson. *The Adams-Jefferson Letters: The Complete Correspondence between Thomas Jefferson and Abigail and John Adams.* Ed. Lester J. Cappon. Chapel Hill: North Carolina University Press, 1959.

Anderson, Benedict. *Imagined Communities: Reflections on the Origin and Spread of Nationalism.* Revised Ed. New York: Verso, 1991.

Bache, Sarah Franklin. Letter to Benjamin Franklin. January 14, 1781. Thomas Paine Papers. The Gimbel Collection, American Philosophical Society.

Bailyn, Bernard. *The Ideological Origins of the American Revolution.* Cambridge: Belknap, 1967.

Baker, Keith Michael. "Public Opinion as Political Invention." *Inventing the French Revolution: Essays on French Political Culture in the Eighteenth Century: Ideas in Context.* Cambridge: Cambridge University Press, 1990.

Barnes, Elizabeth. *States of Sympathy: Seduction and Democracy in the American Novel.* New York: Columbia University Press, 1997.

Beckett, J. V. *The Aristocracy in England, 1660–1914.* New York: Basil Blackwell, 1986.

Berthold, Dennis. "Melville, Garibaldi, and the Medusa of Revolution." *American Literary History* 9.3 (Fall 1997): 425–459.

Botein, Stephen. "Printers and the American Revolution." *The Press and the American Revolution.* Eds. Bernard Bailyn and John B. Hench. Boston: Northeastern University Press, 1980, 11–57.

Breen, T. H. "'Baubles of Britain': The American and Consumer Revolutions of the Eighteenth Century." *Past and Present* 119: 73–104.

Briggs, Asa. *The Age of Improvement, 1783–1867.* New York: David McKay, 1959.

Brown, Richard D. *The Strength of a People: The Idea of an Informed Citizenry in America, 1650–1870.* Chapel Hill, North Carolina University Press, 1996.

Brown, Thomas. *Amusements Serious and Comical: Calculated for the Meridian of London. The Works of Mr. Thomas Brown, Serious and Comical, In Prose and Verse.* 4 Vols, 5th Edition. London: Samuel Briscoe, 1720, Vol. 3.

Browne, Ray B. "Billy Budd: Gospel of Democracy." *Nineteenth Century Fiction* 17.4 (March 1963): 321–337.

Bushman, Richard. *Joseph Smith and the Beginnings of Mormonism.* Urbana: Illinois University Press, 1984.

Burgh, James. *Political Disquisitions.* 3 Vols. London: E. and C. Dilly 1774–1775.

Burke, Edmund. *Reflections on the Revolution in France.* Indianapolis, IN: Hackett, 1987.

Candidus [James Chalmers]. *Plain Truth; Addressed to the Inhabitants of America.* Philadelphia: Robert Bell, 1776.

Carlson, C. Lennart. *The First Magazine: A History of* The Gentleman's Magazine *with an Account of Dr. Johnson's Editorial Activity and of the Notice Given America in the Magazine.* Providence, RI: Brown University Press, 1938.

Certeau, Michel de. *The Writing of History.* Trans. Tom Conley. New York: Columbia University Press, 1988.

Cheetham, James. *The Life of Thomas Paine.* New York: Southwick and Pelrue, 1809.

Cmiel, Kenneth. *Democratic Eloquence: The Fight Over Popular Speech in Nineteenth-Century America.* New York: William Morrow and Co., 1990.

Cohen, I. Bernard. *Science and the Founding Fathers.* New York: Norton, 1995.

Cohen, Lester H. *The Revolutionary Histories: Contemporary Narratives of the American Revolution.* Ithaca, NY: Cornell University Press, 1980.

Conroy, David W. *In Public Houses: Drink and the Revolution of Authority in Colonial Massachusetts.* Chapel Hill: North Carolina University Press for the Institute of Early American History and Culture, 1995.

Conway, Moncure Daniel. *The Life of Thomas Paine.* 2 Vols. New York: Putnam, 1893.

Croxall, Samuel. *Fables of Aesop and Others.* Philadelphia: Aitken, 1777.

d'Entremont, John. *Southern Emancipator: Moncure Conway, The American Years, 1832–1865.* New York: Oxford University Press, 1987.

Davidson, Cathy N. *Revolution and the Word: The Rise of the Novel in America.* Oxford: Oxford University Press, 1986.

Davidson, Edward and William Scheick. *Paine, Scripture, and Authority: The Age of Reason as Religious and Political Idea.* Bethlehem, PA: Lehigh University Press, 1994.

"Declaration of Independence." *Thomas Jefferson, Writings.* New York: Library of America, 1984, 19–24.

Dictionary of American History. Ed. James Trunslow Adams. New York: Scribners, 1942.

Douglas, Ann. *The Feminization of American Culture.* New York: Anchor, 1977.

Eley, Geoff. "Nations, Publics, and Political Cultures: Placing Habermas in the Nineteenth Century." *Habermas and the Public Sphere.* Ed. Craig Calhoun. Cambridge: MIT University Press, 1992, 289–339.

Endy, Jr., Melvin B. *William Penn and Early Quakerism.* Princeton, NJ: Princeton University Press, 1973.

Ferguson, Robert. "The Commonalities of *Common Sense.*" *William and Mary Quarterly*, 3rd Series 57.3 (July 2000): 465–504.

Fliegelman, Jay. *Prodigals and Pilgrims: The American Revolution Against Patriarchal Authority, 1750–1800*. Cambridge: Cambridge University Press, 1982.

_____. *Declaring Independence: Jefferson, Natural Language, and the Culture of Performance*. Stanford, CA: Stanford University Press, 1993.

Foner, Eric. *Tom Paine and Revolutionary America*. New York: Oxford University Press, 1976.

Franklin, Benjamin. Letter to Thomas Paine. September 27, 1785. Library of Congress.

Franklin, Benjamin. *The Autobiography. Writings*. New York: Library of America, 1987.

Fraser, Nancy. "Rethinking the Public Sphere: A Contribution to the Critique of Actually Existing Democracy." *Habermas and the Public Sphere*, Ed. Craig Calhoun. Cambridge: MIT University Press, 1992, 109–142.

Fruchtman, Jr., Jack. *Thomas Paine and the Religion of Nature*. Baltimore, MD: John Hopkins University Press, 1993.

Gaustad, Edwin S. *Sworn on the Altar of God: A Religious Biography of Thomas Jefferson*. Grand Rapids, MI: Eerdmans, 1996.

Golinski, Jan. *Science as Public Culture: Chemistry and the Enlightenment in Britain, 1760–1820*. New York: Cambridge University Press, 1992.

Goodman, Dena. *The Republic of Letters: A Cultural History of the French Enlightenment*. Ithaca, NY: Cornell University Press, 1994.

Greene, Jack P. "Paine, America, and the Modernization of Political Consciousness." *Political Science Quarterly* 93.1 (Spring 1978): 73–92.

Gustafson, Sandra. *Eloquence is Power: Oratory and Performance in Early America*. Chapel Hill: University of North Carolina Press for The Omohundro Institute of Early American History and Culture, 2000.

Gustafson, Thomas. *Representative Words*. New York: Cambridge University Press, 1992.

Habermas, Jurgen. *The Structural Transformation of the Public Sphere: An Inquiry into a Category of Bourgeois Society*. Trans. Thomas Burger. Cambridge: MIT Press, 1991.

Hamilton, Alexander. *Report on Manufactures: The Reports of Alexander Hamilton*. Ed. Jacob E. Cooke. New York: Harper & Row, 1964, 115–250.

Harford, John S. *Some Account of the Life, Death, and Principles of Thomas Paine, Together with Remarks on his Writings, and on Their Intimate Connection with the Avowed objects of the Revolutionsists of 1793, and of the Radicals in 1819*. Bristol [Eng]: Gutch, 1819.

Hatch, Nathan O. *The Democratization of American Christianity*. New Haven: Yale University Press, 1989.

Hawke, David Freeman. *Paine*. New York: Norton, 1974.

Horkheimer, Max and Theodor W. Adorno. *Dialectic of Enlightenment*. Trans. John Cumming. New York: Continuum, 1972.

Hunter, J. Paul. *Before Novels: The Cultural Contexts of Eighteenth-Century English Fiction*. New York: Norton, 1990.

Inglis, Charles. *The True Interest of America Impartially Stated, in Certain Strictures on a Pamphlet Intitled Common Sense.* 2nd Edition Philadelphia: Humphreys, 1776.

James, J. G. "Thomas Paine's Iron Bridge Work 1785–1803." *Transactions of the Newcomen Society for the Study of the History of Engineering and Technology* 59 (1987–88): 189–221.

Johnson, Barbara. "Melville's Fist." *Studies in Romanticism* 18.4 (Winter 1979): 567–599.

Jefferson, Thomas. *Notes on the State of Virginia: Thomas Jefferson, Writings.* Ed. Merrill D. Peterson. New York: Library of America, 1984, 123–325.

Judd, Wayne R. "William Miller, Disappointed Prophet." *The Disappointed: Millerism and Millenarianism in the Nineteenth Century.* Eds. Ronald L. Numbers and Jonathan M. Butler. Knoxville: Tennessee University Press, 1993, 17–35.

Kammen, Michael. *The Mystic Chords of Memory.* New York: Vintage, 1991.

Keane, John. *Tom Paine: A Political Life.* Boston: Little, Brown & Co., 1995.

Kemp, E. L. "Thomas Paine and his 'Pontifical Matters.'" *Transactions of the Newcomen Society for the Study of the History of Engineering and Technology* 49 (1977–78): 21–40.

Klancher, Jon P. *The Making of English Reading Audiences, 1790–1832.* Madison: Wisconsin University Press, 1987.

Knudson, Jerry W. "The Rage Around Tom Paine: Newspaper Reaction to His Homecoming in 1802." *New-York Historical Society Quarterly* 53 (1969): 34–63.

Kramnick, Isaac. *Bolingbroke and his Circle.* Cambridge, MA: Harvard University Press, 1968.

Looby, Christopher. *Voicing America: Language, Literary Form, and the Origins of the United States.* Chicago: Chicago University Press, 1996.

Loughran. Trish. "Virtual Nation: Local and National Cultures in the Early United States." Chicago: University of Chicago, 1999.

Mather, Cotton. *The Christian Philosopher* [London: 1721]. Ed. Josephine K. Piercy. Gainesville, Fl: Scholar's Facsimiles & Reprints, 1968.

McCoy, Drew. *The Elusive Republic: Political Economy in Jeffersonian America.* Chapel Hill: North Carolina University Press for the Institute of Early American History and Culture, 1980.

McKeon, Michael. *The Origins of the English Novel, 1600–1740.* Baltimore, MD: Johns Hopkins University Press, 1987.

Mee, John. *William Blake and the Culture of Radicalism in the 1790s.* New York: Oxford University Press, 1992.

Melville, Herman. *Billy Budd, Sailor (An Inside Narrative).* Eds. Harrison Hayford and Merton M. Sealts, Jr. Chicago: Chicago University Press, 1962.

Montesquieu, Charles de Secondat, baron de. *Persian Letters.* Trans. C. J. Betts. New York: Penguin, 1993.

_____. *The Spirit of the Laws. Cambridge Texts in the History of Political Thought.* Trans. and Eds. Anne M Cohler, Basia Carolyn Miller, and Harold Samuel Stone. Cambridge: Cambridge UP, 1989.

Mott, Frank Luther. *A History of American Magazines, 1741–1850*. New York: Appleton, 1930.

Newfield, Christopher. *The Emerson Effect: Individualism and Submission in America*. Chicago: Chicago University Press, 1995.

Noel, Thomas. *Theories of the Fable in the Eighteenth Century*. New York: Columbia University Press, 1975.

Oldys, Jonathan [George Chalmers]. *The Life of Thomas Pain*. London: Stockdale, 1791.

Oxford English Dictionary. 2nd Edition. Ed. J. A. and E. S. C. Weiner. New York: Oxford University Press, 1989.

Paine, Thomas. *Common Sense: Addressed to the Inhabitants of America*. Philadelphia: Bell, 1776.

_____. *The Complete Writings of Thomas Paine*. Ed. Philip S. Foner. 2 Vols. New York: Citadel, 1969.

Patterson, Annabel. *Fables of Power: Aesopian Writing and Political History*. Durham, NC: Duke University Press, 1991.

Peale, Charles Willson. *An Essay on Building Wooden Bridges*. Philadelphia: Bailey, 1797.

Poor Wills Almanack. Philadelphia: Crukshank, 1776.

Porcupine, P[eter] [William Cobbett]. "Life of Thomas Paine, Interspersed with Remarks and Reflections." *The Political Censor I* (September 1796), 3–49.

Reynolds, David S. *Walt Whitman's America: A Cultural Biography*. New York: Vintage, 1995.

Rice, Grantland S. *The Transformation of Authorship in America*. Chicago: Chicago University Press, 1997.

Rickman, Thomas Clio. *The Life of Thomas Paine*. London: Rickman, 1819.

Ripley, Samuel. Letter to Ralph Waldo Emerson. August 1838. *The Letters of Ralph Waldo Emerson*. 6 Vols. Ed. Ralph L. Rusk. New York: Columbia University Press, 1939, Vol. 2, 148.

Rodgers, Daniel T. "Republicanism: the Career of a Concept." *Journal of American History* 79.1(June 1992): 11–38.

Rogin, Michael Paul. *Subversive Genealogy: The Politics and Art of Herman Melville*. Berkeley: California University Press, 1979.

Rousseau, Jean-Jacques. *Emile, or On Education*. Ed. Allan Bloom. New York: Basic, 1979.

_____. *Discourse on the Origins of Inequality*. Trans. Donald A. Cress. Indianapolis, IN: Hackett, 1992.

Ruttenburg, Nancy. *Democratic Personality: Popular Voice and the Trial of American Authorship*. Stanford, CA: Stanford University Press, 1998.

Sedgwick, Eve Kosofsky. *Epistemology of the Closet*. Berkeley: California University Press, 1992.

Seelye, John. *Beautiful Machine: Rivers and the Republican Plan, 1755–1825*. New York: Oxford University Press, 1991.

Sekora, John. *Luxury: The Concept in Western Thought, Eden to Smollett*. Baltimore, MD: Johns Hopkins University Press, 1977.

Shapin, Steven and Simon Shaffer. *Leviathan and the Air Pump: Hobbes, Boyle, and the Experimental Life*. Princeton, NJ: Princeton University Press, 1985.

Shapin, Steven. *A Social History of Truth: Civility and Science in Seventeenth-Century England*. Chicago: Chicago University Press, 1994.

Sherwin, W. T. *Memoirs of the Life of Thomas Paine, with Observations on his Writings, Critical and Explanatory*. London: Carlile, 1819.

Smith, Adam. *The Theory of Moral Sentiments*. Eds. D. D. Raphael and A. L. Macfie. Indianapolis, IN: Liberty Classics, 1976.

Smith, Frank. "New Light On Thomas Paine's First Year in America, 1775." *American Literature* 1.4 (January 1930): 347–371.

Smith, Olivia. *The Politics of Language, 1791–1819*. Oxford: Clarendon Press, 1984.

Smith-Rosenberg, Carroll. "Dis-Covering the Subject of the 'Great Constitutional Discussion,' 1786–1789." *Journal of American History* 79.3 (December 1992): 841–873.

Solberg, Winton U. "Science and Religion in Early America: Cotton Mather's *Christian Philosopher*." *Church History* 56 (1987) 73–92.

Stewart, Larry. *The Rise of Public Science: Rhetoric, Technology, and Natural Philosophy in Newtonian Britain, 1660–1750*. New York: Cambridge University Press, 1992.

Stone, Lawrence. *The Crisis of the Aristocracy, 1558–1641*. Oxford: Clarendon, 1965.

The New England Almanack, or Lady's and Gentleman's Diary. Providence, RI: John Carter, 1775.

The New Oxford Annotated Bible: The Holy Bible, Revised Standard Edition Containing the Old and New Testaments. Eds. Herbert G. May and Bruce M. Metzger. New York: Oxford University Press, 1962.

The Pennsylvania Evening Post, and Public Advertiser. Philadelphia: Benjamin Towne, 1776.

The Pennsylvania Magazine; or, American Monthly Museum. Philadelphia, January 1775–July 1776.

The Pennsylvania Packet. Philadelphia, December 1778–January 1779.

Thompson, C. Bradley. "Young John Adams and the New Philosophic Rationalism." *William and Mary Quarterly* 3rd Ser. 55.2 (April 1998): 259–280.

Thompson, E. P. *The Making of the English Working Class*. New York: Vintage, 1966.

Traubel, Horace. *With Walt Whitman in Camden*. Vol. 1 (March 28, 1888–July 14, 1888). New York: Appleton, 1908.

Tyler, Royall. *The Algerine Captive: or, the Life and Adventures of Doctor Updike Underhill: Six Years a Prisoner Among the Algerines*. Ed. Caleb Crain. New York: Modern Library, 2002.

Universal Spectator. London. January 30, 1731.

Warner, Michael. *The Letters of the Republic: Publication and the Public Sphere in Eighteenth Century America*. Cambridge, MA: Harvard University Press, 1990.

White, Hayden. *Tropics of Discourse: Essays in Cultural Criticism*. Baltimore, MD: Johns Hopkins University Press, 1978.

Wilson, David A. *Paine and Cobbett: The Transatlantic Connection*. Kingston, Ontario: McGill-Queen's University Press, 1988.

Wolf II, Edwin. *The Book Culture of a Colonial American City: Philadelphia Books, Bookmen, and Booksellers*. New York: Clarendon, 1988.

Wood, Gordon S. *The Creation of the American Republic, 1776–1787*. New York: Norton, 1969.

Young, Alfred F. *The Shoemaker and the Tea Party: Memory and the American Revolution*. Boston: Beacon, 1999.

Index